**Books are to be returned on or before
the last date below.**

This book, taken up in *Inside Schools*, reviews the position of
ethnographic educational research in the light of current issues and of
the author's own experience. The author argues that ethnography is
of teaching itself, being concerned with how teachers and pupils
interact, how meanings are constructed and negotiated, and how this
relates to the experience and practice of research. The approach is
illustrated by rich reference to the author's own research and
research experience, as in examples of teaching-focused events
and teacher-based experience, how to represent such
research, structural features of the research, and the tools used
in that research. Whatever forms
of representation are selected, and whatever audiences researchers will
guide the...

Prominent...

- the p...
- the a... example of representing it, while not forgetting
  the s... of teaching...research...
- resea... method of educational research
- colla...

All those interested in educational research will find a great deal of interest
here, but...research...general relevance within qualitative
research. They bear on such matters as research purposes, research design,
research careers, access, data collection, data analysis, truth criteria, the
relationship between theory and research methods, writing-up and
dissemination.

Peter Woods is Professor in the School of Education at The Open
University.

041 513 1294

Researching the Art of Teaching
Ethnography for Educational Use

Peter Woods

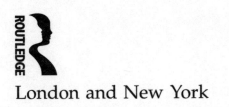

London and New York

For Mickey

First published 1996
by Routledge
11 New Fetter Lane, London EC4P 4EE

Simultaneously published in the USA and Canada
by Routledge
29 West 35th Street, New York, NY 10001

© 1996 Peter Woods

Typeset in Palatino by Routledge
Printed and bound in Great Britain by
Clays Ltd, St Ives PLC

British Library Cataloguing in Publication Data
A catalogue record for this book is available from the British Library

Library of Congress Cataloguing in Publication Data
Woods, Peter.
Researching the art of teaching: ethnography for educational use/Peter Woods.
Includes bibliographical references and indexes.
1. Education–Research. 2. Teaching. 3. Participant observation. 4. Action research in
education. I. Title.
LB1028.W647 1996
370'.78 — dc20   96–21555
                                                                          CIP

ISBN 0–415–13128–6 (hbk)
ISBN 0–415–13129–4 (pbk)

Contents

Preface

This book is a follow-up to *Inside Schools* (Woods, 1986). There, I set out some of the principles and procedures involved in ethnographic research in education as I saw them. Much of that, I would claim, still holds good, but things have moved on in some respects. The major themes of *Inside Schools* remain, though each is taken forward in this book in the light of developments since the mid-1980s. Thus the 'person of the ethnographer' is equally evident here. If anything, this has become even more important in view of increasing interest in subjectivities and in reflexivity. The application to education is also there, in general, but with a particular emphasis this time on the art of teaching – the area of my own research over the last ten years. Again, there has been a growth of interest in this area, under the influence especially of postmodernist researchers. There is more of an emphasis, too, on ethnography for educational use as opposed to more foundational research. The aim is not to lose sight of the gains made in rigour of approach and in the generation of theory, but rather to consider how the benefits of that for education can be brought home.

One way is to seek to identify the conditions that underlie more successful teaching and learning. Another is to make alliances with teachers in the conduct of the research. Thus, the third theme from *Inside Schools* – teachers as researchers – also figures prominently, and here I discuss how we have sought to work collaboratively in my recent research. Much of this has been concerned with 'creative teachers' and 'creative teaching', and I have sought to provide outlets for that creativity in the research, as well as offering what skills we possess to the teachers for use in their endeavours.

Underpinning the book is the loose body of theory known as symbolic interactionism, which in my view continues to offer rich rewards for social and educational understanding. Indeed, I would argue that it has been strengthened by theoretical and methodological developments in recent years, and I try to incorporate some of those in the book.

All those involved in educational enquiry might find something of interest here. But the issues discussed are of general relevance within qualitative research. They bear on such matters as research purposes, research design, research careers, access, data collection, data analysis, the relationship between theory and research methods, writing up and dissemination. I hope the book makes a contribution to the general corpus of work in this area.

Acknowledgements

Many people have contributed to the production of this book. I have learnt a great deal from comments they have made on parts of the content at conferences, at seminars, in informal conversation and in letters, and from the reports of anonymous referees of research proposals, articles and the original book proposal. I thank all those who have contributed in this way. I would like to record a special thanks to Bob Jeffrey, Geoff Troman, Mari Boyle, Nick Hubbard, Peter J. Woods, Peter Wenham, Pat Sikes, Andy Hargreaves and Martyn Hammersley, for long-term and significant input into my thinking. They will not necessarily agree with all that I have written, but the book would have been the poorer without their input.

I have received excellent secretarial services from Sheila Gilks, Aileen Cousins, Yvonne Wooster and Lynn Tilbury, without which my task would have been much harder and taken much longer. Kath, and in the later stages Bronwyn, have sustained my morale. The material in this book draws on research supported over the years by the Open University and the Economic and Social Research Council (grant numbers R000233194, R000235123 and R000236406). I am grateful to these institutions for their support.

Chapters 1, 2 and 5 contain previously published material. Chapter 1 first appeared as 'Is teaching a science or an art?' in Watson, K., Modgil, S. and Modgil, C. (eds) (1996) *Educational Dilemmas: debate and diversity. Vol. 1: Teachers, Teacher Education and Training*, London, Cassell. Chapter 2 is an edited and revised version of 'Symbolic interactionism: theory and method' in LeCompte, M., Millroy, W.L. and Preissle, J. (eds) (1992) *The Handbook of Qualitative Research in Education*, New York, Academic Press. Chapter 5 was previously published as 'Collaborating in historical ethnography', *International Journal of Qualitative Studies in Education*, 7, 4 (1994), pp. 309–321. My thanks to the publishers for permission to reproduce them here. I am grateful to Seamus Heaney and the publishers for permission to quote in Chapter 6 from the author's poem 'Digging', from *Death of a Naturalist*, London, Faber & Faber, 1980.

Introduction
The ethnographer's self

ETHNOGRAPHY AND THE SELF

One might argue that the adoption of research method is simply a matter of fitness for purpose. However, Gouldner has observed that the perception of sociologists comes from two sources: (1) empirical studies and theorizing; and (2) 'personal realities' (Gusfield, 1990, p. 104). The former are usually acknowledged, the latter hidden. Yet they can be the most important, both for the choice and direction of research, and for the researcher. One often does research in part to discover more about oneself. This is not to say that it is self-indulgent, but that it is chiefly through the self that one comes to understand the world. In turn, the discoveries one makes reflect back upon the self, which then feed back into research, and so on.

I begin, therefore, with myself, and some reflections on my own life and research career which seem relevant to my current thoughts and actions.

I was born in the 1930s. My father was a jobbing bricklayer by trade, and an inshore fisherman by pastime. He was a man of great skill and resource, like many of his fellows, who built his own boats, made his own furniture, carved his own ornaments, made his own live music, and produced a great deal of his own food. He had tried, once, as a young man, to work for 'a master', but he did not like it, preferring his independence. This made for an interesting and busy life, but a perilous one, having to bring up a family in the shade of the 1930s' recession and the privations of the 1939–45 war and its aftermath. When no more jobs were available, he would play a special song on his violin to conjure one up, which contains the key phrase, 'my money's nearly spent'. My mother came from a long line of fisherfolk, and, as was the custom with the girls of the family, had gone 'into service' on leaving school. She married my father at the age of 21, and immediately began bearing children – six over a twenty-year period. Most of her time seemed to be spent washing, boiling, mangling and ironing. As she scrubbed, she went through her repertoire of music hall songs ('Have you seen my chap, my chap, my chap, have you seen my chap waiting for me ... '). In the early years of the marriage, she took in washing from others, and provided accommodation and meals for visitors in the summer, to boost the family income. She was first up in the morning to light the fire and prepare breakfast, and last to bed, darning and mending clothes into the small hours. My overall recollection of family life is of a sometimes difficult but happy one. We all got on well together, all went to grammar school and to university. We belonged to an extended family, with numerous characters among them, and a fascinating history. Considerable ingenuity was deployed in self-help and self-sufficiency. However, at times this was not enough, and there were periods of great struggle for my parents. I recall successions of days of heated argument and shouting between them when it was not clear where a necessary resource was coming from. The security of the family seemed to hang on a thread at such times.

On the outbreak of war in 1939, I was evacuated at the age of 5, with my elder sister and two brothers, to a pit village in the north of England. I was billeted, together with one of my brothers, with a miner, his wife and daughter. It was difficult for them, for nobody wanted evacuees. I could not understand the man's speech, and found him unsympathetic and threatening. After a time, my brother left to join my eldest brother in a grammar school in a town several miles away. A period of bed-wetting ensued, and ages passed. One day, I was told at school that somebody wanted to see me. On leaving the classroom I was seized and hugged and kissed by a strange woman. It was, I later discovered, my mother – I had completely forgotten her. I can still remember my incomprehensible pleasure at the meeting. Such visits, however, did not last long. I began to indulge in deviant acts, for which I was severely beaten by the sadistic headmaster, a man straight out of Charles Dickens, whether the deed took place in school or not. After four years, my eldest brother, who used to cycle fifteen miles to visit me on occasions, counselled my parents to take me home, regarding German bombs as less of a threat to my future career.

After the war, I passed the eleven plus and went to the grammar school. My generation was the first to gain access to these selective schools on the grounds of ability following the 1944 Education Act, and they were still full of staff who regarded the new policy as catastrophic. They made their disapproval known in numerous ways. Culturally these schools did not change, at least in the early years, continuing to ape the public schools and to celebrate their middle-class traditions. Half the pupils came from middle-class backgrounds, and blended into this culture. The other half were the new working-class entrants whose own culture clashed with that of the school. At the time it was difficult to understand the personal hostility of some of the teachers, especially when we thought we were doing our best. We made progress academically, my own preference being for the humanities, languages and mathematics, rather than science. Such progress was to the credit of the teachers, but it was against a residual background of bad feeling. The knowledge, skills and resources were rich; the institution, and the roles within it, alienating.

The division within the school was matched by the one outside – between the grammar and the secondary modern school. Several of my friends had failed the eleven plus, some of them to the surprise of our teacher, and had gone to the latter school. From then on, I hardly saw them, or any of their peers at the school. I often wonder what happened to them. The division was quite rigid, between schools, and between lives.

After National Service – compulsory in those days – I went to university. Beyond that I had no idea what I wanted to do apart from being some sort of 'writer', a notion I had had from my teenage years. The popular move among my contemporaries was to go into teaching, but given my alienation as a pupil, this held no attractions for me. I spent two years in and out of temporary jobs, experimenting with various forms of 'writing', without much success, living on the fringes of society. This marginality had its uncomfortable moments, but also provided insights. One of them was that there is no life outside society.

I was then offered another temporary post, this time in a primary school on a working-class estate, taking the place of a woman on maternity leave for the summer term. It seemed a totally different proposition from the secondary school of my youth. I still remember my first experience at the school. Standing at the back in assembly, marvelling at the 300 or so heads of shining hair, and almost gasping in astonishment when they began to sing – one of the most beautiful sounds I've ever heard. As an untrained graduate, I muddled my way through the term, wrestling with such arcane matters as raffia weaving, dishcloth manufacture, and daisy-chain stitch, enchanted and bewildered at the same time. I was captivated by the children, who did most to socialize me into the culture of the school; what to do with them, and how other teachers managed, so capably and easily, was an abiding mystery. Even so, from my vantage point of adult and teacher, and at Collingwood Junior, school now seemed a vastly different place from the class-ridden institution of my youth and studenthood. There was something noble in fact about helping children to learn, and they were so eager to please, to share things with you and to smile at you. I went on from there to train for secondary teaching (it seemed to offer the best career opportunities), and then to ten years teaching in grammar schools – three in all – in various parts of Yorkshire.

'Learning', however, was something different in these schools from that in Collingwood Junior. I was advised by my mentors from the very beginning that 'results' were what mattered. If you achieved good results in the annual public examinations, 'they left you alone for another year'. I was a successful teacher judged purely by examination results. But my teaching became locked into an examination framework, formalized, systematized, assessment-led. 'Question spotting' was part of the teacher's skill. Questions on examination papers came round with predictable regularity, and you could design the year's syllabus on that basis. I would have liked to teach exciting, interactive lessons, but it seemed impossible to break out of the examination gridlock. I enjoyed the company of the students and of my colleagues, but not the more formal aspects of heavily structured and bureaucratized worlds.

When I began to do research, it was invariably into subjects about individuals' struggles within and against those worlds, like deviance and disruption, survival strategies, stress and burnout, teacher and pupil careers. At first, I focused on secondary schools – the area of my most recent experience. Gradually, however, I worked my way back to primary schools, where I have been researching for the past ten years. I see now three main reasons for this. One is that my researches indicated the need to explore earlier stages of the pupil career to understand it fully. Another was the growing desire to research into more positive educational experiences than the largely negative ones that had so dominated sociological research of the 1960s and 1970s, and primary schools are generally recognized as containing more of those. A third was the attraction of engaging with that old mystery of how primary teachers achieved the amazing things they did, which, among other things, might enlighten a key moment in my own life history.

THE ADOPTION OF ETHNOGRAPHY

The discovery of interpretative sociology

There was a large measure of serendipity about my induction into ethnography. I had been teaching for seven years, and had been given a year's sabbatical to take a diploma course in 'secondary education'. The course was interesting enough, but unexciting. It was largely locked into positivistic and quantitative frameworks. There was, however, one hugely exciting event during that year, though it was not picked up in any of the coursework. This was the publication of David Hargreaves' book *Social Relations in a Secondary School* (1967). After the hundreds of widespread surveys, remote analyses, systematic and statistical methods texts, abstruse theoretical works and other depersonalized volumes, here was a book about real people and real life in school. It was rigorous, but also accessible and vibrant. You felt that you knew these boys and their teachers. You had met others just like them. In fact, there was a bit of them in you yourself. 'Clint' and his gang were the terrors of the school. But another refreshing feature of the book was how the problem was not seen as residing in the boys but in the streaming practices of the school. These practices 'differentiated' pupils into groups which then 'polarized' into opposing 'pro' and 'anti' school subcultures. Almost at a stroke, therefore, here was a possibility of a legitimate means of relating to, and sympathizing with, a mass of pupils who in many quarters were regarded as hopeless and rebellious deviants. Some teachers had regarded me like that when I was at school. Hargreaves gave them a voice, afforded them dignity, and pointed the finger at school organization.

Hargreaves' book was an eye-opener, but its lessons for me were not consolidated until two years later, when I enrolled for a masters course (part-time, while still teaching) in which Frank Musgrove taught the sociology. He brought his own brand of sceptical, critical, iconoclastic wit and intelligence to the application of sociology to education, at times standing 'reality' on its head and/or indulging in an outrageous forecast. He 'made the familiar strange', highlighting certain aspects of school life that many had taken for granted as 'normal' and 'unexceptional'. His dry humour, his debunking of pretension, his humanity, were all endearing qualities. From him I acquired a grounding in sociology, and an introduction to the work of Durkheim, Weber and Goffman. More than this, however, were the subtle insights that he made occasionally into the everyday and what had hitherto appeared to me ordinary and sometimes trivial life of the school. Musgrove was intrigued by social interaction and sought to understand conflict, contradiction and inconsistency. The pettiness of the staff room, the strange behaviour of the deputy head, the underlife of institutions, different kinds of discipline, all came under his gaze. It appeared that many things that previously had been explained psychologically had sociological causes, like suicide, vandalism, truancy, bullying, misbehaviour. Musgrove introduced us, too, to cultures and subcultures (putting the Hargreaves work into context). I recall one talk he gave about the 'Hippies', whom he had studied on a recent visit to America. He noted how a prominent, unifying, concept among them was that of 'garbage'. His study of the hippie subculture was typically ethnographic, though he did not call it that, identifying its major interests of purity, naturalism, emotion and immediacy, and its opposition to the bogus, to pollution, to bureaucracy, and to the industrial–military complex. Musgrove had found a means of getting to know a subculture, its values, beliefs, interests and how these were encoded in speech and behaviour. But he also sought to understand them as a product of contemporary society, with changing employment patterns, the growth of automation, and huge, impersonal, companies. Here was an attempt to overcome that classic sociological problem of linking micro with macro. If one could find a way of getting to know this apparently exotic group, why not others, some of which seemed equally beyond the pale of society (or school), but were in fact a product of it?

Not only had these developments provided enlightenment about others, but I had also discovered much about myself. Light began to dawn on some of the mysteries of my childhood and youth, such as the strict gender differentiation of our family structure; the antipathy of some of my grammar school teachers; the pains and pleasures of marginality; the pervasiveness of rhetoric and ideologies masquerading as truth; the fallibility of experts; and the misuse of power. I found out more, too, about myself as a teacher – how much of my activity was alienated through the pressure of the examination system; why some of my great aspirations conceived in the privacy of my home were dashed to pieces in the classroom; how, on occasions, I had been guilty of blaming and 'labelling' pupils (and even head teachers), pushing them in the direction of the label; how different factors and circumstances produced different modes of adaptation among pupils. My view of my colleagues also changed. I recognized their subcultures, patterns of hierarchies, ways of coping. Sociology had opened up a new world. More light now dawned and more complex tools became available through the discovery of symbolic interactionism.

The discovery of symbolic interactionism

Following the course with Musgrove, I took up a position at the Open University. Here in the early 1970s, the radical new course 'School and Society' was being prepared. This was to help disseminate news of the so-called 'new sociology of education'. This was a reaction against the structural-functionalism that had come to predominate in the 'old' discipline. Sociology of education in Britain had only begun in the 1950s, and had been chiefly concerned with measuring input–output factors (that is to say pupil home background and pupil achievement) using mainly survey techniques. Important work was done, but this approach ignored the processes and structures of what lay between input and output, that is the school itself, and its methods were inappropriate for their study. The 'new sociology of education', of which the Hargreaves book was a precursor, focused attention on the social construction of action and knowledge *within* schools and classrooms (as opposed to being 'determined' by external forces).

The 'new sociology' was soon to divide into a more deterministic, Marxist-oriented line, and a more interactionist one. There were divisions within these also, the interactionists developing groups in ethnomethodology (influenced mainly by Garfinkel and Cicourel), phenomenology (of which the main influences were Schutz and Husserl), and symbolic interaction. I was attracted to the last of these. It seemed to me to offer just the kind of intellectual equipment needed to explore some of the mysteries of social interaction in the school that interested me. By this time, my own experience as a teacher and as a researcher had led me to view much teaching as practised in our schools as an art. Teaching, in many of its aspects as practised today, is expressive and emergent, intuitive and flexible, spontaneous and emotional (Woods and Jeffrey, 1996). This is not to say that, in some important respects, teaching is not a science, or that the scientific study of teaching has not much to offer. But teaching as art has, on the whole, received less coverage, perhaps because of the prevalence of scientific paradigms in research. I elaborate on teaching as science and teaching as art in Chapter 1.

Just as the city was a natural social laboratory for the Chicago School of symbolic interactionists (Burgess, 1929), so the school became a natural field centre for those of us interested in this side of the 'new sociology'. It contained a horde of riches, the same kind of 'secret' and 'surprise' that Robert Park had spoken about with regard to the city of Chicago (see Bulmer, 1984). Social organization in this approach is seen as a negotiated order which emerges as people try to solve the problems they encounter in concrete situations. One asks, therefore, what are the problems teachers face as they see them? How are they experienced, what meanings are given to them and what feelings generated? Finally, how are they resolved? Interactionists look at how people 'carve out autonomy despite their lack of formal power' (McCall and Wittner, 1990, p. 70). The emphasis is upon the construction of meanings and perspectives, the adaptation to circumstances, the management of interests in the ebb and flow of countless interactions containing many ambiguities and conflicts, the strategies devised to promote those interests, and the negotiation with others' interests that is a common feature of all teaching situations.

Ethnography, with its emphases on respecting the empirical world, penetrating layers of meaning, facilitating 'taking the role of the other', defining situations and grasping a sense of process, is the natural methodology for such an approach, and for seeking to understand the 'art of teaching'. The practice of ethnography itself, ideally, is both a science and an art. It is an open approach, not pre-determined, inductive more often than deductive, with theory generated and grounded in the data. Ethnographers do not know what they will find. Initial work is typically messy and chaotic, until themes begin to emerge. Ethnography is an act of faith, requiring strong initial commitment. Some prefer the security of more systematic methods.

New directions

During the 1970s and 1980s there were a large number of ethnographic studies in the UK mapping out the interactionist terrain of the school (see Woods, 1990a, 1990b, for summaries). Towards the end of the 1980s, attention turned away from open ethnographic approaches concerned to find out 'what was going on here', and towards nominated problems and issues, such as the effect of examinations, curriculum practice, gender and racial differentiation. The impact of the 'New Right' policies of the Thatcher administrations, culminating in the Education Reform Act of 1988 and subsequent legislation, have effectively directed studies since, and engendered a new branch of the discipline in 'policy sociology', in which ethnography has played its part (Ball, 1990b).

At the same time, some argue that we are undergoing a revolution in approach to qualitative research, matching the developments that are overtaking the postmodernist world. The strongest expression of this is in Denzin and Lincoln (1994). They argue that there have been a number of epochs or 'moments' in qualitative research, depending on shifts in ontological and epistemological orientation:

1   the 'traditional' moment (1900–50) of classical, realist ethnography, as in Chicago School sociology;
2   the 'modernist' moment (1950–70), featuring the attempted integration and systematization of qualitative with quantitative research methods;
3   a 'blurred genres' moment (1970–85), marked by diverse approaches ranging from symbolic interactionism to critical theory;
4   a 'crisis of representation' moment (1986–90), querying the classic objectivist foundations of ethnographic knowledge and calling for a more discursive, reflexive turn;
5   the 'postmodern' moment (1990–now) in which theories are read as multivocal stories focused primarily on social criticism and critique.

I do not see the world in this paradigmatic way. Symbolic interactionism seems to me to provide a sufficiently broad ontological and epistemological base to accommodate most if not all of these approaches, which, over the years, have shown both limitations and new opportunities in the area. While few would still subscribe to a view that there is an objective reality that is totally knowable, the modified view of 'critical', 'analytical' or 'subtle' realism – that is that there is an objective reality, but it can be apprehended only imperfectly – is still persuasive (Altheide and Johnson, 1994). Qualitative research in such areas is interested in both objectivity and subjectivity. How people think and feel, how they interpret and how they construct meanings are integral to the approach. It is exactly the same as 'the avowed humanistic commitment to study the social world from the perspective of the interacting individual', which Lincoln and Denzin (1994, p. 575) see as still one of the prominent features of their view of qualitative research. It is from such material that 'subtle' conceptions of reality are constructed by the researcher. What the new approaches have done is to offer new ways of apprehending those subjectivities, aesthetically and emotionally as well as cognitively; to emphasize the subjects' and readers' engagement with the research and with the text respectively; and to bring more into consideration the researcher's own subjectivity and position as researcher. They enable us to appreciate better the 'art' of teaching. These subjectivities were not totally absent from 'traditional' and 'modernist' moments, and their extension was not debarred by any paradigmatic boundaries, rather simply inhibited by the customary slow and cautious rate of progress. To abandon the gains of those periods, and to concentrate exclusively upon subjectivities, seems to be denying the possibility of a science of teaching. We would be back in the retrogressive position whereby science and art became separated in the first place (see Chapter

1). What we have now is an opportunity to study teaching in the round in both its scientific and artistic aspects, without engaging in specious argument about whether it constitutes exclusively one or the other. As Denzin and Lincoln (1994, p. 577) aver, we are all concerned with 'how best to describe and interpret the experiences of other people and cultures'. And most of us would find a home somewhere among the contributors to the scene-setting *Handbook of Qualitative Research*, who:

> deploy constructivist, critical theory, feminist, ethnic, racial and cultural studies models of interpretation. They locate themselves on the borders between postpositivism and poststructuralism. They use any and all of the research strategies (case study, ethnography, phenomenology, grounded theory, biographical, historical, participatory and clinical) discussed in Part 3 of the Handbook. As bricoleurs, the members of the group are adept at using all of the methods of collecting and analysing empirical materials discussed by the authors of the chapters in Part 4 of the Handbook. And, as writers and interpreters, these individuals wrestle with positivist, postpositivist, poststructural and postmodern criteria for evaluating their written work.
>
> (Denzin and Lincoln, 1995, p. 350)

This could almost be a summary of what is happening within qualitative research generally, and it certainly seems to borrow quite heavily from the previous 'moments' in qualitative research history that Denzin and Lincoln identified. The effect of these recent critiques, therefore, in my view, is not to undermine interactionist ethnography, as some of their advocates claim, but to strengthen it, making it an even more potent methodological force for the issues that now confront the educational world (see Farberman, 1991, for extended discussion of this view; also Luscher, 1990; Schwalbe, 1993; Shalin, 1993; Katovich and Reese, 1993). I hope to demonstrate some of these advantages in the course of this book.

ETHNOGRAPHY FOR EDUCATIONAL USE

My own experiences, background and personality dispose me towards principles of freedom, equality and justice as they are understood in moderate left-wing politics. I am fascinated by the struggle of human agency against the forces of structure and society. I have empathy for those labelled as 'deviants' or 'delinquents', and an interest in the circumstances that produce such actions and reactions. I am excited by the flowering of human capabilities and dismayed at their inhibition. My research is aimed at promoting the first and removing or limiting the effects of the second. The teaching that I believe is best suited to serve these ends is creative, critical and relevant. This does not exclude so-called traditional methods for certain purposes; for example, equipping with basic skills and knowledge in order that children – and teachers – may learn to be creative and critical. The best form of education, in my opinion, is comprehensive. Selective education simply reinforces existing divisions, existing inequalities and injustices. I tend to be supportive of teachers, particularly those who care for children and for the kind of teaching and learning that I have described. I greatly admire charismatic teachers, and much of my later research has been directed towards trying to understand the character and sources of their charisma. But there is something of the sociologist's natural inclination, too, to support the 'underdogs' here (Becker, 1967), teachers having occupied this position vis-a-vis the central government ever since the 'New Right's' rout of the teacher unions in the mid-1980s. There is also a sense of collegiality, not only because of my own experiences, but also because all 'educationists', and a great deal of what they all stand for, have been included in the government's assault. Teachers and researchers at all levels are thus political allies in the struggle for control of the educational agenda. Further, I know how conditions can affect aspirations, and I have seen conditions for teaching deteriorate particularly over the last decade.

My research career has followed two broad phases. In terms of the general research models discussed earlier, my first studies followed an 'enlightenment' model. That is to say, the aim was to contribute to knowledge, and to aid understanding of particular issues or aspects of school life. The most potent form of understanding that I might contribute I saw as coming from sociological theory. The ultimate task, therefore, was to develop theory from the data. How that theory, or even how one's case studies, applied to classroom practice did not lie within my professional boundaries. That was the teacher's concern. However, there is a well-known gulf between teacher activity and academic research, and between teaching practice and theory (McNamara, 1976; Degenhardt, 1984; Day, 1995; Eisenberg, 1995). Also, educational research has little effect on government policy; indeed, it is more often used selectively to fuel government discourse (see, for example, Chapter 7). It all, therefore, seemed remote from teachers' practice and the issues of everyday life in classrooms. This, of course, is exactly the field of play of ethnographic research in schools. If one approach could bridge that gap, and become both a theoretical and practical aid to teachers in their work, surely ethnography could.

I therefore moved into a second phase, one of looking more closely at the implications of my research for teachers and their practice. I hoped that it was still enlightening, but I was becoming more interested in its use. I have discussed some aspects of this in Chapter 1 of Woods (1986; see also Denscombe, 1995). I argued there that ethnography offers teachers access to research, control over it, and results that they consider worthy and of practical use in their teaching. The ways in which I have followed up those points in my own work all rest, in some form or other, upon collaboration between researcher and teacher. The principles that underpin this derive partly from the conviction that if educational improvement is to be made through research, it has to be done by teachers; and partly from the growth in emphasis upon professional development and practitioner reflectivity (Schön, 1983). Also, under the influence of the critical theorists, researchers were becoming increasingly dubious about the ethics of research on, as opposed to with, teachers. I have discussed and included illustrations of collaborative work between teachers and researchers in Woods and Pollard (1988) and Woods (1989). Another major area of development in ethnography along these lines has been the attention given to teacher self-knowledge and identity, through research on teacher careers (Sikes et al., 1985) and teacher life-histories and biographies (Woods, 1987a; Woods and Sikes, 1987; Woods, 1993c). In this book, I give some examples of how collaboration has worked in my recent research.

In some ways, this might seem to represent a departure from sociology's traditional concern with critique. For those researchers whose chief aim is educational improvement (in contrast, for example, to the 'pursuit of knowledge', or more distinctly political aims), a continuing concentration on shortcomings and failure in schools and classrooms has limitations (though there have been notable advances through teachers and some local authorities, in areas, for example, of gender and racial differentiation). From more general and open ethnography, through research more directed at problem issues, it is a small step to research on educational successes. If these can be identified within existing conditions, there is considerable merit in portraying their nature in the detailed and intimate terms that ethnography permits, and in analysing the conditions in which they arise. This is a bottom-up, grounded approach, which first locates the empirical cases, taking care to specify the criteria by which they are selected, and then employs a range of theories to portray and explain them. However, the concentration on educational successes by no means entails the abandonment of criticism. They are researched with the same attention to rigour and/or quality as any other activity. This kind of study might be seen as a distinctive contribution to school effectiveness and school improvement research, areas largely characterized so far by quantitative approaches.

These, then, are some of the 'personal realities' that have guided me in my research.

ORGANIZATION OF THE BOOK

In Chapter 1, I consider the nature of teaching. Is it a science or an art, or, perhaps, some of each? In some ways, though a popular topic, this is a false question. We cannot consider this as a culture- and value-free zone, for the activity is what a teacher makes it. I take as a baseline manifestation of teaching in Western societies in recent years, and the major theories and approaches that have informed it. But mainly I am guided by what teachers actually do in classrooms, how they carry out the act of teaching. I argue that it does contain a large artistic component.

Symbolic interactionism, especially in conjunction with some postmodernist techniques, provides excellent opportunities to research both the science and the art of teaching. Interactionism places emphasis on the role of the self and the hidden assumptions behind appearance. It questions the nature of knowledge and concentrates on process. In Chapter 2, I spell out the basic principles of symbolic interactionism and their methodological implications. I trace the involvement of the researcher's self through various stages of data collection and analysis, and show how, in this approach, the whole research process, including theory building, is grounded in the empirical world.

Some potential benefits to ethnography emerging from the current interest in postmodernism are discussed in Chapter 3. The keenest advocates of a postmodernist approach argue for a new epistemology, abandonment of Enlightenment principles embodied in traditional scientific enquiry with its emphasis on reason, purposive rationality and ultimate truth, and a completely new order involving redefinition or abandonment of traditional principles of research as 'validity'. A. Hargreaves (1993, p. 22) argues

> In the postmodern world, multiple rather than singular forms of intelligence are coming to be recognized . . . multiple rather than singular forms of representation of students' work are being advocated and accepted . . . .Many ways of knowing, thinking and being moral, not just rational, 'logical' ones, are coming to be seen as legitimate.

My own view is to see these largely as an extension of method and of modes of representation within the interactionist field, rather than an alternative paradigm. In particular, there appear to be exciting chances of developing methods for researching the art of teaching. I rehearse some of these in Chapter 3. Chapter 4 then consists of an extended example of the application of such methods in our current research on the effects of school inspections on primary teachers and their work.

One of the new emphases in research is on collaboration, on giving teachers and students 'voice', and on 'democratic validation'. Dadds (1995, p. 115) argues that the latter becomes 'less a competition for power and the ultimate dominant judgement, more a reflective exploration of worthwhileness as viewed from several exchanged positions of interest'. In my research on 'critical events' in education, I engaged in collaborative work with teachers and students, and employed some democratic evaluation. Since such events bring radical change and development in both pupils and teachers, I saw them as the best judges of just what change had occurred; and I also valued their views on how I had represented that change in the text. In Chapter 5, I discuss some of the prominent features of my research on such events. Basically, the exercise was one of 'historical ethnography', using a range of qualitative techniques on things that had happened in the recent past. The work was collaborative, with teachers, pupils and other critical agents combining with the researcher to reconstruct and analyse the event. Evaluation focused on expressive outcomes, the report using a large measure of teachers' and pupils' own articulations. Respondent validation was considered important, though within the context of other tests of validity. One of these is the ability of the research to strengthen the participants in their work, and to influence other practitioners – in other words, for the research to share in the criticality of the event.

It seemed appropriate that one chapter in the book should be on the writing process itself. There are now several excellent texts available on this subject (for example, Becker, 1986; Wolcott, 1990a; Richardson, 1990), and I have written before on the subject (Woods, 1986). But it seemed to me that there was more to be said about the psychological processes involved in connection with the use of the tools that we choose to use in our work. The link between these and the researcher's self and identity, and the ability to work artistically, has been little explored, yet it is crucial to this most difficult stage of the research process. It seems even more topical since the business of research and writing has become revolutionized through the introduction of computers and word processors, but most of the discussion of this is concerned with technical application (see, for example, Tesch, 1990). There has been little discussion of the general influence of writing implements on research, yet, as I argue in Chapter 6, these – and indeed word processors – are very much more than instrumental conduits from the researcher's mind to the paper on which he or she writes.

Finally, in Chapter 7 I turn to dissemination, though I do not consider the delivery of research so much as its reception. The chapter is a reminder that researching teaching, whether as science or art or both, does not take place in a political vacuum, both in a macro and micro sense. What happens to work when it is finished and published – and even, sometimes, before, when differing influences are brought to bear? How is it interpreted and used? No matter how we might strive for 'contributing to knowledge' or 'educational improvement', different interest groups can use research for different purposes to those intended by the researcher. Education and politics are frequently inseparable, and the latter often predominates in unforeseen, uncomfortable and educationally counter-productive ways. However, the responses of diverse audiences to one's work can be very instructive for a researcher. It can alert the writer to the different meanings that can be attributed to it. In turn, those can enhance one's understanding of events, as well as the chosen means of representation.

1 The art and science of teaching

INTRODUCTION: THE ISSUE

Is teaching a science or an art? The question, in one form or another, has long intrigued educationists. In essence, the debate is about whether teaching is an activity where some general laws or principles can be identified, and which can be understood in scientific terms, facilitating planning or prediction; or whether it is largely an individualistic, intuitive, spontaneous process, involving so many factors that it is impossible to specify general lines of direction, and producing work of creative imagination. It is a small step from here to another popular, intriguing question: are teachers born or made? If teaching is knowable in scientific terms, it can be taught. We can build on knowledge, cumulate wisdom, get better and better. If it is to do chiefly with inherent abilities, instinct, imagination and emotion, then it might be argued that people either have these abilities or dispositions or they do not.

The debate, too, might be identified, to some extent, with the progressive–traditional issue, which reveals some implications for teacher practice. The former approach favours learning by discovery and through play, creative activity, learning through doing, holism and integration; the latter emphasizes instruction, factual knowledge organized by academic discipline, systematization, structured learning, clear objectives, formal testing (Bell, 1981). In some respects this is a false dichotomy, for most teachers appear to show aspects of both. But the tensions are still there. For example, in the debate leading up to the 1988 Education Reform Act, there were complaints about the loss of teachers' artistic qualities (Brighouse, 1987; Barker, 1987).

Educational aims and methods are inevitably value-led, concerned with the kind of society we wish to promote, and the kind of education best suited to that aim. We might ask whether, over and above the values, there is a purer heart of education. Whatever the ends, are they best promoted by scientific or artistic means? I shall examine the cases for teaching as a science and as an art, before trying to draw a conclusion.

TEACHING AS SCIENCE

The objectives model

To say that teaching is a science is to say that it is a rational activity, subject to general principles and laws, that are discoverable through research. As we come to know them, so teaching can become more systematic, structured and stable. Our aims are inevitably value-oriented, but, as J.S. Mill observed, we have to 'hand [our ends] over to science' for the best methods of achieving them. The more clearly we can specify our aims, the better. In one form, such thinking promotes the rational planning of a curriculum by objectives, which are harder-edged and more precise than general aims, and which, preferably, can be measured. This 'behavioural-objectives' model is the most prominent example of this approach, defining education as the 'changing of behaviour' (which includes thinking and feeling). As Sockett (1976, p. 17) points out, 'By eliminating the value aspect from the definition, the processes of education can be tackled by science. Furthermore, by making objectives measurable, you can see exactly what has been achieved, and what more needs to be done.'

Some have felt that these techniques are more appropriate for 'training' than for 'education', that they form a constraining strait-jacket on teachers, and ignore the educational worth of processes as opposed to ends (Stenhouse, 1975). They are about efficiency more than educational quality. Nor can they so easily be separated from values. Specifying objectives is useful for teacher accountability as well as assessing student achievement. The whole framework seems ready-made for the marketing ideology that has informed government policy in the 1980s and 1990s (Ball, 1993). In short, the objectives model may represent a scientific means, but in respect of a highly specific and limited view of education.

The knowledge base of teaching

In an attempt to conceive of teaching in a more comprehensive way and from the point of view of the teacher, for the purposes of teacher training, Shulman (1986, 1987) advances a 'knowledge-base' model. The knowledge base, in summary, consists of content knowledge, general pedagogical knowledge, curriculum knowledge, pedagogical content knowledge, knowledge of learners, educational contexts, educational ends, purposes and values. To take one example, pedagogical content knowledge includes

The most useful forms of representation of those ideas, the most powerful analogies, illustrations, examples, explanations and demon-strations – in a word, the ways of representing and formulating the subject that makes it comprehensible to others. Since there are no single most powerful forms of representation, the teacher must have at hand a veritable armamentarium of alternative forms of representation, some of which derive from research whereas others originate in the wisdom of practice.

(1986, p. 9)

Shulman maps out the area rather like early cartographers, who knew where to look and could sketch outlines, though without precision. The next part of the enterprise will be for researchers to 'collect, collate and interpret the practical knowledge of teachers for the purposes of establishing and codifying its principles, precedents and parables' (1987, p. 12). Shulman is keen that the 'knowledge-base approach does not produce an overly technical image of teaching, a scientific enterprise that has lost its soul' (p. 20) – as perhaps it did under the objectives model. He clearly recognizes the circumstantial nature of teachers' knowledge. Some feel that, in practice, he has 'begun to build a new educational science, a new foundational knowledge-base for teaching' (Hargreaves, 1994a, p. 19).

A socio-historical explanation

If Shulman points to the possibilities, why has it not been done before? Both teaching and science have been around for some time. Simon (1988) provides an historical answer. In an article entitled 'Why no pedagogy in England?' (where 'pedagogy' means 'science of teaching'), he argues that such a concept has become 'alien to our experience and way of thinking' (p. 336). He is critical, for example, of the now defunct Schools Council (1964–81), whose work he asserts was informed by no science of teaching, no theories of the child or learning, and was in consequence doomed. Why is the concept of pedagogy shunned in this way? It is not because of any intrinsic defects or inadequacies in science, nor because of poor teaching, but, argues Simon, because of social and political factors. In the nineteenth century, one of these was the influence of the dominant elite institutions – the ancient universities and the leading public schools – which saw the profession of teaching as a gentlemanly one, not requiring training as such, but learning through experience for those with the 'appropriate social origins' (p. 337). The main purpose of these schools was socialization, and the formation of character. Teachers, students and parents of these schools formed a common, self-perpetuating culture. Also, in the two leading universities of Oxford and Cambridge, education, until recently, has had a low profile – low prestige, few resources for research, lack of quality output.

Simon feels there was a great opportunity towards the end of the century, with the publication of Alexander Bain's book *Education as a Science* (first published 1879, reprinted sixteen times before 1900), where a programme was laid out for the scientific study of such things as child development, the purposes and principles of curriculum, motivation and discipline. However, the early 1900s saw the demise of the elementary school (which might have made a good forum for the development of pedagogy) as a vehicle for mass education, and the rise of the local authority secondary schools, which required children to be differentiated at the end of elementary education. Elementary education became a matter of containment; and the emphasis on selection bred a preoccupation with mental measurement, and psychometric theories which laid stress on inherited ability.

Simon goes on to specify conditions for a science of teaching – mainly a recognition that the process of learning is similar for all human beings, and that therefore there are some general principles that can be identified. This should be our starting point – identifying what children and teachers have in common (see also Galton, 1989). Unfortunately, he argues, we have been diverted in the past twenty-five years into concentrating on children's differences. This has been due to a large extent to the overwhelming influence of the Plowden Report (1967), which stressed the uniqueness of every child. However, instead of revolutionizing teaching in the romantic way envisaged therein, it has been argued that child-centredness developed into an ideology which came to exert a constraining influence on teachers' careers and cultures (Alexander 1984, 1992). Alexander explains:

> Ideology – a group's array of central ideas, values and beliefs – is a key element in any culture because it serves to define, justify and control a culture's members . . . properly to belong one needed to accept and enact the ideology.

> (1992, p. 169)

The grip of this ideology on primary teachers illustrates again the nature of teaching as a socially constructed activity. Many teachers felt that they had to pay it allegiance (careers and jobs depended on it), while practising pragmatically (and unscientifically and unartistically) in their classrooms (Simon and Willcocks, 1981).

Private troubles, public issues

Similarly, we have laboured under the idea that teaching is an individual activity. Until recently, autonomy in one's own classroom was a central feature of teacher culture (Hargreaves, 1980). Here one could develop the practices and strategies that marked one's own individual adaptation to the demands of teaching. We have a tendency, too, to celebrate the idiosyncratic, charismatic teacher. All the great teachers of the past were of this kind. Features in popular educational papers, such as the 'My Best Teacher' series in the *Times Educational Supplement*, encourage this mode of thought. However, we need to look at what teachers have in common. What are the regularities and patterns in their behaviour that permit us to see them as members of particular groups? What forms of reciprocal interaction take place between the teacher and these groups? What is there in a teacher's background, such as upbringing, schooling, home life, peer groups, personal experiences, that helps explain a teacher's behaviour? The 'charisma' of exceptional teachers might then be demonstrated as something learned and acquired, and available to others. Similarly, it might be shown that teaching weaknesses that might seem due to individual traits have other, stronger explanations. Societal and institutional factors, for example, can contribute to discipline problems within classrooms, though they are experienced as an individual concern. Social science reveals that what is a private trouble is a public issue (Mills, 1959), and it is at that level that it has to be tackled.

In yet another scenario, a teacher might appear to be giving a highly skilful and artistic performance. He weaves a spell with words, takes up the pupils' spontaneous questions, puts disparate things together imaginatively, uses space, timing and cadences of the voice, creates a suspenseful atmosphere, and most of the children seem to be enjoying the lesson and respond. However, systematic observation reveals that he has twice as many interactions with the boys as with the girls, that his examples and encouraged answers from the children in a multiethnic class are mono-ethnic, that the questions he asks favour middle-class pupils, that the pupils are not internalizing the teaching but engaging in coping strategies. This may be artistic teaching, but artistic for whom? The reality is less exciting, more uncomfortable and disturbing. We don't want to believe it. It threatens to take the edge off our own enjoyment. At worst, it threatens to undermine our own hard-won positions. These are all reasons why scientific explanations may be resisted. There are other reasons.

Opposition to science

The social and educational sciences are still young, and much of their early history has been taken up with a struggle for status in the universities. Philosophical bases have to be explored, methodological development and refinement set in hand. They are imperfect sciences (though it might be claimed that they are improving as the search for rigour and relevance goes on), and there have been questions raised about the failure or inconsequence of much educational research (Anning, 1986). Also, there has been a great deal of political opposition. Under the 'New Right' regime of the 1980s and early 1990s, 'educationists' have been branded as the villains in the alleged 'declining educational standards' saga. 'They've had their say, and they've had their day', announced Prime Minister Major at the Tory party conference of 1992. It is not difficult to account for such opposition. Sociology, for example, adopts a critical approach, identifies as ideologies (such as the 'New Right') what politicians regard as truth (often expressed as 'common sense'). Sociology shakes received, unsubstantiated opinion, and identifies and exposes questions of value. The best way of teaching, good teaching, the purpose of it, what pupils should learn – these are all issues on which people hold strong views. That they are questions of value is not always appreciated where they are held as articles of faith.

If some object to the social sciences' debunking and demystifying tendencies, there are others who claim that the social sciences, at times, do exactly the opposite. Thus Olson (1992, p. 91) has argued that science is often used to apply a dead hand to justify existing practices and policies, which are based on the 'best social science available'. Thus, the 'mystique of science is used to defend the reputation of the schools against criticism'. However, this will not work, for the simple reason that 'experts do not know the whole story; only a small part of it. Teachers know more.' This may be so, but it can be argued that it is still, in time, 'knowable' to others through scientific means. This kind of criticism is more, perhaps, one of how science is used, rather than against science itself.

Above all, perhaps, is the so-called 'two-cultures' mentality which continues to pervade society. Science, despite its enormous contributions and potential, remains the second culture. The public at large have little scientific understanding, more students still opt to study arts subjects at university, and the teaching of science itself in schools has a low reputation (*Guardian*, 25 September 1994, p. 23).

The promise of science

What then are the gains of seeing teaching as science? As a complex and difficult activity, teaching generates a great deal of myth, mystery, and homespun, pragmatic advice to new recruits. 'Never smile until Christmas' is a common recipe for coping through one's first term. Much rests on intuition and instinct which defy rational explanation: 'It just seemed right to do it that way.' However, social science demystifies and enlightens. It establishes the nature and purpose of myths like 'never smile', showing them to contain a kernel – but only a kernel – of truth, but functioning as warnings and guides to action, and appealing to emotional states. It offers to explain the apparently unexplainable. In some ways teaching may be not unlike primitive societies in the guarded mysteries of its culture, standing to gain in similar ways from systematic study:

> In arriving at an understanding of how such societies work, anthropologists have inevitably thrown a flood of light on general principles of social organization and have enabled us to see how, on the one hand, apparently exotic customs are simply ways of coping with common human problems that we handle in different ways.
>
> (Worsley et al., 1977, pp. 30–31)

Similarly, sociologists show how the daily lives of individuals are connected to broader systems of organization in wider society, and how those lives are distinguished by order and regularities, rather than adventitious, unconnected events. As Worsley et al. note,

> In order to understand these interconnections in the world 'out there', we need a body of theory which itself is systematic. We cannot, in social science, operate effectively with bits and pieces of ideas unconnected to each other, as we often tend to do in everyday life.
>
> (ibid., p. 54)

Science depoliticizes, identifying values, ideologies, the micro-political nature of school life, and the strategies deployed in the furtherance of aims. It provides information, explanation, and intellectual tools for understanding social action, for delineating and solving problems, and for planning according to our preferred choices. Used in the service of human understanding it is a creative, imaginative activity that sometimes reveals something surprising, and can energize and inspire. There is nothing cold about the descriptions of warmth and care for their children experienced by primary teachers (Nias, 1989); or in the excitement and inspiration felt during particularly promising or rewarding teaching (Woods, 1993a); or in the analyses of humour as a teaching accessory (Stebbins, 1980). Science is not the only factor involved, since

> decisions, in the end, will be made as the outcome of sets of complex pressures from many kinds of people: idea-mongers, power-wielders, organized citizens, etc., not social scientists alone, and not only on the basis of knowledge or reason.
>
> (Worsley et al., 1977, p. 69)

But it provides a good basis, and offers a means of assessing the consequences of those decisions.

TEACHING AS ART

The limitations of science

The view of teaching as a rational and stable activity amenable to scientific methods is one that has been created by social scientists; but it is not one that has been recognized by teachers. Indeed, teachers' views have sometimes directly contradicted research, even that involving very large samples (see, for example, Denscombe et al., 1986). Eisner (1985, p. 91) speaks of the 'yearning for prediction through control' and the 'drive to discover the laws of learning' in the quest for effective schools that has characterized many of the approaches to educational evaluation this century. He argues that this was based on a particular, nomothetic view of person. Science has undoubtedly made important contributions in education, but it has also had some bad effects. In particular, it has oversimplified complex situations; prioritized the future (in the form of objectives) over the present (process); objectified knowledge, seeing it purely as cognitively grasped and quantifiably measurable; and bred standardization and uniformity. However, teaching is a socially constructed activity (Adelman, 1988). Schooling itself is a cultural artifact, and education a process whose features may change from individual to individual, context to context (Eisner, 1985, p. 91).

Science also, in large measure, is a socially constructed activity. Consider, for example, the cold-eyed, disembodied, male-oriented scientism that characterized prominent approaches to teaching during the 1960s and 1970s (Casey and Apple, 1989). These saw the improvement of teaching being reliant on developments in technology, and held a deficit view of teachers. Such accounts, still widely regarded as classics, hardly penetrate the surface of the complex activity of teaching. More recent studies of teachers, and particularly women teachers (for example, Acker, 1989; de Lyon and Migniuolo, 1989), have shown the barrenness of those approaches. But are not more modern attempts at scientific appraisals, like Shulman's, more promising? Not according to A. Hargreaves. For him, such attempts

> conjure certainty from uncertainty. They build a science from a craft. They answer a modern problem (threatened professional status and peripheralization from the university) with a modern solution (reinvention of scientific certainty as an aspiration to higher-order foundational knowledge). What we can claim to know about teaching becomes defined by what we wish to regulate and control.
>
> (1994a, p. 19)

Elsewhere (1994b), Hargreaves heralds the demise of 'reason and purposive rationality'. Disillusionment with them has set in with 'the uncertainties, complexities and rapid change of the postmodern world, along with growing awareness of the perverted realizations of science in war, weaponry and environmental disaster' (1994b, p. 28). Science has made important contributions to our understanding of teaching, but in relation to current realities, it can only reach a part, and not necessarily the most important part, of the activity.

Features of an artistic approach to teaching

What, then, does that activity consist of? The following are prominent features.

Multiple forms of understanding and representation

Eisner argues that 'rationality has been conceived of as scientific in nature, and cognition has been reduced to knowing in words; as a result, alternative views of knowledge and mind have been omitted in the preparation of teachers' (1993, p. 264). Such alternatives exist in 'poetry and pictures, literature and dance, mathematics and literal statement'. Abbs (1989, p. 15) adds 'our quite remarkable abilities to sequence narratives, to construe analogically, to conceive figuratively, to consider tonally, to think musically, to construct maps and diagrams, to make signs and symbols with our bodies' (see also Gardner, 1983; Noddings, 1992). Highet (1951) points to the irrationality of some of this:

> Painters do not copy what they see, but select very carefully, and the elements which they choose to select carry a meaning, all the more powerful for being sometimes irrational....What visual artists like painters want to teach is easy to make out but difficult to explain. They can hardly ever explain themselves, because they put their experiences into shapes and colours, not words.
>
> (p. 243)

This seems to be at the opposite extreme to scientific certainty. It would appear, therefore, that an important part of teaching is 'not knowing'. Moloney (1994) expresses this well in his treatment of a poem by Walter de la Mare:

> We had been reading 'The Listeners'. It's a wonderful poem to look into with children of any age. So much mystery. So many unanswered questions. And the eerie heart of the poem, the throng of phantoms ranged in tiers on the stairway of the empty house utterly unmoved by the mortal banging on the door.... It's an image to enrich the subconscious and stay with you for a lifetime.
>
> (p. xii)

Would it be useful to have the poet appear to clarify the mystery? No, because if he did 'explain the enigma, then he'd kill the poem stone dead': 'Doubt, ambiguity, uncertainty, unspoken implication, innuendo, it's these imprecisions, these echo chambers which breathe life into literature... leading us to the edge of what we know' (ibid.).

In these areas, explanation closes down, whereas it is important to convey to students' minds how much we do not know, leaving 'the imagination free to create and fill the dark spaces' (ibid.). Perhaps the art of teaching here lies in the teacher's professional judgement in circumstances where there is no 'right answer' (Tripp, 1993), and where we 'get to know' through all our senses, not just mind. (On the more general application of 'poetic thinking', see Bonnett, 1991.) Egan (1994, p. 203) consequently suggests we think less of 'efficiency in teaching' and more of 'imaginative engagement in student learning'.

Expression and emergence

In describing teaching as an art, Stenhouse (1985, p. 105) said that he meant that it was 'an exercise of skill expressive of meaning .... It expresses in a form accessible to learners an understanding of the nature of that which is to be learned.' It is essentially a 'personal construction created from socially available resources and it cannot be imparted by others or to others in a straightforward manner' (p. 106). The teacher's art is expressed through performance:

> There is in education no absolute and unperformed knowledge. In educational research and scholarship, the ivory towers where the truth is neglected are so many theatres without players, galleries without pictures, music without musicians. Educational knowledge exists in, and is verified or falsified in, its performance.
>
> (p. 110)

Carr (1989), discussing the work of Schwab (1969), elaborates on what is involved in performance:

> Teaching is primarily a 'practical' rather than a 'technical' activity, involving a constant flow of problematic situations which require teachers to make judgements about how best to transfer their general educational values ... into classroom practice. Interpreted in the language of the 'practical', 'teaching quality' would have little to do with the skilful application of technical rules but instead would relate to the capacity to bring abstract ethical values to bear on concrete educational practice – a capacity which teachers display in their knowledge of what, educationally, is required in a particular situation and their willingness to act so that this knowledge can take a practical form.
>
> (p. 5)

This is similar to Eisner's (1985) point about 'connoisseurship'. For Eisner, educational improvement comes not from the discovery of scientific methods that can be applied universally, or from particular personalities, but 'rather from enabling teachers ... to improve their ability to see and think about what they do' (p. 104), or in other words, their 'art of appreciation', a subtle ability to discriminate. This contributes to what Polanyi and Prosch (1975) describe as tacitly held practical conduct knowledge, or what Tripp (1993, p. 129) calls 'practical professionalism'. Tripp contrasts this with scientifically verified knowledge, which is still important, but cannot account for the expertise of all successful teachers. He writes, 'Is this not expertise which comes from intuition, experience and "right-mindedness" rather than scholarly disciplinary knowledge?' (p. 128).

Such teaching is expressive and emergent, and cannot be set up in advance through, for example, objectives. Some situations may call for this, but employed as a general framework it forecloses on so many possibilities and opportunities for educational advancement. Teaching requires ends to be created in process, in the 'course of interaction with students rather than preconceived and efficiently attained' (Eisner, 1979, p. 154). Such interactions

> are like jazz improvisations; you don't necessarily know who is going to play what, but when you hear it you have to follow on to make the music flow. Responses to the 'music' of classroom discussion are often a matter not of reflective practice – reflection here is much too slow – but a matter of instantaneous response to the qualitative immediacy of the events themselves.

Stenhouse (1985, pp. 80–81) elaborates on why he feels the objectives model is inappropriate in some areas. Objectives tend to be oversimplified and self-fulfilling; militate against teacher and student creativity; distort the intrinsic value of content and process; render problematic the investigation of exploratory areas; and discount the possibility of teacher development. While objectives may serve the acquisition of skills and information, they 'do not work in respect of knowledge, which is the heartland of the school curriculum'. This requires teacher judgement, but the objectives model treats the teacher as a kind of 'intellectual navvy, working on a site plan simplified so that people know exactly where to dig their trenches without knowing why' (p. 85).

Tom (1988), in consequence, argues that the effective teacher needs to be flexible, that is able to adapt her or his behaviour to the teaching situation, which is changeable and frequently unpredictable. In fact, 'the dynamic nature of teacher adaptability, mediating processes, and the teaching situation itself, means that we can recognise teaching effectiveness, if at all, only after the fact' (p. 49). There is not much hope here for the identification of general principles and regularities that Simon (1988), as discussed earlier, thinks is such an essential task. Indeed, that is a misconceived idea since it applies a 'purely technical perspective to phenomena intimately connected to underlying human purposes'. Tom concludes that research-based prescriptions do not make an effective teacher, but rather that such a one

> is able to conceive of his or her teaching in purposeful terms, analyse a particular teaching problem, choose a teaching approach that seems appropriate to the problem, attempt the approach, judge the results in relation to the original purpose, and reconsider either the teaching approach or the original purpose.
>
> (pp. 49–50)

He quotes Dewey in this context: 'Judgement and belief regarding actions to be performed can never attain more than a precarious probability.... Practical activity deals with individualized and unique situations which are never exactly duplicable and about which, accordingly, no complete assurance is possible' (Dewey, 1929, p. 6). Eisner (1979, p. 161) also notes that 'to say that excellence in teaching requires artistry implies that the teacher is able to exploit opportunities as they occur. It implies that goals and intentions be fluid' – in contrast to the single-mindedness and clarity of objectives required by rational planning. Teaching involves freedom to try out new ways, new activities, different solutions, some of which will inevitably fail. It is important that education provides that kind of opportunity and disposition to play, and to take it to the limit, for 'to be able to play with ideas is to feel free to throw them into new combinations, to experiment, and even "to fail"' (Eisner, 1979, p. 160). Play stimulates the educational imagination and increases the ability to see and take advantage of new opportunities.

Creativity

Best recommends what he calls the 'Personal Enquiry' approach, which involves developing qualities such as 'curiosity, originality, initiative, co-operation, perseverance, open-mindedness, self-criticism, responsibility, self-confidence and independence' (1991, p. 275). This is what makes a creative individual, imbued with the spirit of creative enquiry.

> What this means for students is not so much that they should know *about*, but that they should *know*, physics, mathematics, biology, history, etc. And this will include developing a feel, a sensitivity, a grasp, and a love for a subject, entering creatively into the *spirit* of an area of enquiry....In short, students...should be creative scientists.
>
> (Best, 1991, p. 269)

There are some who feel teaching is far removed from this kind of activity. For example, Willard Waller (1932), in his classic and widely influential text, painted a grim, unrelenting, depressing view of 'what teaching did to teachers'. It 'deadened the intellect', 'devoured its creative resources' (p. 391), made teachers 'inflexible' and 'unbending' (pp. 381–382), and 'reduced their personalities' (pp. 431–432). Though this text was written in the 1930s, there are echoes for some in current times with the trend towards the intensification of teachers' work, and the deskilling and deprofessionalization of teachers (Apple, 1986). However, while this may represent the reality for some, it is wide of the mark for others. Jackson (1992), for example, does not recognize Waller's description from his experience. He is convinced that teaching has made a big difference in his, and in others', lives. He cannot verify this against some external reality or conventional indicators. In considering what teaching has done for him, Jackson relies not on scientific evidence, but on intuition, what 'feels right' to him. This is far from being a matter of guesswork, and involves a host of factors to do with such things as principles, knowledge and experiences. It is to do, in short, with the sort of person he has become. It is clear that this is one with distinct artistic leanings.

Jackson notes that we must guard against excessive sentimentality, just as against Waller's extreme cynicism and despair. If we think in terms of the sort of person we wish to be and the kind of life we wish to lead, scientific objectivity is completely the wrong approach. What is needed is 'something more like a kindly bias, a forgiving eye, an attitude of appreciation, a way of looking that promotes the growth of sympathetic understanding' (p. 88). We must look at the minutiae of school life through an interpretative frame, cultivating 'a heightened sensitivity to the nuances of schooling' (p. 90).

Thus equipped, we would be better able to appreciate the beauty of teaching. Lincoln and Guba (1990, p. 55), in elaborating 'the art of craftsmanship', write of the 'power and elegance of a narrative, its grace and precision'. The same kind of description can be used of teaching. Highet (1951, p. 79) argues that teaching 'demands a good deal of artistic sense, and those teachers who plan their teaching best are usually marked by strong aesthetic sensibilities'. He mentions one who 'cannot utter a sentence without shaping it beautifully' (ibid.). We can expand that idea usefully to a whole lesson, or part of a lesson, which, as observers, we can marvel at as objects of beauty. The way a lesson unfolds, how a teacher creates atmosphere, uses a range of tones (Jeffrey and Woods, 1994), orchestrates conflicting elements in his or her role (Lieberman and Miller, 1984), balances priorities, dilemmas, pressures, and his or her own aims through exercising a complex and demanding skill (Nias, 1989), involves his or her whole self and the pupils likewise in situations where they realize their full identity – all of this involves teachers giving an 'aesthetic form to their existence through their own productive work' (Foucault, 1979).

Emotion

In contrast to the emphasis on rationality, teaching has an 'emotional heart'. A. Hargreaves (1994c) represents this as 'desire', which is

> imbued with 'creative unpredictability' and 'flows of energy'.... In desire is to be found the creativity and spontaneity that connects teachers emotionally... to their children, their colleagues and their work. Such desires among particularly creative teachers are for fulfil-ment, intense achievement, senses of breakthrough, closeness to fellow humans, even love for them .... Without desire, teaching becomes arid and empty. It loses its meaning.
>
> (p. 12)

Highet (1951, pp. vii–viii) makes a similar point. Teaching involves emotions, which cannot be systematically appraised and employed, and human values, which are quite outside the grasp of science.... 'Scientific' teaching, even of scientific subjects, will be inadequate as long as both teachers and pupils are human beings. Teaching is not like a chemical reaction; it is much more like painting a picture or making a piece of music.... You must throw your heart into it.

Some even feel strongly emotional about the issue. Carl Rogers (1983), for example, regrets that he cannot be 'coolly scientific' about the point, but 'can only be passionate in my statement that people count, that inter-personal relationships are important'. Better courses, curricula and technology can never release full human potential. 'Only persons acting like persons in their relationships with their students can ever begin to make a dent on this most urgent problem of modern education' (pp. 132–133). Such an approach involves

a transparent realness in the facilitator, a willingness to be a person, to be and live the feelings of the moment. When this realness includes a prizing, a caring, a trust and respect for the learner, the climate for learning is enhanced. When it includes a sensitive and accurate empathic listening, then indeed a freeing climate, stimulative of self-initiated learning and growth, exists.

(p. 133)

This does not mean that the use of emotion is undisciplined. As in drama, artistic teaching and learning provide opportunities for a range and depth of emotional expression, and these are associated with the search for truth and sincerity (Stanislavski, 1972). Teachers must mean what they say and do, and be clear in the expression of their emotions, thus encouraging similar responses and emotional discoveries among their students (Collingwood, 1966). Like a good story, they 'evoke a feeling that is best described as aesthetic; we are moved by what we hear just as we are moved, when the text is really good, by what we read. Great teachers, like great books, show us new vistas' (Eisner, 1995a, p. 11).

The emotional aspect of teaching is thus important in its own right. But it is also important for cognition. Mackey (1993) argues that

there are occasions when the emotions cause the senses to be heightened such that sights, sounds, smells, tastes and the tactile send stronger images to the brain.... Our grasp on the real world is deepened by the intensity of these images.

(p. 250)

She gives, as an example, her own experiences on reading William Golding's *Inheritors*, describing the intensity of her emotion, simulta-neously sparking the insightful cognition as 'vision' and awareness, which she could formulate in words only in subsequent reflection. Through his work of art, Golding had caused deep appreciation in this reader of basic faults in humanity because of her heightened emotionality. Similarly, she had been involved in a play that had generated an uncommon amount of community spirit possibly unattainable in the real world, but casting new light upon it: 'It was during the "high" emotional points of the show that this cognition was reached, when you were transfigured, most vulnerable and receptive to issues of universal interest' (p. 253).

What Mackey was experiencing here has been described by D. Hargreaves (1983) as a kind of 'conversive trauma'. Teaching has tended to be dominated by incremental theories of learning, involving the gradual, cumulative acquisition of knowledge and skills. This is no doubt relevant for some learning, but misses out a crucial aspect. Bolton (1994, p. 95) has referred to how art has 'always challenged the boundaries of our existence', how artists are prepared to suspend the 'conventional orderliness of their everyday systems of thinking'. Art is risk-taking and potentially rule-breaking, and cannot be predicted by theory. Rather, art informs theory, which promotes sound practice until challenged again by artistic thinking. This is not an easy area to study, but Hargreaves has developed a 'traumatic conception of learning' which goes some way towards describing the cathartic experience involved. In studying adults' experiences of art, he found them to include some not unlike religious conversions. He detected four elements in 'conversive traumas': the powerful concentration of attention; a sense of revelation (a 'new and important reality is opened up'); inarticulateness ('feelings drown the words'); and arousal of appetite (for more of the experience). The last is the most significant for education, being a powerful motivator. Abbs (1994, p. 54) similarly found among a group of arts teachers that, for them,

aesthetic experience is overwhelming;
it engages powerful sensations;
it involves feeling;
it brings a heightened sense of significance;
but it cannot be adequately communicated in words;
and it leaves one with a desire for others to share it.

I have tried to develop these ideas and situate them within a theory of learning which combines the virtues of sudden traumatic change and gradualness (Woods, 1993b). Full educational benefit requires pre-trauma preparation in the form of confidence building, sensitivity sharpening, skill development, and acquiring control and powers of expression. During the trauma, personal change occurs, with new discoveries about the self, realization of new skills and abilities, formation of new attitudes, and new levels of appreciation. There is also social development, leading to new knowledge and awareness of others, and a sense of community spirit rising above the restrictions of institutional roles and statuses. The 'critical events', which provided the data for this analysis, were all characterized by a constructivist teaching style; charismatic personal qualities of teachers and others involved; naturalistic context; co-operation; and grounded and open enquiry.

Though the above analysis was applied to arts subjects, there is no reason why it should not also apply to science. Scientists too experience the thrill of discovery or invention, marvel at the wonder of the natural world, experience the thrall of involvement, witness the dramas that are enacted in the chemical, physical and biological world, appreciate its beauty, work within naturalistic contexts – all essentially artistic accomplishments. That these might not yet have been realized in school teaching is more to do with levels of resource and tradition than with the intrinsic nature of the subject.

TEACHING AS SCIENCE AND ART

Social scientists tend to see teaching as a rational and stable activity amenable to science. Artists tend to view it as more variously expressive. Both groups would probably agree that there is no such thing as 'real' or 'genuine' teaching. Rather, it is a product of a set of relationships, situated within historical time and particular conceptions of space (Hargreaves, 1994c). It is also a political activity, never more so than in the struggles in education over the last decade. Some (for example, Apple, 1986) relate these developments to theories of intensification and the proletarianization of educated labour, which they see resulting in teachers acting little more than technicians, operationalizing others' requirements. Some (for example, Powell and Solity, 1990), though, feel that many teachers are still in control to some extent, and that pedagogy is a matter of individual resolution.

What is clear, however, is that teaching is a complex activity that defies any single form of characterization. We would be likely to find examples of science, art, technical and clerical work, intensification and many others in the course of a typical teacher's day. Teachers are faced with many problems and dilemmas; they have their own interests and beliefs; yet they are at the centre of a number of competing values and ideologies; they are situated within a network of inter-relationships and expectations. Viewing teaching as a science represents a lifeline through this maze of activity, breeding a questioning spirit, seeking evidence for claims made, looking for explanations and alternative explanations, for general applications and commonalities. As the educational sciences develop, we can hope for improved understanding, and ultimately a better practice based on secure foundations. If 'some of the subtlest qualities of good teaching will always elude research' (Chanan, 1973, p. 7), this should not obstruct the attempt to discover and understand them. What is subtle and mystical in one generation may become common knowledge in another.

In the end, it has to be recognized that the division into science and art is something of an artificial one. Abbs (1989) traces back to Descartes this 'mental schizophrenia', which 'broke the world into the harsh polarities of objectivity and subjectivity, reason and unreason, cognition and affect, science and the arts' (p. 15). Richardson (1990) points to the division between literary and scientific writing from the seventeenth century, which had become complete by the nineteenth (see also Clifford and Marcus, 1986). 'The search for the unambiguous was the "triumph of the quest for certainty over the quest for wisdom"' (Rorty, 1979, p. 61, quoted in Richardson, 1990, p. 14). Nisbet (1962), also, in discussing 'sociology as an art form', points to how myths formed in the nineteenth century – namely that art involved 'genius or inspiration' and was concerned with beauty, while science was concerned with rigorously controlled method and objective truth. However, both, he argues, are concerned primarily with reality and with understanding, and both depend upon detachment. But it is the artist, or the artist in the scientist, that provides the 'leap of the imagination'. Science and art, therefore rely on the same kind of creative imagination. Where art is defined out of science, the latter loses a great deal of its creative stimulation. Equally, where science is defined out of teaching, teachers sacrifice a wealth of rigorously acquired and tested knowledge. This reveals the poverty of debating whether teaching is a science or an art – as with most dichotomies and polarized thinking (Alexander, 1992).

Gage (1978), in a book entitled *The Scientific Basis of the Art of Teaching*, agrees with this. He does not believe it possible that some day good teaching might be achieved by 'closely following rigorous laws that yield high predictability and control' (p. 17). But scientists, when doing research, are practising an art. They use 'judgement, intuition, and insight in handling the unpredicted – contingencies of the same kind that arise when a painting, a poem, or a pupil is the target of an artistic effort'. As far as teaching is concerned, Gage concludes,

> Scientific method can contribute relationships between variables taken two at a time and even, in the form of interactions, three or perhaps four or more at a time. Beyond say four, the usefulness of what science can give the teacher begins to weaken, because teachers cannot apply, at least not without help and not on the run, the more complex interactions. At this point the teacher as artist must step in and make clinical, or artistic, judgements about the best ways to teach.
>
> (p. 20)

In a similar way, Brown and McIntyre (1993) predict that the results of their investigation 'will not be a set of standardized teaching behaviours; they will be personalized to the individual teacher, but there are likely to be certain over-arching generalizable features which are common across teachers' (p. 19). They prefer to see teaching as a craft, involving complex skills learned from both study and experience (see also Marland, 1975;

Tom, 1988; Cooper and McIntyre, 1996). However, it is not just about skills and knowledge, but involves also 'issues of moral purpose, emotional investment and political awareness, adeptness and acuity' (Hargreaves, 1994c, p. 6; see also Olson, 1992). This does not mean, to return to a question posed at the beginning of this chapter, that teachers are born, not made, as they 'learn through the critical practice of their art' (Stenhouse, 1980, p. 41; see also Rudduck, 1985). Nevertheless, some of these issues identified by Hargreaves have hardly been touched on here, or indeed elsewhere. Clearly, teaching is both a science and an art – and more besides.

2 The promise of symbolic interactionism

INTRODUCTION

One of the main approaches for the exploration of teaching in the latter half of this century has been that of symbolic interactionism deriving from the Chicago School of the 1920s and 1930s. In this chapter, I aim to explore its underlying rationale, its sociological relevance, its methodological apparatus, its approach to theory, and its continuing relevance.

PRINCIPLES OF SYMBOLIC INTERACTIONISM

I will concentrate here on the 'main' line of interactionism deriving from Mead and as popularized by Blumer, Becker, Glaser, Strauss and others.

The self

At the heart of Mead's thought is the 'self'. Mead is centrally concerned with the inner experience of the individual and how the self arises within the social process (Mead, 1934, pp. 7–8). Much activity is symbolic, involving construction and interpretation, both within the self and between the self and others. In the case of a child's misbehaviour, for example, if the teacher assumes a stern countenance, moves nearer to the child, or produces a detention book from a drawer and places it on the desk, these activities are symbolic. They convey meaning that is interpreted in the other's experience – in this case, 'I know from my own past experience and by observing and listening to others that the detention book is used to record the names of pupils who behave in a certain way for detention after school. As the teacher looked at me as he placed it carefully on the desk, this is probably a warning to me as to the consequences of my present actions.' One mind communicates to another. For joint activity to ensue, it is necessary that the same meaning is attached by the participants in the act to the symbol. An important component of this activity is that individuals have developed the ability to respond to their own gestures. Thus, the teacher knows from her or his past experience that the same consequences ensue as those inferred by the pupil; furthermore, each knows that the other assigns the same meaning to the act. This construction of meaning in interaction occurs by means of the ability to take the role of the other, to put oneself in the position of the other, and to interpret from that position. Thus, people imaginatively share each other's responses. This sharing and the mutual imbuing with meaning makes the behaviour truly social, as it would not be if it were mere response.

Symbols can be non-verbal, as in the preceding example, but the most important are verbal, as expressed in language. The internalization of symbols and meaning patterns and the stimulation of thought through language increase the human being's powers of reflectivity and the ability to see one's self as an object, to make indications towards one's self, and to act as one might towards others.

Defining the situation

Social interaction, therefore, is a process of construction, not a mere response to factors playing on the person such as personality factors, psychological drives, social norms, or structural or cultural determinants. Human interaction is not a neutral mechanism that operates at the instigation of external forces but, rather, a formative one in its own right. The teacher in the earlier example must consider many things, such as the behaviour of the pupil; the consequences for the pupil, the teacher and others; the implications for the achievement of aims; and how this action might be received. Social life is composed of many such transactions. Schemes of interpretation become established through use but require continued confirmation by the defining acts of others. For example, a pupil might challenge a teacher's symbolic warning to test the resolve behind the meaning. The teacher must then act to confirm the initial definition and to sustain the continuing framework. But the interaction is open to redefinition. By 'testing out' the teacher, the pupils may find new degrees of latitude. Similarly, the teacher may discover pupil interests and values, not to mention power, that have an influence on his or her teaching style.

Interaction can be built up through different constructions of reality and conflicting definitions of the situation, leading to a breakdown in order. The definition of situations lays the basis for how we perceive and interact with others, and it guides the orientation of our conduct. For smooth interaction to occur, it is necessary that all interpret situations in the same way.

Socialization

The basis for the adult self is laid in childhood, notably during play and taking part in games. As the child acquires language, she or he can label and define objects in terms that have shared meaning. Others designate the child by name, facilitating the child's view of self as social object. At the play stage, however, the child relates to others as individuals, not as a group or groups. 'Significant others' – parents, teachers, friends, perhaps – have particular influence on the emergence of the child's self, but, as yet, it is a segmented, unco-ordinated self. Co-ordination, and the ability to adopt the perspectives of a number of others simultaneously, develop during 'the game stage'. Games have sets of rules, and to take part successfully the individual must be able to take the role of all the other participants simultaneously. This is different from the segmented and specific orientation to the particular attitudes of individuals. What this means, in effect, is that individuals can see their own behaviour not only from the point of view of significant others but also in terms of generalized norms, values and beliefs. Mead called this 'the generalised other', and it is a crucial element in how he saw the relationship between self and society. Social organization provides a framework inside which people construct their actions. Structural features such as 'social class' 'set conditions for their action but do not determine their action' (Blumer, 1962, pp. 189–190). People do not act towards social class or social systems; they act towards situations. Social organization may shape situations to some extent and also provide 'fixed sets of symbols which people use in interpreting their situations' (ibid.). This may be more rigid in primitive societies, but in modern societies, where social interaction is more complex, new situations arise more frequently, requiring more flexibility in schemes of interpretation.

We may take as an example the process of socialization. Some view this as largely a one-way process, by which the individual learns a set of meanings and values that are shared by members of society and that the individual is required to learn if he or she is to participate in society. Some theories emphasize identification with role models (see Becker, 1971); some 'social learning', which rests on a system of rewards and punishments (Bandura, 1969); some 'cognitive development', which argues that appropriate conduct is inferred from early knowledge that one is male or female. The symbolic interactionist would see the role not as a prescriptive list of behaviours to be selected from, or as offering a how-to-do-it manual for all occasions, but, rather, as a more abstract model, offering general guidance. Appropriate conduct is worked out by an interpretative and interactive process.

Recent debate about 'sex role socialization' theory provides an example. Such theory, which became the most prominent explanation of gender differentiation, holds that boys and girls learn and internalize the appropriate attitudes, beliefs, mental sets and behaviours of males and females. The very way in which they assign meaning and make interpretations is dictated by their sex. The range of their symbolic universe is delimited by such activity. However, this view has been strongly attacked. Neither girls nor boys are passive recipients of existing culture but, rather, create their own responses in interaction with it. The point is well illustrated with respect to 'passive' or 'quiet' girls. On the face of it theirs may be taken as typical female behaviour, in line with cultural prescriptions, but research has shown that, in some cases at least, this is a considered strategy in response to one kind of situation. It is not a release of propensities in line with any *natural* feminine behaviour, or a response directed by social conditioning, but an active adaptation to the circumstances they find themselves in. It may be a form of resistance (Anyon, 1981) or it may represent the most expedient means to an end, and it may be variably deployed (Stanley, 1986).

Similarly, Mac an Ghaill (1994) shows how, in one comprehensive school, masculinities are not just counterparts to femininities, but are developed in particular institutional contexts, and in relation to each other. Certain groups of boys in his research showed very different attitudes and behaviours. Some were seen as an anti-school male subculture, displaying all the 'macho' elements traditionally associated with masculinity. Another group were more academically positive and upwardly mobile. They became interested in the traditionally 'feminine' arts subjects, attracting ridicule from other male students and from some male teachers. Another group negotiated a new form of masculinity through the new vocational career route. Yet another group, of middle-class background, saw themselves as possessing high-status cultural capital, and gave high value to personal autonomy and to communication strategies which they used to negotiate with teachers to good effect. Mac an Ghaill goes on to discuss some of the major influences external to the school operating on new forms of gender identity, notably changes in the labour market, in family life and structure, and in ethnicity, racism and sexuality. He illustrates the barrenness of approaches claiming sex-role socialization in any simplistic sense, arguing that gender identities are multiple, not singular, that they are not necessarily fixed, or even consistent, and that they are subject to a range of powerful influences.

Sex role socialization is more appropriately seen as a *factor*, therefore, in gender differentiation, not a determinant. Moreover, socialization is not an unmediated internalization of norms and values but a developed capacity to take the role of others effectively. Through this process, the individual learns an enormous number of meanings, values and, thus, actions through the communication of symbols with others. This is done through the interplay of the two aspects of the self – the 'I' and the 'Me'.

The 'I' and the 'Me'

The 'I' part of the self is the more spontaneous, impulsive initiator of action. The 'Me' is the product of viewing oneself as object, as one would be viewed by another. The 'I' and the 'Me' are in constant interaction with each other. Mead described the relationship in these terms:

The 'I' is the response of the organism to the attitudes of the others; the 'Me' is the organized set of attitudes of others which one himself assumes. The attitudes of the others constitute the organized 'Me'; one reacts towards that as an 'I'.

(quoted in Rose, 1962, p. 12)

We can never know the 'I' as we can the 'Me'. The 'I' is embodied in present action. As soon as the action is complete and we reflect on it, it becomes part of the 'Me'. Thus, the 'I' can only be inferred from observing the 'Me'. 'It is only after we have done the things that we are going to do that we are aware of what we are doing' (Mead, 1934, p. 203). For this reason, we can never know ourselves or others completely. The nature of and reasons for our behaviour are only partially known and may be reconstructed in the light of new experiences over time (Mead, 1929).

The two parts of the self complement each other, both for the individual and for society. The creative 'I' is the source of initiative, novelty and change; the 'Me' is the agent of self-regulation and social control. Creative acts add interest to personal lives and are the main ingredient of social change and adaptation. However, they might not all be beneficial or useful. The 'Me' acts 'to evaluate the innovations of the "I" from the perspective of society, encouraging socially useful innovations while discouraging un-desirable actions' (Baldwin, 1986, p. 118). The 'Me' is part of a social group, holding the values of that group, and those values are used to assess the initiatives of the 'I' through reflection, whereby the individual chooses a course of action.

People develop different propensities for using the 'I' or the 'Me'. The conventional form of the 'Me' may be reduced in some cases. Mead gives the example of the artist, where 'the emphasis upon that which is unconventional, that which is not in the structure of the "Me", is carried as far, perhaps, as it can be carried' (1934, pp. 209–210). Reformers, radicals and revolutionaries are others pursuing unconventional courses, although in all these cases, as with artists, they are sustained by reference groups with their own norms and values, providing the parameters of their own 'Mes'.

On the other hand, some people may suppress the 'I' and be guided almost entirely by the dictates of the 'Me'. In general, however, a mixture of the two is regarded as efficacious for both self and society. Neither could survive without a measure of routine, but the health of both depends on the abilities and freedom of people to 'think their own thoughts', 'express themselves' and 'be original' (Mead, 1934, p. 213). These thoughts, however, must feed back into the group if they are to be useful. People are never fully socialized in the sense that they know how to respond appropriately to all events and stimuli. However experienced we become, new problems and situations calling for new solutions and adaptation always arise.

METHODOLOGICAL IMPLICATIONS OF SYMBOLIC INTERACTIONISM

Respecting the empirical world

The most important premise is that enquiry must be grounded in the empirical world under study. By the 'empirical social world' is meant the minute-by-minute, day-to-day social life of individuals as they interact together, as they develop understandings and meanings, as they engage in 'joint action' and respond to each other as they adapt to situations, and as they encounter and move to resolve problems that arise through their circumstances.

Blumer (1976, p. 13) argues that 'every part of the act of scientific enquiry... is subject to the test of the empirical world and has to be validated through such a test'. Research methods are the means to discover that reality; they do not themselves contain it. They should respect, therefore, the nature of that reality – hence the emphasis on 'naturalism' (Matza, 1969), on 'unobtrusive methods' (Webb et al., 1966) and on 'grounded theory' (Glaser and Strauss, 1967). The last of these is a reminder that the entire research process, not just data collection, should keep faith with the empirical world under study. The research design, the problems formulated for study, the specification of categories, the relationships among the data, explanatory concepts and interpretative frameworks all must be tested for closeness of fit. They all received special emphasis from Blumer, writing at a time when, in some approaches, a considerable disjuncture often existed between some of these processes and the empirical world. Problems selected for study in these approaches might have been prominent in the mind of the researcher but not necessarily of major importance in the situations studied. Abstract concepts were devised with little attempt to trace through their linkage with the reality to which they were purported to relate. Theories were formulated to 'explain' the data, being imposed on it *post hoc*, with the linkages not fully explored (see Hargreaves, 1980).

Respecting the empirical world means making as few assumptions in advance of the study as possible. Mac an Ghaill (1989) gives an example of the desirability of this. The predominant 'race-relations' viewpoint in the 1970s and 1980s saw black pupils' educational achievement in terms of 'cultural deficit'. That is to say that black pupils' adaptation to school was hindered by features in their own culture. While he started with this viewpoint, however, Mac an Ghaill came to reformulate the research problem. As he accumulated material from his observations of and interviews with teachers and pupils, he went 'beyond the white norm'. The problem, he concluded, was racism, not cultural deficit (see also Mac an Ghaill, 1988 – though see the discussion on involvement and distance later). Sociologists, in short, must 'make' their own problems, 'among which may be to treat educators' problems as phenomena to be explained' (Young, 1971, p. 2). The basis for 'making' such problems will be experience in the empirical world. It was his growing, deep acquaintance with this experience that persuaded Mac an Ghaill that he had the wrong research design.

Layers of reality

Social life is not only complex in its range and variability; it is also deep, in that it operates at different levels. Berger (1966, p. 34) talks of social reality having 'many layers of meaning. The discovery of each new layer changes the perception of the whole.' Blumer (1976, p. 15) talks of 'lifting veils'. Thus, a school typically presents a 'public face' to outsiders. A researcher who stays for one or two weeks might discover more than a casual visitor about how the school really works, because public façades cannot be maintained for long. But a longer stay is needed and much work is necessary to develop the knowledge, skills and trust that will permit entry into those innermost arenas and confidences required for first-hand understanding of the situation.

Methodologically, this means, first, maintaining a certain openness of mind, not prejudging the matter under investigation or necessarily settling for first or even second appearances. As in all research, curiosity should be fostered, to see beyond to the next layer or 'veil'. What is presented is carefully noted, but the status to be attached to it is temporarily suspended. However, guesses might be made, tested along the way and abandoned, and changed or revised in the light of later discoveries. Second, this kind of exploration cannot be undertaken in a day or a week. Nor can it take place outside the actual situation of the object of study or by proxy. Depending on the area under investigation, it can take months or years of working 'in the field'. Third, this mode of study has implications for the relationships the researcher fosters with subjects in the research. People are unlikely to allow total strangers into their private and confidential gatherings or to tell them their innermost thoughts and secrets without certain guarantees. They must be backed by a certain trust in the researcher and reflected in the 'rapport' traditionally developed between researcher and subjects.

Taking the role of the other

If we are to understand social life, what motivates people, what their interests are, what links them to and distinguishes them from others, what their cherished values and beliefs are, why they act as they do, and how they perceive themselves and others, we need to put ourselves in their position and look out at the world with them. Their reality may not be our reality, or what we think theirs is.

Taking the role of the other would allow researchers to obtain 'inside' knowledge of the social life under study. If they are to understand people's outlooks and experiences, researchers must be close to groups, live with them, see them in various situations and in various moods, appreciate the inconsistencies, ambiguities and contradictions in their behaviour, explore the nature and extent of their interests, and understand their relationships among themselves and with other groups – in short, if possible, to adopt their roles. To these ends, researchers have joined such groups as delinquent gangs (Patrick, 1973; Parker, 1974), the teaching staff of a school (Hargreaves, 1967), and groups of hippies (Yablonsky, 1968), bikers (Willis, 1978) or pupils (Llewellyn, 1980).

We need to know, therefore, the subjects' viewpoint, whether it be that of a disruptive child, a truant, a schizophrenic pupil, an anarchic pupil or, indeed, a 'conformist' one. This information is important for teachers, not just researchers. Pupils are not just receivers or consumers of knowledge, but constructors of shared meanings in a combined exercise with teachers. Quicke (1992; see also Quicke and Winter, 1993) has pointed out that these meanings are an aspect of 'metacognition' – knowledge *about* learning processes, about strategies of learning, and about people who are involved with them, like teachers. We might include in this a host of factors, notably the emotional, which affect the whole character of the learning enterprise and pupils' disposition towards it (Elbaz, 1992). If we are concerned to produce autonomous, critical and reflective learners, and to improve learning, we need to know what sense pupils are making of what is offered to them, and how they view and feel about the circumstances in which it is being offered. It might then be possible to improve the pupil's metacog-nitive knowledge, and the context in which it is constructed.

In summary, to understand social interaction, it is necessary to witness it as closely as possible and in depth, in all its manifestations and all the situations in which the form under examination occurs. Because social interaction is constructed by the people engaged in it, one should try to see it from their point of view and appreciate how they interpret the indications given to them by others, the meaning they assign to them, and how they construct their own action. In addition, because this is a process, it must be sampled over time.

Appreciating the culture

Groups in interaction develop a large number of symbols imbued with inter-related meaning that collectively constitute a culture or subculture. Often, symbols that seem of the least significance to outsiders are the ones most redolent with the meaning for participants. Such symbols may possess some alternative cultural significance for an observer, enabling reasonable, but false, interpretation. The observer, therefore, must attempt to see these symbols from the standpoint of the culture, rather than imposing on them the frameworks and understandings of other cultures within which the same symbols may have different meanings. The task, then, is to capture the meanings that permeate the culture as understood by the participants. The consequences of not doing so have been occasionally illustrated in teacher–pupil studies. Moore (1992), for example, in a study of Bangladeshi pupils' experiences of English lessons, shows that even where teachers are adopting a declared multicultural policy, their view of reality can still be firmly rooted in their own culture. This ethnocentrism prevents their appreciating what a minority ethnic bilingual pupil has to offer, and leads them to challenge not only surface features of writing such as grammar and punctuation, but also substantive content and style. They treat their own approach as the only 'correct' one. This unconscious attempt to enculturate in the example Moore gives did not succeed, and may only have helped alienate the child from his work. In a more successful example, the teacher was more reflective and multiethnically oriented, could distance herself from her own cultural forms, and situated the style and content of the pupil's writing within his own culture. She made surface feature corrections, but built on the pupil's reality and encouraged emergent skills. The pupil responded with improvements in his writing, some totally unexpected. Dubberley (1988a, 1988b) has shown how the middle-class culture of teachers impacts heavily against the working-class 'pit' culture of children from a mining community in the north of England. Unsuccessful teachers asserted their own culture as dominant, and gave offence with sarcasm and insults. More successful teachers had the knack of accommodating the contradictions between school and the culture of the community.

A group culture often has a certain ambience or ethos which the researcher needs to grasp. The best commendation one can receive perhaps about the accuracy of one's attempts to understand a group's ethos is from the group members. They, after all, are the ones who generate the meanings involved. Lincoln and Guba (1985) argue that the standard for qualitative research, where the objective is to reconstruct events and the perspectives of those being studied, is the demonstration that the findings and the researchers' interpretations are credible to those who are involved. Thus Willis (1977) showed various drafts of his book to the 'lads' who were the subject of his research, and included their reactions as an appendix. Mac an Ghaill (1988) showed what he had written to the black pupils he had been studying. One of them said, 'It's really good. I've read through most of it. I think that you have really captured what it's like for black kids at school' (p. 142).

This is not to say that 'respondent validation' (that is, insiders confirming the correctness of analyses) is always appropriate or desirable. For example, where the subject of study is school processes rather than perspectives, the subjects' view of the research may be strongly influenced, if not completely dominated, by their role within the institution (see, for example, Scarth, 1985). Also, we need to distinguish between everyday conceptions of reality and the sociological theory through which it may be interpreted (Denzin, 1978). Such theory may bring a result not recognized and/or not liked by insiders. As Denzin (1978) puts it,

> Sociological explanations ultimately given for a set of behaviours are not likely to be completely understood by those studied; even if they prove understandable, subjects may not agree with or accept them, perhaps because they have been placed in a category they do not like or because elements of their behaviour they prefer hidden have been made public. An irreducible conflict will always exist between the sociological perspective and the perspective of everyday life.

(p. 9)

Learning the symbols

One of the first requirements of symbolic interactionist research is to understand the symbolic meanings that emerge in interactions and are attributed in situations over time. Methodologically, this means learning the language of the participants, with all its nuances and perhaps special vocabulary. Other means of communication – gestures, looks, actions, appearance, and the whole area of 'body language' or non-verbal communication, which are intended to convey meaning to others – are also important. These symbolic expressions must be linked to observed behaviour and the situations in which they occur, because they can vary among them and over time. Ideally one needs to show how meanings emerge in interaction. Thus, pupils might complain in interviews or on a questionnaire of being 'picked on' or 'shown up' by teachers. However, it is difficult (1) to understand fully what these events actually mean and (2) to know how to interpret them without seeing them occur.

Scenes must be closely monitored if we are to identify their inner mysteries. Understandings between pupils and teacher can become extremely recondite, triggered by the briefest of signals among them, which are inaccessible to outsiders. For example, Delamont and Galton (1986) refer to a 'Horace' joke. A child spelled 'horse' 'horace', and this was picked up by another child who called 'Look! There's a horace outside the window eating the grass.' Thereafter misspellers were referred to as 'Horace' or described as 'doing a horace'. This may seem unremarkable – simply an inside joke – but basically it is a reminder both of group identity and of underlying rules, very important ones concerning correct spelling, which are both dramatized and made more acceptable by being displaced in humour and by being deeply embedded within the classroom culture. Thus, the group collectively 'owns' the mystery. It is something they have generated and that belongs to them and them alone as a group. The more impenetrable it is to outsiders, the more successful it is in these respects.

The inter-relation between behaviour and language and its embeddedness within the social structure of the classroom is well illustrated by Werthman (1963), who describes how 'looking cool' emerges from inter-action wherein teachers transgress certain unwritten but tacitly agreed upon rules. The heavy but ingenious symbolism of the behaviour is expressed here:

> Of all the techniques used by gang members to communicate rejection of authority, by far the most subtle and most annoying to teachers is demeanour. Both White and Negro gang members have developed a uniform and highly stylized complex of body movements that commu-nicate a casual and disdainful aloofness to anyone making normative claims on their behaviour. The complex is referred to by a gang member as 'looking cool', and it is part of a repertoire of stances that include 'looking bad' and 'looking tore down'. The essential ingredients of 'looking cool' are a walking pace that is a little too slow for the occasion, a straight back, shoulders slightly stooped, hands in pockets, and eyes that carefully avert any party to the interaction. There are also clothing aides which enhance the effect such as boot and shoe taps and a hat if the scene takes place indoors.
>
> (p. 221)

The beauty of this behaviour lies in its superb efficacy. Its message is clear, unmistakable and hurtful, but gives little chance for counter-attack. Werthman's point of entry was the boy's references to 'looking cool', which the researcher then 'unpacked' by observations. Subjects' own references cue one into important aspects of their culture, whether it is 'dossing or swatting' (Turner, 1983), 'blagging or wagging' (Willis, 1977), 'bunking off' (Furlong, 1977) or 'having mates' (Mealyea, 1989).

Distinctive argot is not the only clue, however. Subjects may use the same terms as the researcher but intend very different meanings. Cues indicating a term of special significance might be frequency of use, emphasis and generality. Thus, pupils' references to 'work' have been shown to have varying meaning among different groups (Woods, 1990b). Furthermore, what various pupils understand by 'work' may be consider-ably different from the researcher's understanding. The words themselves are not enough, even though they may be the same as those of the researcher. They must be interpreted. The researcher aims for 'shared meanings', when one 'feels part of the culture and can interpret words and gestures as the members of that culture do' (Wax, 1971, p. 11).

Similarly, we need to know what meaning is attributed to actions by participants. Wilson (1977) gives the example of 'student hits other student' in a study on 'inter-student aggression in the classroom'. If we were using preconstructed categories, all observed instances of the action would have to be included (although there could be some difficulty over what constituted 'hitting'). The interactionist, however, would want to know how the action was understood by those involved:

How do the various participants (the hitter, person being hit, onlookers, teacher) perceive the event?
Do they even see it as aggression?
Do the hitter and person being hit concur on the meaning?

(p. 252)

Wilson goes on to point out that hitting may not even be an act of aggression. It could, in fact, be the reverse – an act of affection or part of subcultural norms that indicate 'playful demonstration of strength'. It could also be a means of annoying the teacher or causing classroom disruption. Even if it is aggression, there are many subtleties involved. For example,

> The event could be an initiatory first act, or it could be a retribution for previous acts of aggression not necessarily linked immediately in space, time, or kind. The event could be part of a personal relationship between the two students involved, or it could be part of a larger interpersonal network of relations – for example, intergroup hostility.

(ibid.)

There are many other possible meanings for such an act, not all of them readily explainable by the participants. Although it may be impossible to comprehend them all, the researcher aims to uncover as many as possible through long-term observation of, and close discussion with, the actors.

Situating the interaction

To understand the interaction under study, one must also understand the context within which it occurs. This is because (1) the situation can affect perspectives and behaviour, and (2) perspectives can affect situations. One of the best examples of the situation affecting perspectives is the transformation that comes over teachers when they enter the classroom. Lacey (1976, p. 60) noted in his research that many of the teachers in the school of his research were 'sincere in their desire to help and encourage their pupils to learn'. However, on occasion, these 'reasonable, kindly men' turned into 'bellowing, spiteful adversaries. They left the staffroom in good order; it was in the classroom that things went wrong.' Keddie (1971) also noted this phenomenon of teacher change and advanced an explanation based on the difference between two contexts. In the 'educationist' context, which prevailed outside the classroom, teachers employed theoretically led definitions. For example, streaming (tracking) by ability was seen by teachers as an institutional reinforcement of class-determined inequalities. However, in the 'teacher' context of the classroom,

> what a teacher knows about pupils derives from ... streaming, which in turn derives from the dominant organizing category or what counts as ability. The 'normal' characteristics ... of a pupil are those which are

imputed to his band or stream as a whole.... This knowledge of what pupils are like is often at odds with the image of pupils the same teachers may hold as educationists since it derives from streaming, whose validity the educationist denies.

(Keddie, 1971, p. 139)

Thus, teachers are constrained by the circumstances of their work – large classes, examination pressures, mandated curriculum – which might bring about a profound transformation of their views, attitudes and behaviour (see also Gracey, 1972). Clearly the research methods need to be sampled across as many situations as possible if perspectives are to be understood fully.

Alternatively, perspectives can help determine situations. Thus, Denscombe (1980) shows how teachers, faced with an unpopular new policy of 'open' classrooms, subtly 'closed' them again. Pupils' understanding of the school situation can be vastly different from teachers' (Corrigan, 1979; Willis, 1977). For example, they may see it as not a 'place of learning' but an 'arena for socializing', for which learning may be counter-productive. Several studies have shown how pupils transform situations to be more in line with their own interests. Turner (1983) describes how a pupil who conformed in some lessons was disruptive in others. This was because the school did not always meet his own ideal of wanting to do well by providing good teachers. Bad teachers did not give 'proper lessons', therefore, but such lessons were functional in providing him with an opportunity to respond to peer group pressure and 'mess about a bit'.

Much teacher–pupil conflict appears to be produced by opposing definitions of the situation. The 'blazer-ripping incident' at a school of my research (Woods, 1979) is an illustration. Here, the school blazer was a prime symbol of school authority and pupil oppression. The rules of school uniform were enforced with rigour in the interests of maintaining order – another illustration of the symbolic value of appearance. On the last day of term, it was traditional for a certain amount of 'blazer-ripping' to occur – symbolic of pupils gaining their freedom. However, one year a boy's blazer was ripped to shreds early in the last week of term. This precipitated a major crisis. The teachers launched a big offensive to apprehend and punish the culprits. The boys simply could not understand what all the fuss was about. 'They'd been writing all over blazers, writing their names on them, it's a traditional activity at the end of your school days' (Woods, 1979, p. 119).

The symbols here are clear: the school uniform, the 'ideal pupil' appearance and behaviour. Unsurprisingly, at the end of compulsory schooling, the desecration of these symbols is a prominent part of the celebrations, part of the rites of passage that mark transition into the world of work. Such desecration is recognized, too, by teachers as legitimate activity – but only at the proper point of the passage, that is, the end of the week. The beginning of the week was still 'school', requiring business as usual, governed by school rules. Hence, competing teacher and pupil definitions of the situation were the cause of misunderstanding, which precipitated conflict.

Clearly, the methods employed must be sensitive to both interpretations. Research methods must pick up the interaction between perspectives and situation to see how they bear on each other. Researchers must sample across time also, because the same props may mean different things on different occasions. If the research took the teacher's perspective, the pupils would be judged 'deviant'. If it took the pupils' perspective, the teachers would appear unreasonable. Neither deviance nor lack of reason was at the heart of the problem here.

Interaction as process

In their interaction, people are continually interpreting the indications of others and constructing their behaviour accordingly. It is not something that is done once according to some set pattern. There may be some general guidelines, but this does not alter the fact that social interaction is a moving process, with people defining, assigning meanings, aligning and realigning their actions, seeing how they can best satisfy their interests, comparing and contrasting them with others, adjusting them if necessary, and devising strategies. Interaction and interpretation do not remain static, governed by determining features like group norms. An overemphasis on such norms was indeed a criticism of some of the early work on pupil subcultures (see Furlong, 1976). Pupil cultures are still there, but pupils have an active engagement with them. Davies (1984, p. 57) puts this well in her study of a group of 'problem' girls in a secondary school when she says 'sub-cultures are not a kind of superglue where pupils must instantly "adhere" to the rules of the group, but at most a cavity foam filling with plenty of air space to manoeuvre'.

Research methods can also strongly influence the outcome. This is well illustrated by studies of pupils' interethnic association. The great majority of work in this area, using predominantly sociometric techniques, had previously found pupils preferring their own ethnic group and not forming many interethnic friendships (for example, Davey and Mullin, 1982). However, Denscombe, Szule, Patrick and Wood (1986) state that this finding was contrary to many teachers' observations in the schools of their research. They studied two multiethnic classes, using a range of methods including extended fieldwork observation of free association in the classrooms and in the playground. They indeed found a high degree of racial integration, which supported the teachers' own observations. While this, of course, may be a product of those particular schools, it is also quite likely that the quantitative techniques of the earlier studies failed to capture the complexity of the situation, in which there could have been many forms of interaction, both conflictual and consensual, both between and within ethnic groups, varying among situations and over time and in nature and degree of 'friendship'.

The research methods, therefore, need to grasp a sense of social flux. They may reveal that some forms of behaviour are fairly stable, others variable, and others emergent and developmental. Some forms of interaction proceed in stages: the methods need to encompass each stage and its place in the whole. Consider, for example, the process of 'labelling' deviants (Becker, 1963). Labelling may begin with some comparatively insignificant deviation from one's customary, law-abiding role, which in itself is easily normalized. This is primary deviance (Lemert, 1967). Secondary deviance arises out of the social reaction to the former. As D.H. Hargreaves, Hester and Mellor (1975) put it:

> The labelling creates, under certain conditions, problems for the person who committed the deviant act which can be resolved by the commission of yet further deviant acts and by a self-designation as a deviant person. The paradox is that the social reaction which was intended to control, punish or eliminate the deviant act has come to shape, stabilize and exacerbate the deviance.
>
> (p. 6)

Consider the stages of the labelling process in this hypothetical example:

1 A girl in a class of schoolchildren likes socializing with her peers during lessons and often talks to her neighbours.
2 She is perceived by the teacher as a chatterbox and a bit of a nuisance.
3 She is disciplined, perhaps through sarcasm. The sarcasm stings and promotes feelings of revenge and antagonism, which encourage her to increase her deviant behaviour.
4 Meanwhile, the teacher discusses the girl with colleagues, some of whom feel that they have noted similar tendencies, and they collectively apply the label of 'nonconformist' to the girl, so that she is treated similarly by all her teachers.
5 The girl responds with more persistent deviant behaviour, which becomes habitual. Eventually, the role becomes internalized and the girl acts out her teachers' expectations; this role may be reinforced by her own peers' reactions to her. She has become a 'real' deviant.

The initial reaction by the teachers has been crucial in this development. The 'primary' deviance, if treated in a different way, might have remained at a low level, marginal to the girl's otherwise completely acceptable behaviour (see Hargreaves, 1976). Clearly, it is necessary for the research methods to encompass the whole of this process and to delineate each part of it and their interconnections. If only one part is sampled, the wrong conclusions may be drawn.

Researching the self

If we are to understand the 'I', we must explore people's innermost feelings, their impulses and passions, their hunches and risk taking, the things they would like to do but cannot, what prompts them to act in certain ways, and what gives them pleasure and what causes pain. Some of this clearly addresses the affective and subconscious rather than the cognitive and conscious domains. Nias (1989) is one of the few to tackle this area. She argues that

> no account of primary teachers' experience is complete if it does not make room for potentially dangerous emotions such as love, rage and jealousy, on the one hand, and intermittent narcissism and outbreaks of possessive dependence on the other. Although much of this book focuses upon teachers' socially-regulated 'selves', their own descriptions of their feelings about pupils, and their relationships with them and with their colleagues, reminds us that the regressive, passionate and unruly aspects of human nature are always present in the classroom and may sometimes escape from rational control.
>
> (p. 203)

In our research on creative teaching (Woods and Jeffrey, 1996), we have explored how teachers who regard pupils as whole selves rather than as institutionalized clients make 'emotional connections' with pupils in order to maximize their teaching, and to 'bring home' knowledge to their personal fields of relevance. Teachers themselves have emotional needs – to be inspired, motivated, enthused, reassured, and what one described as 'renewed' – in other words to have an active and vibrant self at the heart of their practice. Sensitive teachers create atmospheres and moods in the classroom, seeking conditions in which the 'I's of their pupils may flourish.

The 'I' also indulges in hunches, impulses, ideas, guesses and risk taking, much of it consigned to the subconscious and instantly monitored and conditioned in the immediacy of the moment. It produces what Schön (1983) has described as 'knowledge-in-action'. It also involves innovation, inventiveness and creativity, not just in planning major exercises, but also in minute-to-minute activity, demanding a number of varied decisions that characterize the teacher's work. Some of these may be based on routine and a well-formulated 'Me'. Others bring the 'I' into play. Because we cannot put ourselves in another's skin and 'know' what he or she 'knows' (Laing, 1967; Schutz, 1967), we would need to be actively involved ourselves to understand them fully. Otherwise, a very close monitoring of these processes is required, working beside a teacher as she or he deliberates, considers, weighs up the pros and cons, seizes upon a decision, makes a gesture, acts on impulse, or does something unexpected.

A focus on the self also demands a consideration of the person's interests and biography. Interests are an expression of the self, not a requirement of the role. Role requirement may vary with personal interests, although not necessarily. Thus, while we might assume a teacher's primary interests to be giving instruction and keeping order, Pollard (1985b) has shown these to be secondary interests. The primary ones are, he claims, maximizing enjoyment (the affective element again), controlling the workload, maintaining one's health and avoiding stress, retaining autonomy, and maintaining one's self-image. In some circumstances, these primary interests may dictate behaviours other than instructing and controlling, such as that of 'coping', which may involve a range of strategies designed to manage severe pressures and constraints (Hargreaves, 1978).

The fact that the self is a process with a past and a future as well as an ongoing present requires some attention to the formulation of the self. Frequently what one sees is only a small portion, with hidden layers of meaning and reality both laterally across the here and now and longitudinally back in time. A full understanding of the present 'self' requires knowledge of its construction over time, of the formative years of primary socialization, of the influence of 'significant others', of decision points and 'critical incidents' (Strauss, 1959), of the search for means to ends and the reformulating of ends, of the identification of reference groups, and of the laying down of 'side bets' (Becker, 1964). Consequently, pupils' and teachers' lives and careers have become a popular subject for study in interactionist research (Ball and Goodson, 1985; Sikes et al., 1985; Acker, 1989) and 'biography' and 'life-history' popular methods (Hatch and Wisniewski, 1995; Thomas, 1995).

Symbolic interaction and society

Symbolic interactionism typically deals with small-scale, everyday life, seeking to understand processes, relationships, group life, motivations, adaptations and so on. In so doing, and because it places such emphasis on the importance of the empirical world, it has attracted criticisms of being 'idealist', 'situationist' and 'empiricist' (Whitty, 1974; Sharp and Green, 1975; Troyna, 1994). Critics claim that it is unable to theorize the larger system and to see how the 'everyday' is affected by it; however, although this might be a legitimate criticism of some studies, it is not an essential feature of the approach.

Symbolic interaction does have a view on wider concerns – on social structures and system. In some approaches (for example, structural-functionalism or economic Marxism), the imperatives of the system are acted out directly in people's behaviour. But people do not merely respond to imperatives in this manner; they construct a response, which in some respects might vary from what the wider system might lead us to expect. Thus, the broad claims of correspondence theory – that schools simply correspond to the structures and attitudes of the wider society (see, for example, Bowles and Gintis, 1976) – have been shown by a number of interactionist studies to be invalid. Schools do not reproduce docile workers for the labour force. There are too many rebels among them (see for example Willis, 1977). Similarly, the theory of intensification, derived from Marxist theories of the labour process, claims that teachers' work has become more overloaded, routinized, all-consuming and externally directed; but A. Hargreaves (1994c) shows that this can only be a partial explanation of what teachers do. Indeed, some of their practice shows contrary tendencies. Thus, interactionism can be said to have a 'corrective' function inasmuch as it can submit some of the claims of such theories to empirical test. In the process, the theory becomes modified (in the case of correspondence theory, to one that recognizes the 'partial and relative autonomy' of the school), lays emphasis on 'cultural production', and begins to formulate theories of 'resistance' (Willis, 1977; Aggleton, 1987). Interactionist studies can continue to monitor these for accuracy of representation – for example, with respect to the types of behaviour defined as 'resistance' (Hargreaves, 1984a). The point can be applied more generally. A detailed interactionist study can be used for comparative purposes in any area – for example, the study of black students may test some more traditional studies of the schooling of white youth (Mac an Ghaill, 1989, p. 186).

This is one way, then, in which the approach bears on wider concerns, as a commentary on, or test of, broader theories about society and systems. However, interactionism can also approach society and social structure from below. By monitoring the attribution of meanings as well as how these sustain situations and processes, and how people define and redefine each other's and their own perspectives, patterns may be identified that exhibit both personal creativity and external constraint. This has been conceptualized in such devices as 'coping strategies.' These require the study

> of the situational constraints in response to which they are fashioned, and of the relation (present or past) of such constraints to wider structural concerns. While the language of strategy analysis has so far been confined to interactionist research, this need no longer be the case. All too frequently, the *situation* [italics in original] has been regarded as the outer limit of constraint upon teacher and pupil behaviour. Concerns which have normally been thought to be the proper province of interactionist research should now be linked with and included in theories about the operations of social structure.
>
> (Hargreaves, 1980, p. 193)

Strategies are not only two-dimensional (micro–macro); they have historical referents. Pollard (1982) has pointed to the importance of personal biography and institutional history in their formulation. In recent years, this has further renewed the interest among some in 'life-histories'.

These have the advantage of monitoring a developing self within the context of local factors such as home life, parents, school and teachers, and significant others, as well as wider concerns, which the passage of time has brought into focus, such as social class, religion, and social, political and economic climate. Sensitively handled and portrayed, the influences of these can be seen in the acted-out life of the formulating self (see Dollard, 1935; Goodson, 1980; Bertaux, 1981).

Interactionist studies have produced many rich studies of cultural formation and intergroup conflict and division that serve a potentially productive basis for macro studies. Similarly, the 1988 Education Reform Act provided a good opportunity to trace through the interconnections between political framework and school and classroom structure and process. Studying the interconnections helps to cultivate the 'sociological imagination', which

> enables its possessor to understand the larger historical scene in terms of its meaning for the inner life and the external career of a variety of individuals. It enables him [*sic*] to take into account how individuals, in the welter of their daily experience, often become falsely conscious of their social positions. Within that welter the framework of modern society is sought, and within that framework the psychologies of a variety of men and women re-formulated. By such means the personal uneasiness of individuals is focused upon explicit troubles and the indifference of publics is transformed into involvement with public issues.
>
> (Mills, 1959, pp. 11–12)

The sociological imagination enables us to grasp history and biography and the relations between the two within society. Life-histories are clearly conducive to this, but so is qualitative research in general.

Mac an Ghaill (1989) argues that qualitative research is useful to the sociological imagination because it enables us 'to bring into focus the three-dimensional social world of biography, culture and history' (p. 185). His own study of black youth revealed to him that much previous traditional research was 'distorted, de-racialised and degendered' (p. 186). This 'sociological refocusing' is necessary because it offers some micro–macro interconnections. In his case,

> In studying the schooling of black youth, student–teacher classroom survival strategies can be seen to be linked to the wider framework of racism and sexism, thus acknowledging that 'race', class and gender are constitutive elements in the maintenance of hegemonic domination. Consequently, the transformation of these power relations requires a theory of social change that includes these interrelated elements.
>
> (p. 186)

RESEARCH METHODS AND THE RESEARCHER'S SELF

The research methods most appropriate for symbolic interactionism fall under the general term 'ethnography'. Several texts discuss the approach and its techniques (for example, Glaser and Strauss, 1967; Lofland, 1971; Schatzman and Strauss, 1973; Bogdan and Taylor, 1975; Burgess, 1984a; Woods, 1986; Strauss, 1987; LeCompte and Preissle, 1993; Hammersley and Atkinson, 1995) as do many articles (including the collection in McCall and Simmons, 1969; Becker, 1970; Burgess, 1982, 1984b, 1985a, 1985b; Sherman and Webb, 1988). I consider here the chief research instrument – the researcher – and how it interacts with theory and method. This applies symbolic interactionist principles to the research process itself. The researcher does not stand above and outside the research. The research is contextualized within situations and definitions of situation; research activities are constructed and interpreted in distinctive processes; and the researcher's self is inextricably bound up with the research. Reflexivity – the need to consider how one's own part in the research affects it – is therefore an essential requirement. This is illustrated by referring to some of the basic techniques.

Initial commitment

Interactionist research needs the involvement of the researcher's self. This means that knowledge of 'how to do it' can only come from 'going out and doing it'. This was the basis of Park's (1920) advice to his students to 'go and get their hands dirty in real research' and of Becker's to his to 'get in there and see what's going on' (Atkinson, 1977, p. 32).

The initial guidance comes from the predisposition of the researcher to the approach and commitment to interactionist principles. The techniques follow generally from the methodological implications traced out in the previous section, but they flow directly from the self. This is not to say that things are done instinctively and to perfection but, rather, that one 'learns on the job'. Nor is it to say that research manuals are not important. Indeed, they are as essential as in any other approach, but their use is coterminous and interactional, rather than sequential. They only begin to make sense when one is involved, engaging with similar issues and situations. The 'empathy' that is so important in one's feelings for the subjects of the research is also important for one's engagement with methods' texts. The excitement of discovery, the boredom of the 'nothing happening' syndrome, the pleasure of meeting and interacting with people, the problems of effecting access and 'coming up against brick walls', and errors and inadequacies, as well as finding new ways of doing things or providing a new slant on a particular technique, are all part of the endeavour, and the messages from others are seen to best advantage when placed on the comparative basis of one's own research processes and situations. The texts themselves were produced from experience in the real world. In this way, the methodology *and* its study are grounded in the empirical world.

Researcher skills

The ethnographer, thus, works to develop research skills *in situ* and to 'fine-tune' the self. So much depends on what one sees and hears that much rests on one's powers of observation and listening. The kinds of skill that are involved are those of social management – interpersonal skills that facilitate the negotiation of access into both private places and private thoughts and that develop the kind of trust and rapport that encourage people to relax, be 'natural', go about their everyday business in the researcher's presence in their usual way, and hold nothing back in interview. Good social management helps to ensure that some things to be seen and heard are worthwhile. To this end, some researchers have cultivated the 'good guy' image, one sympathetic to the group under study (Lacey, 1976). Where two or more groups are in conflict under study, considerable personal skills are required to handle the consequent role conflict engendered in the researcher.

Although 'naturalism' may be a keynote, things do not just happen and unfold before one's eyes, nor are important situations immediately revealed nor access offered. One's right to witness and take part in slices of other people's lives must be worked for and earned. Although just 'hanging around' is not an uncommon activity among ethnographers, and quite appropriate in some circumstances, at other times one must make things happen in the sense of effecting entry to an important event or meeting, arranging interviews, or approaching people with a view to converse with them. For this, one needs interpersonal skills and fine judgement as to when to bring them into play and when to leave them alone. Without this kind of ingenuity, one fails to penetrate beyond the outer layer of reality.

If entry is achieved, one then needs observational skills. These involve, in the first place, *vision* – the ability to see and take in a wide range of activity over a period of time. Vision consists of a cultivated power of scanning, which ensures that as wide a portion of activity as possible is covered. Scanning will include the less as well as the more obvious places, people and activities. At the same time, the ethnographer needs powers of *discernment* – selecting specific aspects for more concentrated scrutiny and greater definition (the criteria for which I discuss later) – which inevitably means letting other aspects go by. Once these are detected, one must consider how to record material. Filming and taping are useful aids where they do not intrude, but in many situations this is neither possible nor appropriate. The ethnographer therefore cultivates the art of memorizing key words and images for commitment to written record as soon as possible. He or she notes key aspects or comments on scraps of paper or even a sleeve, summarizing incidents with 'key words' that will recall whole incidents, speaking into a dictaphone, punctuating the period of observation with 'recording slots' to ensure against 'drowning' in the data, performing all these activities smoothly in a seamless web both for efficiency and so as not to intrude on the action.

Similarly, special skills are needed for interviewing, at their centre a certain persona showing understanding of and empathy with the interviewee. Once this is started, other skills are brought into play, notably active listening, which shows the other that you hear and react and construct interpretations occasionally, both with a view to maintaining the interpretative frame and keeping the other 'warmed up'; focusing – that is, keeping the interviewer to the subject; in-filling and explicating where material is incomplete, unclear or ambiguous; checking for accuracy by pressing points, seeking evidence, rephrasing, summarizing, playing devil's advocate, seeking contrary instances (Dean and Whyte, 1958). The interview, therefore, is not just a device for gathering information. It is a process of reality construction to which both parties contribute and by which both are affected. Some of the interviewer's own self is put in – some contrasting or complementary experiences perhaps, or some indications of own persona; or at the very least the interviewer acts as a sounding board – and the interviewer comes out reflecting on how the interview has affected his or her thoughts, ideas, viewpoints and theories.

The researcher as a person

Thus the researcher is a finely tuned instrument with considerable skills, but is a person no less, with values, beliefs and a self. The researcher's own background, interests and values will be influential in selecting a topic for research. However, other criteria are also brought into play. These include balance, which will direct one to areas and subjects as yet uncovered; refinement and development, where previous studies have not 'saturated' the topic (Glaser and Strauss, 1967); and relevance – that is, the research is deemed to be directed towards some social good.

The research subject is then identified partly by personal interests and values, as are a number of choices within the study, such as what to concentrate upon, whom to see and talk to, what one sees and notices. The conduct of the research, however, is subject to checks and balances. One of these is representative sampling, or what Ball calls 'naturalistic sampling' (Ball, 1990a, p. 102). This covers places, times and persons. Thus, if one were studying teachers' or pupils' perspectives, or the culture of a group, one would consider them in different settings, since it is well known that behaviour can differ markedly in different situations. The same point applies to time. Weekly and yearly cycles, for example, are critical in schools. If the research is sampled at just the beginnings and ends of terms, weeks or days, it might discover situations untypical of other occasions.

Again, if seeking to represent a whole group, the research would ensure that it had sampled across that group according to some appropriate criteria, which might be, for example, age, gender, ethnicity or subject specialization.

Systematic sampling on this scale cannot always be fully achieved in qualitative work because of (1) its initially largely unsystematic, exploratory nature; (2) problems of negotiating access; (3) problems of gathering and processing data through one set of ears and eyes. Some unrepresentativeness is almost inevitable, therefore. Often, one has to make do with an 'opportunity sample' in those areas where access is offered; or a 'snowball sample', where the sample is developed through personal contact and recommendation. There is nothing wrong with this as long as undue claims about generality are not made.

However rigorous the methods used, the research is always a construction. This is because researchers must put their own selves into the research and interpret what they see or hear. This is so, however much one tries to disguise one's presence. King (1978) took refuge in the 'play house' in an infants' classroom so that he could better observe activity unaffected by his presence. Everyone knew he was there, however, and he had to make sense of what was happening. He would do this by observing, taking notes, talking to the teachers involved, writing up field notes after the event, reflecting on them and doing some initial analysis, which might then guide further investigations, and so on. The research is thus gradually constructed over time. The people concerned, the researcher included, are continually making indications to each other, attributing meanings, interpreting symbols. How researchers do this depends, again, on the kind of self they bring to the interpretation – experiences undergone, interests and values, personal reference groups, affective disposition toward those studied, commitment to causes involved in the research.

DILEMMAS OF THE RESEARCHER ROLE

The fact that the researcher has a self, engages in interaction, and interprets and imbues meaning gives rise to a number of dilemmas in the researcher role. If handled sensitively, however, these can be a source of strength.

Objectivity or subjectivity?

Some deny the possibility of objective study, and argue that all research is inescapably subjective; others maintain the contrary – that is, that the proper quest of social scientific research is objective truth. There are also those who believe that both aspects are involved, and far from being oppositional, they are, in fact, complementary, simply opposite ends of a spectrum (Giddens, 1986; Barone, 1990a). I prefer this approach.

At the objective end, there are matters the truth of which can more easily be established to most people's satisfaction than others. These include facts like a person's age, height, weight, place of birth; movements over time, which can be logged; what happened in an actual event; and how cultures are constituted. This may represent an escalating scale of difficulty, but in principle, the truth can be teased out, using some of the methods discussed in this chapter.

A second aspect is the development of general laws, concepts or theories from the data. I discuss this in more detail later. The data may not be generalizable, but the theory is, and it is open to modification by future research. As Glaser and Strauss (1967) put it:

> Even if some of our evidence is not entirely accurate this will not be too troublesome; for in generating theory it is not the fact upon which we stand, but the *conceptual category* (or a *conceptual property* of the category) that was generated from one fact, which then becomes merely one of a universe of many possible diverse indicators for, and data on, the concept.
>
> (p. 23)

Some have argued that a number of subjectivities can constitute a general truth, as when Dilthey points to 'what is shared by all' (in Jansen and Peshkin, 1992, p. 690). This is one postmodernist defence against the charge of nihilism and/or relativism. As Emihovich (1995, p. 45) puts it in discussing the merits of narratives in social research, 'The key...lies in collaboration, of constantly testing our meaning against that of others, building consensus around shared meaning, and ensuring that as many voices as possible are included.' However, as Phillips (1990, p. 290) points out, group consensus does not necessarily constitute a general truth – the collective view can be wrong.

Interactionism is interpretative, mainly interested in how people see things and construct their meanings. The emphasis is on agents grappling with the structures, with society and institutions, and with general laws. Structures exist, but do not have a determining influence. Theories may be sound, but do not explain every single case, nor do they predict what will happen in every case. The multiplicity of factors that abound in every case make that level of accuracy impossible. It becomes even more difficult when exploring people's views or feelings, especially those which they only know and/or can articulate partially themselves. It exists within them, but 'objectifying' the knowledge or feeling is such a problem that it may invalidate the product. Giddens (1986) calls a person's presentation to the world 'practical consciousness'. He believes that it can only ever be partial, and that part of it is not available to discursive awareness. However, this does not mean that we should not attempt to explore these hidden recesses.

Teaching, for example, is a highly personal process, and feelings enter strongly into the teacher's repertoire (Nias, 1989). The question of teacher

motivation – as of pupil motivation – is paramount. Teachers, like everybody else, have to 'feel right' in order to do their job properly (Riseborough,
1981). How, then, do they engage with their work? What is it that motivates
them? From what do they derive their greatest satisfaction? What is it like
to teach well, or teach badly, and what are the attendant conditions? What
is it like to experience stress, and how can that inform us about its causes
and consequences? What causes teachers anger, pain, elation, sense of
achievement, reward? Such reactions can help reveal the meaning of an
event (Jansen and Peshkin, 1992, p. 705). How do they employ their own
and their pupils' emotions in achieving their aims, and how does this
actually work? In this connection there have been considerable advances
recently in understanding pupil cognitive development (see, for example,
Edwards and Mercer, 1987; Mercer, 1995); but again, the part played by
pupils' feelings in this has been underplayed (Woods and Jeffrey, 1996). All
of this area is ripe for investigation, as are matters like school ethos
(dominated hitherto by mainly quantitative approaches – see, for example,
Rutter et al., 1979; Mortimore et al., 1988), classroom climate and atmosphere, the aesthetics of teaching, and the teacher's self. We have hardly
begun to understand these subjects, though anybody who has been
involved in teaching knows that they are crucial to educational advance.
The omission has been due mainly to lack of an appropriate methodology.
Bloom and Munro (1995, p. 110) argue that we must 'allow the complexity,
ambiguity, and contradictions of lived experience to disrupt the traditional
coherence of the text'. We need to understand those subjectivities. But I
would be looking across those to develop or interrogate theory as well, or
to formulate new concepts. These are all part of the same world.

Validity or understanding?

What, then, are the criteria of adequacy? Traditional scientific approaches
which acknowledge the possibility of objective truth and thus emphasize
the importance of validity and reliability have come under severe
challenge in qualitative research in recent years from those who prefer to
seek ends like 'understanding', 'fidelity' and 'trustworthiness'. Others,
and I count myself amongst them, argue the relevance of both. An
approach along these lines is what Altheide and Johnson (1994, p. 489)
call 'analytic realism', and Hammersley (1992) 'subtle realism'. Both reject
traditional dichotomies and dualisms, such as realism/idealism or
universalism/relativism. They deny that we have direct access to an
external objectivity, though there are 'independent, knowable phenomena'. These are human constructions, and cannot be known with absolute
certainty. But we must do our best to get as close to them as possible.
Analytic realism assumes that

   the meanings and definitions brought to actual situations are produced through a communication process. As researchers and observers become increasingly aware that the categories and ideas used to describe the empirical (socially constructed) world are also symbols from specific contexts, this too becomes part of the phenomena studied empirically, and incorporated into the research report.... The process by which the ethnography occurred must be clearly delineated, including accounts of the interactions among context, researcher, methods, setting, and actors.

(Altheide and Johnson, 1994, p. 489)

Hammersley (1990, p. 61) opts for principles of plausibility (is a claim likely to be true given our existing knowledge?) and credibility (does a claim seem warranted 'given the nature of the phenomenon concerned, the circumstances of the research, the characteristics of the researcher etc.'). If neither of these applies, we shall require evidence to be convinced, and this evidence must also be put to the test of plausibility and credibility. How much evidence is required 'depends on the relationship between the conclusions drawn and what the audience takes to be beyond reasonable doubt' (Hammersley, 1993, p. 32).

Similar criteria to those of Altheide and Johnson and of Hammersley, however, find resonance with others, though they may emphasize different aspects. Lofland (1995, p. 49) refers to 'theoretical candour' (the researcher's views of the sources of their analysis); the 'ethnographer's path' (an account of with whom the researcher interacted, in what order, and how); and 'fieldwork evidence' (procedures of assembling and processing data, and practices of presenting data). These are all largely within the traditional ethnographic mould. Some (for example, Lincoln and Guba, 1985) speak of 'trustworthiness', which readers judge in ascertaining the fit between what they read and what they know and have experienced. 'Trustworthiness', according to Lincoln and Guba (1985, p. 300), consists of 'credibility, transferability, dependability and confirmability', established by the constant comparative method of analysis (which I discuss later). As they point out in a later article (Guba and Lincoln, 1994, p. 114), these largely parallel positivist criteria.

These days, Guba and Lincoln prefer the concept of 'authenticity' (see below), and, like some others, would claim to be working to a completely different epistemological approach. If the above are working within a scientific frame of reference, these are more concerned with the artistic side of teacher practice. Some lay emphasis upon whether the account recreates, reawakens, evokes, 'rings bells', 'strikes a chord' in, evokes the spirit and feel of situations, or brings a penetrating insight to respondent and/or reader. Eisner (1991, p. 30) talks about the 'ability to craft text so that what the observer has experienced can be shared by those who were not there'. Elsewhere, Eisner talks of 'educational criticism', which is striving to 'articulate or render those ineffable qualities constituting art in a language that makes them vivid' (1985, p. 92). The task of the critic is

> to adumbrate, suggest, imply, connote, render, rather than to attempt to translate. In this task, metaphor and analogy, suggestion and implication are major tools. The language of criticism, indeed its success as criticism, is measured by the brightness of its illumination. The task of the critic is to help us to see.
>
> (ibid., pp. 92–93)

Similarly, others (for example, Blumenfeld-Jones, 1995) speak of 'fidelity', which, like a painting, is about capturing a likeness of the subject of study. Such a likeness is not something that can be portrayed by simple photography, but requires construction, scene setting, mood inducing, character composition. It will not be a complete picture – that is impossible – but it will present an important aspect in a striking form (see Simons, 1994). Denzin (1994, p. 505) speaks of 'verisimilitude'. This comes from 'thick description' (Geertz, 1973), which, in contrast to straightforward description of facts, 'gives the context of an experience, states the intentions and meanings that organized the experience, and reveals the experience as a process' (Denzin, 1994, p. 505).

What these authors propose is an artistic pursuit, and requires the same kind of appreciative approach by the reader. It may induce what Greene (1978) calls 'wide-awakeness' or Denzin (1989b) an 'epiphany'. Eisner (1995b) argues that this kind of research can 'make aspects of the world vivid and generate a sense of empathy', and heighten awareness of previously unseen qualities (p. 2). Simons (1994), too, drawing on Stake and Kerr (1994), claims that 'research has the power to stimulate thinking as much as express conclusions, and crucially, that research, like Magritte's paintings, if portrayed in problematic ways can provoke us to think differently' (p. 8). Such studies also 'generate awareness of particularity' (Eisner, 1995b, p. 3) and further, through the particular, what is general (as discussed above). MacDonald and Walker (1975, p. 3) argue that 'case study is the way of the artist, who achieves greatness when, through the portrayal of a single instance locked in time and circumstance, he communicates enduring truths about the human condition'. This is similar to Lofland's (1995, p. 40) point about the aim of 'analytic ethnography' being similar to trying 'to see the universe in a grain of sand'. Further, such studies 'possess a sense of wholeness, a coherence, a kind of organic unity that makes both aesthetic experience and credibility possible' (Eisner, 1995b, p. 4).

Wolcott (1994) does not find the concept of 'validity' very useful, and aims to 'understand rather than to convince'. Eisner (1995b, p. 3) also believes that the 'primary tactical aim of research is to advance understanding'. Wolcott (1994) aims not for 'objectivity' but for 'rigorous subjectivity', involving accurate recording and accurate writing or 'wordsmithing' (p. 355). We should try to be as 'credible, balanced, fair, complete, sensitive, rigorously subjective, coherent, internally consistent, appropriate, plausible, and helpful as possible' (Jackson, 1990, p. 154). In some instances there is no one correct interpretation, and to search for it is a wasteful distraction.

> What I seek is something else, a quality that points more to identifying critical elements and wringing plausible interpretations from them, something one can pursue without becoming obsessed with finding the right or ultimate answer, the correct version, the Truth.
>
> (Wolcott, 1994, pp. 366–367)

The example Wolcott uses to make his point is one in which he himself was deeply implicated. He had never been able to sort out his own thoughts and feelings (p. 365). The quest in this particular case, therefore, is not perhaps just understanding, but self-understanding. In clarifying things a little more we not only contribute to knowledge and others' awareness, but come to know our own selves a little better.

The kind of understanding aimed for is one that moves the whole person. As Denzin (1995, p. 16) expresses it: 'Understanding is visceral. The fully interpretive text plunges the reader into the interior, feeling, hearing, tasting, smelling, and touching worlds of subjective human experience.' This puts a strong emphasis on feelings. However, these can both enhance and distort our perceptions. In the research process, Smith (1980, p. 8), for example, using an instance from her own experience in which she became very angry because of what she perceived to be gross injustice to a child, concludes that 'rage is not a dependable emotion with which to interpret experience', but the feeling helped to reveal the meaning of the event to her better than any 'facts' from conventional sources. Clearly, we should not allow our feelings to run riot, but should monitor them reflexively, as Peshkin (1988, p. 21) does when looking for the 'warm and cold spots'. In this way, feelings serve the research instead of swamping it.

Others are more interested in 'usefulness' to the reader, even to the extent of 'empowering' them. Thus Guba and Lincoln's (1994, p. 114) notion of 'authenticity' involves criteria of fairness, enlarging personal constructions, improved understanding of the constructions of others, stimulating to action, and empowering action. In similar vein, some ask whether research is useful or persuasive. Barone (1990b) sees reality as a negotiation between the subjective mind of the observer and the objective external world, with no fixed boundaries between. Certain works of art, to which research studies might aspire, could be catalysts for observers or readers for reflections on, or reconstructions of, their views of reality (as argued in Chapter 1), or, in other words, to reinforce their 'practical consciousness'. Articulating another kind of 'use', Day (1995, p. 358) states quite clearly, 'I am for research which is useful and useable', noting that much research has 'become captured by its own agenda', remote from the concerns of practising teachers. While this foundationalist research might still have a place, he argues, it is no longer entitled to the pre-eminence it has held in the past (see also Guba and Lincoln, 1981; Fullan, 1992). Hargreaves (1995, p. 15) takes this argument further, claiming that 'the postmodern information age is blurring the boundaries between teachers' knowledge and university-based knowledge'. He points to the political (as well as epistemological) aspects of these fields of knowledge utilization, and argues the need for teacher empowerment, and for teachers to 'reclaim the discourse of education'.

Scientific ethnographers would argue the merits of naturalism (subtle), respondent validation and triangulation as aids in establishing validity (see Woods, 1986; Delamont, 1992). However, for some postmodernist researchers, this is too limited, for the triangle is fixed and two-dimensional. Richardson (1994b, p. 522), for example, prefers to talk of 'crystallization', for the crystal 'combines symmetry and substance with an infinite variety of shapes, substances, transmutations, multidimensionalities, and angles of approach. Crystals grow, change, alter, but are not amorphous.' One example she gives is of Valerie Walkerdine's *Schoolgirl Fictions* (1990), in which she displays how the fictions of masculinity and femininity become fact through using in the textbook journal entries, poems, essays, photographs of herself, drawings, cartoons and annotated transcripts.

This is altogether a more ambitious project. It makes great demands upon the researcher's imagination and powers of creativity; and engages the researcher's feelings, in passion and commitment. Hargreaves (1994a, p. 23) has described 'good teaching' as being 'rooted not just in knowledge, skill and competence. It is also ignited by passion, challenge, creativity and joy.' We need a method to engage with this. The same might therefore be said of the 'good researcher'. As Eisner (1991, p. 37) puts it, 'Why take the heart out of situations we are trying to help readers understand?'

My own position is a combination of these approaches. I would be concerned to know: (1) is the subject telling the truth as he or she feels/sees it?; and (2) where referring to events and incidents, is the subject's account accurate? This second is less important where the subject's interpretation is the key issue – for what is seen as real is real in its consequences (Thomas, 1928); in other circumstances, the actual facts could be crucial. For the researcher, there is some verification work here, and this is where the usual practices of triangulation, immersion, respondent validation and so on apply. There is also exploratory work, seeking to understand both the 'practical consciousness' that the agent works with, and some of its more hidden supports. This calls for an array of methods for the purpose of gaining new insights and new understandings.

Exploration is more of an artistic task, verification scientific, a conjunction that is not unusual in qualitative enquiry. Telling the story of these events through the perceptions of the participants is part of this tradition. Langer (1967) draws the contrast between 'generalizing abstraction' (p. 155) through the attempt to develop theory which may have general application beyond the particular circumstances of its generation; and 'presentational abstraction', which involves 'the symbolic transformation of subjectively known realities into objective semblances that are immediately recognized as their expression in sensory appearances' (p. 157). This also involves exactness, but it is more important that it creates something that is lifelike and develops 'feeling within the form' to produce 'believability' (Blumenfeld-Jones, 1995, p. 31).

In recent years, the area of ethnographic interest in schools has expanded beyond the cognitive, and into aesthetics and the emotions. The basic situation has not changed. There are still people interacting within situations, and within cultural and subcultural groups; they are still devising strategies and negotiating. We are in a position now to cast more light on these activities. Some new methods, therefore, are required, without totally abandoning the old. With the postpositivists I agree with a form of 'subtle realism', but I would not want to see enquiry bound and dominated by a stringent application of plausibility and credibility criteria, and the requirement to test results formally in a narrowly defined way. This seems to me to squeeze all the interesting material, which is not susceptible to that form of test, out of account (see the discussion in Hammersley, 1987a, 1987b; Woods, 1987b). This includes a great deal of the expressive behaviour I included in Chapter 1 as illustrative of the art of teaching. For this kind of material, we need more of an appreciative approach aiming towards understanding and forms of expression that will adequately describe it and convey it successfully to the reader. I discuss some of these in the following three chapters.

Involvement versus distance

An associated methodological problem for qualitative researchers is that between involvement, immersion and empathy on the one hand, and distance and scientific appraisal and objectivity on the other. The former is necessary to understand others' perspectives as they see them, to see how they see others, to identify their problems and concerns, and to decode their symbolic behaviour. It involves negotiating access, developing rapport, trust and friendship, sociability, inclusion, identification with the others involved, sensitivity to their concerns, and ability to appreciate their feelings as well as cognitive orientations. However, the more one succeeds in taking the role of the other, the greater the danger of the researcher's perspective being taken over by the subjects in the well-known syndrome of 'going native' (Paul, 1953), or 'going over to the other side' (Thomas, 1995). A frequent criticism of some ethnographers is that they romanticize their subjects, seeing them through 'rose-coloured glasses', representing them with great sympathy as well as empathy, while others who figure in the subject's world appear as pale shadows (this criticism has been made of Willis, 1977). There is also the risk of distortion – of letting the part represent the whole.

To guard against the dangers of going native, one is advised to cultivate some social distance. The researcher is, after all, different from the subjects of the research. She or he is there to research, to plumb the depths and 'get to the bottom of things' certainly, but of all groups involved in any specified interaction and in a way that recognizes put-ons, power positions, 'line shooting' and fairy tales. She or he is also there to analyse, to advance explanations, and to represent material in ways that might not otherwise occur to the inmates. Establishing comparative bases in and among groups, cultivating rapport with other groups, triangulation of methods to increase validity, reflectivity outside the situation, the consideration of material *post hoc*, the writing up of field notes and diaries all aid this process and enable the researcher, if involvement and distance are cultivated in a judicious mixture, to have the best of both.

Creativity versus evaluation

This dilemma reflects the tension in the researcher between the 'I' and the 'Me'. To what extent should the 'I' be given free rein; to what extent checked and disciplined by the 'Me'? In 'discovery' research, the 'I' has to be given a certain licence. As Mead (1934) argues, we do not know what wonders lie within its capabilities. The 'I' is important in several respects. First, in the realm of feelings, the 'I' is responsible for the stirring of excitement, curiosity and motivation so indispensable for any kind of research. This does much to counter the physical and mental fatigue one experiences during the intensive fieldwork period. It keeps the mind alert to a range of possibilities, in several situations and in interaction with a number of people throughout the day, often including 'rest' periods (because these are (1) interesting in themselves and (2) useful for making up notes). It keeps one going in writing up field notes at night. It supplies the drive and impulsion that keep sloth and ennui at bay during difficult periods or that win over them when promising openings beckon but one's stamina wilts. Secondly, the 'I' creates opportunities for interaction. Some may feel they can witness things as they naturally happen with 'fly-on-the-wall' techniques (although flies can be very distracting!). Others may feel the need to make things happen, at least with respect to creating openings and making appointments. There is always a tension here between 'naturalism' and 'arrangement', but access must be organized. Sometimes it is not clear where one goes next – the 'I', unleashed, should come to the rescue. Openness of mind, willingness to follow hunches and take risks, and a certain stoicism if they do not work are all part of this. Thirdly, it is the 'I' that creates ideas, conceptualizes, identifies patterns, notices a relationship where no relationship was suspected before, detects a missing factor, recognizes a problem, and worries at its resolution.

All this is indispensable. But somewhere along the way the 'I' must be subject to checks and discipline. The 'Me' embodies the scientific community, the canons of social scientific research, and existing literature in the area. It will carry out tests, looking for negative cases and seeking contrary evidence. Some ideas will prove ephemeral and, thus, be discarded for lack of evidence or reshaped to fit that which exists. The 'Me' will spot weaknesses in the use of only one method or only one informant and qualify findings accordingly. It will monitor for inadequate sampling and repair it. It will reveal ambiguities, inconsistencies and lacunae, and point to the need for more research. It will reveal leading questions and other errors on the tape transcript and, thus, condition one's approach. It will show how one's research is similar and dissimilar to others' in the area. Thus, the 'I' scanning freely detects critical items and themes for study; the 'Me' locks them into place. The 'I' and the 'Me' are not phased in this neat way but are more or less in continuous interaction, although the 'I' probably has more licence in the earlier, discovery, and scene-setting part of the research. The conditioning of the 'Me' helps to identify the worthwhile features of the research, sifting out elements that do not stand up by agreed criteria and highlighting those that do. It helps to make more 'solid', as opposed to 'indulgent', sense, 'scientific' as opposed to 'personal'.

The dilemma is sometimes represented as intensive examination of one particular area, kind of interaction or process, or subject versus extensive examination of many. Ethnography involves intensive study of the subject under examination, putting social life under the microscope, seeing the myriad details of everyday life in fine relief, and leaving no stone unturned in the search for deeper focus and sharper definition. Critics have sometimes complained that this leads to myopia, tunnel vision, and getting bogged down in detail. However, the myopia is counteracted and even made a virtue by attention to sampling; triangulation of sources, of researchers or of methods; historical and social contextualization (for an example, see Lacey, 1970); and the search for formal theory (see next section).

Covert versus overt research

This is the main ethical problem in ethnography and reflects the tension between the public's right to know and the subject's right to privacy (Bulmer, 1980, 1982; Burgess, 1985a; Soltis, 1989). Such problems are most acute in ethnography, which rests on the deep personal engagement of the researcher and relationships established and developed during the study. Consider, for example, the ethical implications of researching in repressive institutions, such as a concentration camp or an authoritarian and punitive school, or in criminal activities, or in racist or otherwise biased institutions. It might be thought difficult for a researcher committed to principles of equality and social justice, for example, to work 'overtly' in such institutions. There might be greater problems in access being granted in the first instance or being sustained once the purpose of such research was discovered. Yet it is important that such institutions be researched.

Such features might come to light in the course of the research. The researcher is then faced with the problem of whether or not to expose such injustices. This might run against the terms of his or her negotiated contract and the human decency implied by the relationships developed during the research. It might also be counter-productive in terms of promoting the cause (producing, for example, confrontation rather than conversion) and to the cause of research generally, in prejudicing other researchers' opportunities. On the other hand, to say nothing might be to condone the wrong or injustice reinforcing the prevailing system. Worse, the researcher might act as a 'provocateur', subjects rehearsing morally dubious activities possibly in exaggerated form in the belief that they are doing the researcher a service.

Participant observation has, on occasion, been likened to 'spying' or 'voyeurism', activities more in keeping with intelligence services and perversion than academic research. There is an unsavoury feel to such a role so conceived. The researcher effects entry, carries out what observations are required, persuades subjects to 'spill the beans', and then 'cuts and runs', writing up the account in private in the service of humanity in general. The question is, do the ends justify the means? If we accept that, are we any better than those studied? Is there a moral code that we should accept? How far would that prevent the truth from emerging?

Bulmer (1982) has argued strongly against covert research. It runs against the principle of 'informed consent' (people agreeing to take part in research on the basis of knowledge of what it is really about); invades privacy, 'contaminating private spheres of the self' (p. 220); involves deception, which is inimical to the qualities of trust, rapport and friendship; breeds more and more problems, for example, of where to stop; harms sociology and sociologists; and carries a number of practical problems (such as the difficulty of sustaining such a front over a long period).

However, as Bulmer acknowledges, research is hardly that clear-cut. There are some who seek to justify covert research they have conducted (Humphreys 1975; Homan, 1980; Holdaway, 1982) and others who see *some* as unavoidable (Denzin, 1968; Roth, 1962; Burgess, 1985a; Gans, 1968). 'Consent' is not a straightforward business. As Dingwall (1980, p. 878) points out, in stratified settings there is a 'hierarchy of consent', senior personnel acting as 'gatekeepers' and subordinates possibly being forced to participate. Also, one encounters so many people during a typical study, often casually, that it is impossible to secure the consent of all. The researcher is faced with a complexity of choices and is subject to a number of situational constraints. Public and private spheres are not always sharply defined, and 'total openness' is probably unachievable. One cannot always predict the courses qualitative research will take or what surprises it will turn up. Covert methods in some instances, too, *have* advanced our understanding of society (for example, Rosenhan, 1982; Festinger et al., 1956). In large, complex organizations, covert observation is perhaps more acceptable, the self being cushioned here by bureaucracy. Douglas (1970) argues that the powerful hide behind secrecy, manipulation and deceit, and require similar methods to penetrate their armour.

Bulmer (1982) is not impressed by these arguments, feeling that 'sociologists need to think creatively about ways in which access may be gained other than by outright deception'. He quotes from the *American Sociologist*'s (1968) *Toward a Code of Ethics*:

Just as sociologists must not distort or manipulate truth to serve untruthful ends, so too they must not manipulate persons to serve their quest for truth. The study of society, being the study of human beings, imposes the responsibility or respecting the integrity, promoting the dignity and maintaining the autonomy of these persons.

(Bulmer, 1982, p. 318)

It should be noted, too, that open fieldwork *has* been done with sociologically unsympathetic groups such as the National Front (Fielding, 1981). These ethical problems set up conflicts in the researcher's self. Whyte (1955) experienced considerable personal anguish over the deception he felt compelled to use in his study of 'Cornerville'; Patrick (1973) felt obliged to conclude his research on a Glasgow gang because his covert involvement was pressing him into criminal activity; Humphreys (1975) later regretted the various deceptions he had deployed in his study of homosexual encounters.

The moral conflict arises from elements grating against each other in the self. The researcher engaging in joint action with subjects sets up an interpretative and moral frame that rests on a certain code of conduct involving certain mutual expectations. The interaction, in other words, is rule-bound, although most of the rules are implicit, just as the interaction being observed. It is constructed over time and reinforced by many interactions. The other's behaviour towards you as researcher, as already noted, rests on the perception of who and what you are, why and for whom you are doing the research, what your interests are, your view of them, and your relationships with them and others. As Dean (1954) states,

A person becomes accepted as a participant observer more because of the kind of person he turns out to be in the eyes of the field contacts than because of what the research represents to them. Field contacts want to be reassured that the research worker is a 'good guy' and can be trusted not 'to do them dirt' with what he finds out.

(p. 233)

If most of this relationship is based on a sham, one is deceiving not only the subjects, but also one's self. If it offends one's own values and runs contrary to principles ingrained through years of socialization, not to mention allegiance to a professional code of ethics (all represented in the 'Me'), one risks a damaged self, a 'spoiled' project and possibly a spoiled research career. In the course of a research study, many such issues will need to be confronted. The 'I' will seek a creative resolution of them. Where partial deception is involved, the 'Me' will monitor how, and with what justice, it is encased in a greater good, and, if it concludes 'not much', the 'I' in turn will seek early repair and recompense. If there are no such opportunities or the deception is too great, the researcher may experience agonies of conscience and a personal crisis. The appreciative element of symbolic interactionism, taking the role of the other, and seeing the world through other's perceptions all take place in a moral context. So, too, do the indications one makes to oneself. Reflexivity involves a constant monitoring of the rightness of what one is doing. It may also involve a change in the researcher's self. Taken-for-granted beliefs and assumptions, views on the world, and comprehension of one's own interests, abilities and aspirations may all come under review.

Ethnographers will continue to debate these matters keenly. And, while general ethical parameters will be worked out in codes of professional ethics that apply to the community, there will be many particular instances requiring individual adaptations that depend on the construction of self. As Dingwall (1980, p. 888) acknowledges, 'competent fieldwork requires a clear conscience'. In Soltis' (1989, p. 129) opinion, this basically involves observing the 'non-negotiable' values of 'honesty, fairness, respect for persons and beneficence' – markers laid down by the professional community for personal struggles. But while they are 'non-negotiable' in principle, in practice many decisions must constantly be made that contain the dilemma that observing these values in one form means not doing so in others (see, for example, Burgess, 1985a). At the same time, the underlying purpose of the research, which is usually to produce generalizable statements and theory, provides some ethical safeguards through close attention to how this theory is produced. It is to this subject that I now return.

THE GENERATION OF THEORY

Grounded theory

During the 1970s and the unproductive debate about 'positivism' versus 'interpretivism', it was customary to draw the contrast between the hypothetico-deductive method and the 'testing' of theory on the one hand and the qualitative inductive method and the 'generating' of theory on the other. However, qualitative techniques can be used both to generate and to test theory, though the emphasis in fieldwork research to date has been on the first, largely guided by the work of Glaser and Strauss (1967).

Their criticism of much verification work was not because verification of existing theories was not important but, rather, because many of the theories that were being tested were not 'grounded' in the empirical world and were unsound in the first place. They were poorly generated in the social activity they sought to explain. They would, thus, have poor predictive value and be of little use in practical applications.

Generating theory

Much qualitative work has been criticized for being merely descriptive, for being limited to 'how' rather than including 'why' questions. But these distinctions are not as clear-cut as they might seem. Ethnographic description is theory-laden in several senses. The researcher inevitably interprets what she or he finds through certain theoretical frameworks. The same applies to the subjects she or he studies in how they make sense of the world. The representation of findings, too, is no ordinary 'description' that anybody could provide. In the rich detail of several 'layers of reality', classifications, categories, typologies and conceptual refinement, representation amounts to what Geertz (1973) has called 'thick' description, already heavily theoretically informed. That many ethnographies stop at this point may be an indication of the inferential difficulties in proceeding further or, of course, sheer exhaustion. Another possibility is that it could be the limit to which the researcher feels that 'theoretically informed description' can go. But the research does not have to stop there, because theory is process, an 'ever-developing entity, not a perfected product' (Glaser and Strauss, 1967, p. 32). Analysis also is not a separate stage of the research but is done in interaction with ongoing fieldwork from the very beginning. One may be reluctant to 'take' rather than 'make' problems (Turner, 1962) or to specify the issue or problem to be examined in advance of the study. But then no ethnographer begins absolutely with a blank page. From readings, discussions and experience, ethnographers will have developed a notion of the research. It may be a 'foreshadowed problem' (Malinowski, 1922) derived from lacunae in the literature, either empirical or theoretical. It may involve some 'mapping' of previously uncharted territory. The Chicago School excelled at this, with their fascination to understand the city in all its social aspects. The same applies to British ethnography of the 1970s and 1980s, which 'mapped out' the field of the school and classroom and, in time, rectified certain imbalances, such as the early 1970s favouring of boys as a research interest over girls, the neglect of black people, the emphasis on deviants and on older, secondary school pupils, and a period of 'teacher-bashing'. Theoretically guided research may be used to test an existing theory or to modify or elaborate upon it. One of the best examples is the development of differentiation–polarization theory (see Woods, 1990b, pp. 29–36).

In these various ways, the research is theoretically driven from the start. Once in the field, the search begins for new theory. Theory often is represented as being in the situation one studies or emerging from it. It is actually constructed in the researcher's head, but is rigorously checked and rechecked against the ongoing data. It is not the product of some preconceived idea. In so far as it 'emerges', it does so from the strength of the indicators one identifies. The sheer weight and apparently disparate nature of data prompts motivation to structure and synthesize. Nias (1991, p. 162) observes that

> the extent and quality of the information I collected challenged me to search for and eventually find connections and relationships between apparently isolated ideas. In seeking not to drown in the data, I found unexpected reefs under my feet.

What form do these indicators take? They are signs that alert one to the fact that 'something is up', that there is something odd about what is being witnessed, or that there is a connection between events previously unsuspected or a pattern that is gradually, over time, revealed. Inconsistencies and contrasts also arouse interest, such as those mentioned earlier concerning radical changes in teacher behaviour between situations (Waller, 1932; Keddie, 1971; Lacey 1976; Hargreaves, 1978b). Why do teachers behave with such irrationality and such pettiness on occasion? Why do pupils 'work' with one teacher and 'raise hell' with another (Turner, 1983). From this latter observation, Turner came to certain conclusions about pupil interests and school resources and refined notions of 'conformity and deviance'.

The investigation of key words is a common method for unpacking meanings. Becker et al. (1961) gave the example of 'crock', a common term used by physicians about their patients, which the researcher used as a way of understanding medics' perspectives. Similarly, the identification and comprehending of pupil argot is a *sine qua non* of understanding pupil culture. Why did Willis' 'lads' refer to another group of pupils as 'ear'oles'? (Basically, it was because they were always 'listening' and never 'doing'; but the term carries a wealth of meaning that stands in contrast and thus highlights the 'lads'' own beliefs and activities.) Other research has turned up 'dossers' (idlers) and 'swots' (hard-working pupils) (Turner, 1983). Beynon (1985) found the boys of his research indulging in an activity they described as 'sussing-out'. This was a sophisticated set of linked activities, which at first glance seemed anarchic and meaningless (cf. Cohen, 1968), but which were part of a 'process of establishment' during the crucial phase of 'initial encounters' (see also Ball, 1980). The pupils studied by Werthman (1963) and Rosser and Harré (1976) laid great emphasis on 'looking cool'. Sharp and Green's (1975) 'progressive' teachers wanted their children to be 'busy', which led them to formulate their concept of 'busyness' as an organizing feature of such teachers' perspectives.

The construction of typologies and theoretical models

After the identification of key topics, one proceeds to investigate their types and properties. What kinds of sussing-out, for example, are indulged in? Beynon (1985) classified the major types – group formation and communication, joking, verbal and non-verbal challenges, intervention, and play – with subtypes within them. Some qualitative studies stop at this point, incurring the criticism that all they do is construct typologies. But typologies are not lacking worth in themselves, nor is cessation of analysis at this point an inevitable product of the method. What this activity does is ensure that the notion of sussing-out has substance and delineates its major forms. We would want to go on from there to consider how sussing-out works. How do teachers and pupils modify their behaviour toward each other? Why does it take this particular form?

To answer these questions we would need to consider three things. First, we would need to act upon the interactionist axiom of seeking to understand events from the point of view of the participants, and try to discover the pupils' intention. The second factor is incidence. One would want to know when and where this kind of activity took place and with whom. Was it limited to initial encounters? If it were occurring at other times, another explanation would be required. Under what sort of circumstance did it occur, and with what kinds of teacher and what kinds of pupil? Were all pupils involved, or only some? What proportion of total pupil behaviour was taken up with this kind of activity? This is the contextual aspect. Comparisons need to be made with other sections of activity. Theory and methodology interact, the emerging theory guiding the next part of the investigation. If there were similar activity elsewhere, then the theory might have to be revised – although there might be another explanation for that activity. Third, what would the consequences of the activity be? The theory would lead us to expect that where the required knowledge was ascertained, where teachers justified their claims to being able to teach and to control, different, more 'settled' behaviour would ensue; where it was not, the behaviour would presumably continue and perhaps intensify, because the boundaries of tolerance would be seen as lying further and further back. If this were not the case, again the theory might have to be revised.

It is also necessary to explore alternative theories. In the case of sussing-out, one would need to consider the possibility that the behaviour was a cultural product (for example, of male, working-class or ethnic culture) or an institutional behaviour (that is, a function of a particular kind of school organization). Some of these elements, of course, might also be involved – that is, the behaviour might be and probably is multifunctional.

Comparative analysis

The development of the theory proceeds in a rigorous way, primarily by means of comparative analysis. Instances are compared across a range of situations, over a period of time, among a number of people, and through a variety of methods. Attention to sampling is important if the theory being formulated concerns a particular population. Thus, comparisons are made among a representative set. Negative cases are sought for these and perhaps may invalidate the argument or suggest contrary explanations. These comparisons may be made both inside and outside the study. These kinds of comparison, however, can also be used for other purposes – establishing accurate evidence, establishing empirical generalizations, specifying a concept (bringing out the distinctive elements or nature of the case), and verifying theory (Glaser and Strauss, 1967).

Theorizing begins from the first day of fieldwork with the identification of possibly significant events or words. Field notes are not only recorded but coded, in a number of ways. There are alternative ways of doing this (Glaser and Strauss, 1967; Lincoln and Guba, 1985; Grove, 1988). I largely follow the Glaser and Strauss model. The first coding may arise directly from the data, taking subjects' classification. For example, in a study of 'pupil perspectives', 'being picked on', 'being shown up' and 'being made to do hard work' are some pupils' claims about their treatment by teachers that could form the initial classification. Re-examination of the material might reveal that some might be placed under several codes, as well as force consideration of material that has not yet been but that must be coded, if the theory is to be all-inclusive – all aspects of pupil perspectives revealed by the research must be included.

Some provisional rules are now established for allocating to categories, and these become more refined, more clearly demarcated and firmer as the research proceeds. These codes may have sufficient theoretical purchase to form the basis of the theory. This is true of 'being shown up' and 'sussing-out'. Or they may be translated into higher-order constructs, as with 'teacher strategies' and 'pupil strategies'. Such concepts should be analytic – 'sufficiently generalized to designate *characteristics* of complete entities, rather than the entities themselves' (Bulmer, 1979, p. 666) – and *sensitizing*, which means more forward-looking and offering direction (Blumer, 1954).

Glaser and Strauss (1967, 1968) give the example of 'social loss' generated in their study to explain nurses' differential treatment of the dying. Sikes, Measor and Woods (1985) developed a theory about different kinds of teacher commitment and how movement among them depended on socioeconomic circumstances in their study of teacher careers; A. Hargreaves (1984c) abstracted his notion of 'contrastive rhetoric' as a political strategy in school policy discussions (for his account of the generation of this concept, see Hargreaves, 1987). All of these are based in the first instance on initial coding arising directly from the data. The whole process ensures the groundedness of the ensuing theory (for more detailed examples, see Strauss, 1987).

As categories and codes are suggested by the data, so they pre-figure the direction of the research in a process known as 'theoretical sampling'. This is to ensure that all categories and codes are identified and filled or groups fully researched. Thus, Mac an Ghaill (1989) followed the observation of an anti-school group, the 'Warriors', with the collection of material from school reports and questionnaires on their attitudes towards school, enabling him to build case histories. This is a good illustration of how theory and methodology inter-relate, leading to an 'escalation of insights' (Lacey, 1976). Investigation goes on until 'saturation' occurs – when no new theoretical forms are being generated and new data does not add to existing ones.

To aid this process, the researcher becomes steeped in the data but, at the same time, employs devices to ensure breadth and depth of vision. These include the compilation of a field diary, a running commentary on the research with reflections on one's personal involvement; marginal comments on field notes as thoughts occur on reading and rereading them; comparisons and contrasts with other material; further light cast by later discoveries; relevance to other literature; notes concerning the adequacy of data and analysis; and aides-memoire, memos and notes, committing thoughts to paper on interconnections among the data and some possible concepts and theories. Consulting the literature is an integral part of theory development. It helps to stimulate ideas and to give shape to the emerging theory, thus providing both commentary on and a stimulus to study. Consulting colleagues is also helpful, for their funds of knowledge and as academic 'sounding boards'. The sounding board is an important device for helping to articulate and shape ideas. What may seem to be brilliant insights to the researcher may be false premises to others. The critical scrutiny of one's peers at this formative stage is very helpful. It may be obtained by discussion (the mere fact of trying to articulate an idea helps to shape it), by circulating papers, or by giving seminars.

Where appropriate, those featuring in the research may engage in 'respondent validation', as discussed earlier. Although not always as applicable for the reasons given, this can be useful in testing the salience of higher-order constructs. For example, explaining their relevance to respondents on matters of close concern to them can be particularly instructive (see also Ball, 1984). In one such life-history study, I was persuaded to discard some concepts that I thought illuminated some aspects of the life, but that the subject saw as obfuscatory (Woods, 1985). More discussion ensued on the points in question, and as more empirical details emerged it became clear that he was right. The result was a tighter analysis more firmly grounded in the 'life'. For Mac an Ghaill (1988, 1989), the involvement of the pupils in his study in his analysis was crucial:

> There was continual critical discussion, among the students and myself, of the descriptions and interpretations of the data. More specifically, we were concerned primarily with the inter-relationship of the three dimensions of 'race', gender and class. For the Black Sisters, racism was the main determinant of their lifestyles outside the domestic situation, though the interaction of class and gender with racism was acknowledged.
>
> (Mac an Ghaill, 1989, p. 182)

Another important factor is time. The deeper the involvement, the longer the association, the wider the field of contacts and knowledge, the more intense the reflection, and the stronger the promise of groundedness. Nias (1991) remarks:

> The fact that I have worked for so long on the material has enabled my ideas to grow slowly, albeit painfully. They have emerged, separated, recombined, been tested against one another and against those of other people, been rejected, refined, re-shaped. I have had the opportunity to *think* a great deal over 15 years, about the lives and professional biographies of primary teachers and about their experience of teaching as work. My conclusions, though they are in the last resort those of an outsider, are both truly 'grounded' and have had the benefit of slow ripening in a challenging professional climate.
>
> (p. 162)

Nias reminds us that a great deal of *thinking* must go into this process and that this is frequently *painful*. Wrestling with mounds and mounds of ever-accumulating material; searching for themes and indicators that will make some sense of it all; taking some apparently promising routes, only to find they are blind alleys; writing more and more notes and memos; rereading notes and literature for signs and clues; doing more fieldwork to fill in holes or in the hope of discovering some beacon of light; presenting tentative papers that receive well-formulated and devastating criticisms – all these are part and parcel of the generation of theory.

The criteria for a good grounded theory include a strong degree of fit with the data it purports to explain; explanatory power, accounting for the relationships among the elements under specific conditions, thus being able to predict outcomes under particular circumstances; relevance, in being directed towards central concerns of the area under examination; flexibility, in being capable of taking into account new and different material; density, where the theoretical constructs are few but encompass a large number of properties and categories; and integration, indicating a strong relationship among the constructs (Glaser and Strauss, 1967, 1968; Hutchinson, 1988; Strauss and Corbin, 1994).

THE PROMISE OF SYMBOLIC INTERACTIONISM

D.H. Hargreaves (1978a) has drawn attention to the following strengths of symbolic interactionism:

1 its appreciative capacity, or its ability to explore social action from the point of view of the actor;
2 its designatory capacity, or its ability to articulate taken-for-granted, commonsense knowledge, thus providing a language for discourse about these areas;
3 its reflective capacity, or its ability to provide members or inmates with the means to reflect on their own activity;
4 its immunological capacity, or its ability to inform policy by providing knowledge and understanding of the everyday life of school, thus helping to protect the policy from failure;
5 its corrective capacity, or its ability to offer a critique of macro-theories that may be incorrect in their empirical assumptions – and, hence, serving as a means of strengthening them. Some of these were mentioned earlier.

We might add to these four others:

6 Its illuminative capacity, or the range, depth and richness of detail it provides on individuals, groups, institutions and issues. Interactionist ethnography has opened up and illuminated the 'black box' of the school. It will be prominent in the investigation of issues – for example, in the United Kingdom, in monitoring the consequences of the 1988 Education Reform Act, such as the impact of testing pupils and teachers, the induction of new governors, how teachers adapt their subject, teaching and their selves to the new imperatives, the repercussions for teacher careers, and the experiential consequences of institutional change. On all such issues, and others, there will be a continuing need for the kind of information the interactionist approach provides.
7 Its theoretical capacity. Symbolic interactionism has considerable theoretical possibilities. It can generate theory inductively, leading to strongly grounded theory. It can exert strong influence on macro-theory and lead to its reformulation, as in resistance theory. It also offers good chances of conceptualizing the micro–macro interface. As well, it

affords a means of testing theory, as in the line of work associated with differentiation–polarization.

8 Its policy-making capacity. Finch (1986) points out that the researchers of the Chicago School of the 1930s were not directly concerned with policy. Their work, however, did have direct policy implications, although 'not of a kind which could be straightforwardly applied within the dominant political framework' (p. 132). Much interactionist work since has been similar. There are signs, however, that some interactionists are becoming more directly policy-minded. This was certainly true of the Manchester studies of Hargreaves (1967) and Lacey (1970), which conceivably had an impact on school organization policy. It is vividly illustrated by A. Hargreaves (1988), who shows how an analysis of classroom teaching drawing attention to the effects of such things as large classes, full timetables, examination pressures, and poor career prospects leads to vastly different policy implications from those promoted by the Department of Education and Science (1983), which was arguing that the most important factor in teaching was the teacher's 'personal qualities'. It is much to the fore also in studies of pressing social issues such as gender and 'race'. Such studies would be expected to inform whole-school policies on these matters (see, for example, Stanley, 1986, 1989; Gillborn, 1990, 1995; Measor, 1983, 1989; Wright, 1986, 1992; Foster, 1990; Mac an Ghaill, 1994).

9 Its collaborative capacity. Interactionism provides opportunities for researchers and teachers to join together in doing research, thus promoting professionalism and helping to effect change from within the school. The researcher's theoretical and methodological knowledge and the teacher's practical knowledge of teaching make a strong combination, the one enriching the other (Pollard, 1984; Woods, 1985, 1986, 1989; Hustler et al., 1986; Woods and Pollard, 1988; and see Chapter 5). This entails a model of teacher as 'reflective practitioner' (Schön, 1983), theoretically aware, and seeking ways of applying scientific knowledge to practical problem solving. This is consonant with the 'transformative', 'emancipatory', 'empowering' (of members) approach of critical ethnography (see Lather, 1986; Anderson, 1989; Troyna and Carrington, 1989). We might expect collaborative work to increase, therefore, in the future.

Interactionist ethnography continues to be relevant because:

1 We are still a long way from understanding the nature of the art of teaching.

2 It has its part to play in the general monitoring of teachers' lives and cultures, which undergo continual change. In the restructuring of schools currently in progress, there are new forms of institutional organization, new roles and careers among the personnel, new perspectives formulating. These changes and their effects need monitoring in

themselves. However, policy is not just put into practice in linear fashion. A number of studies have shown that implementation, to some degree or other, is negotiable (Ball and Bowe, 1992; Vulliamy and Webb, 1993; Woods, 1995a; Webb and Vulliamy, 1996). It is in such areas that ethnography is particularly strong.

3 Teaching requires, for many, heavy investment of the self. Teachers feel strongly about their work, and fortify their pedagogy with sophisticated use of the emotions. This manifests itself in innumerable ways in the course of a lesson. These 'expressive dimensions' of a teacher's conduct, especially in the minutiae of classroom life which are often overlooked because they appear trivial and mundane, exert considerable moral influence on students.

4 Interactionist ethnography can contribute to a sociology of learning. Pollard (1990), for example, has argued for an amalgamation of symbolic interactionism and social constructivism in considering how pupils learn. The whole area of metacognition (Quicke, 1992) needs exploring, and pupil perspectives and cultures require continuous monitoring.

5 There are many ways of describing practice and progress. Our understanding of classroom life has been enhanced by labelling, deviance and subcultural theories; by concepts such as coping strategies, collaborative cultures, contrived collegiality, testing out, and initial encounters; and by the explication and unpacking of key inmate terms, such as 'having a laugh', or 'keeping 'em quiet'. There will always be a demand for new concepts and new ways of seeing in the interests of raising our understanding of school life. This is not only because such work is never finished, but more importantly because things are rapidly changing – as in point 2 above.

6 There are too some current issues that have become more or less a preserve for psychologists, but which demand the attention of sociologists. I have mentioned deviance (which includes disruption, school exclusion and bullying) and learning. There is also teacher stress, a growing problem in England and Wales since the 1988 Act. Teacher stress has been looked at almost exclusively in psychological terms, but it is a social fact. This can be demonstrated by statistics, but to understand its nature and origins, detailed qualitative work involving teacher narratives and perhaps life-histories is indicated.

7 Interactionist ethnography will also continue to map out the micro end of the micro–macro continuum, and explore agency in its ongoing relationship with structure. It can both describe subjective experience and act as a test of theory, as in A. Hargreaves' (1994c) research on Canadian teachers' experiences of intensification. It can show how social class (Dubberley, 1988a, 1988b), race (Wright, 1986, 1992) and gender (Draper, 1993) are acted out in the minutiae of day-to-day classroom life.

8 Interactionist ethnography can play a part in the life of the area or subject being researched to its advantage, or to those of other people involved. It is a very accessible method, particularly to teachers, both to use and to read about, and can play a strong role in teacher development (Woods, 1986; Denscombe, 1995). Through its articulating, designatory and illuminative qualities, it can lend strength to teachers in a political capacity. This is not to say that ethnographic research should not retain its critical edge, using its capacity to 'get to the bottom of things', to cut through rhetoric and ideology, and to recognize strategy and contrivance. Some of its findings, therefore, may at times be uncomfortable for teachers.

We have noted how interactionism can help bring together cognition and affectivity, and micro and macro. It also amalgamates art and science. This manifests itself in various ways – the 'brilliance of the prose', which 'has to creep around inside our own belief systems and dig these elements and objects out and present them to our gaze' (Goffman, in Taylor, 1987, p. 155), 'poetic eloquence' (McLaren, in Newman, 1989), and the graphic, almost alive, evocations of interaction in Willis (1977), Riseborough (1981) or Beynon (1985). Further examples follow in Chapter 3. More important than these end products is how art and science combine in the production of research. The one inspires to represent culture, biographies and activities as they are lived and experienced in, sometimes, almost poetic terms; the other ensures that there is no poetic licence, that this is really what happened. The one facilitates the identification of patterns, themes and connections that will assist the emergence of concepts and theory; the other monitors these ideas, rejecting those that are unsatisfactory by scientific criteria, ordering and arranging others, and comparing them with others elsewhere.

This, some might argue, is no more than an expression of the 'I' and the 'Me' and their essential dialectic for the unity of the self. If art and science do need to be brought together, interactionism has good qualifications to promote the amalgamation and to help produce a most human science.

3   Seeing into the life of things

While with an eye made quiet by the power
Of harmony, and the deep power of joy,
We see into the life of things.
>   (Wordsworth, 'Lines Composed . . . Above Tintern Abbey')

INTRODUCTION

As noted earlier, traditional notions of validity, including that advanced in Chapter 2, have come under increasing criticism in the last decade or so. One particular line of attack has followed from what Tyler (1986) describes as the 'postmodernist turn'. This has gathered pace in the 1980s and 1990s to such an extent that Richardson (1993, p. 706) can assert that 'We have an historical opportunity to create a space for different kinds of science practice.' I think this is true, but I see these new techniques and approaches as enriching our existing research methods armoury, rather than replacing it. In this chapter, I look at some new ways of seeing and of presentation which aim to emulate Wordsworth in various ways in constructing words and actions that live on themselves in 'the life of things'.

These approaches are, as yet, experimental. There is a danger that an 'experimentalist' *Zeitgeist* will promote a belief that 'anything goes', spawning a mass of ill-founded, shoddy, dilettante studies. Yet postmodernist developments could be quite the reverse of this, contributing to better understanding and better-founded knowledge. For the quest is for accuracy of, and depth of, understanding, and for ways of conveying that to others which keep faith with that accuracy and depth. There is a view that verification studies have put a strait-jacket on research, and that they, in their way, *because* of a misplaced attention to a particular form of rigour, have restricted the achievement of new understanding through experimentation.

The search for 'new ways' has involved 'passionate criticism' and emotional involvement (see Emihovich, 1995; Wolcott, 1990b; Hargreaves, 1994c). Much has been missed in the use of conventional methods, particularly in the area of emotions and feelings, atmospheres, climates, moods and tones. Customary academic writing is unable to reach these areas. Rose (1990, p. 46) urges us to 'break frames, disciplinary rules, received notions, and the conventions of fieldwork with its repetitious intellectual labours'; A. Hargreaves (1995, p. 32) to 'diversify what are to count as legitimate forms of knowledge about teaching and education' and 'broaden the forms of discourse through which research knowledge is presented'. Richardson (1994b, p. 523) argues that there is no one 'right' way to present a text, but many different ways depending on our aims and audience. 'Material' is a constant in mass if not in form in her discussion, like 'wet clay for us to shape'.

There is a range of possibilities. Denzin's (1992, 1993) deconstructions of films suggest a new way of understanding a lesson. In an attempt to convey feeling with succinct precision some are experimenting with poetry (Johnson, 1993; Richardson, 1994b), or with poetically crafted narrative (Eisner, 1993) or drama (for example, Becker et al., 1988; Paget, 1990). Some use literature as a model, or employ narrative, story, fiction (Rowland, 1991; Winter, 1991; Bolton, 1994), or polyvocal, heteroglossic, multigenre constructions (Barone, 1990b; Rose, 1990; Quantz, 1992; Richardson, 1994b). Marcus (1994) recommends co- or multi-authorship and 'messy' texts. Others recommend film, video (Myerhoff, 1978; Rollwagen, 1988), photography (Walker, 1993; Schratz and Walker, 1995; Preskill, 1995), art (Simons, 1994) or computer multiple displays. Richardson (1994b, p. 521) records further experimentation in 'narratives of the self', fiction, poetry, drama, 'performance science', 'responsive readings', 'aphorisms', comedy and satire, visual presentations, and more. Becker (1994) recommends the use of 'hypertext' – a text whose parts are linked multiply (as in Joyce, 1990) rather than in linear progression. Artistic activity requires artistic methods both to explore its qualities, and to represent them. However, as Richardson (1994a, p. 8) points out, most of these retain the narrative tradition of ethnography while challenging the traditional format.

These are exciting possibilities. I shall review here some alternative approaches and presentational formats as they relate to my own research (for more comprehensive reviews, see Richardson, 1990, 1994b; Grant and Fine, 1992).

LIFE-HISTORY, BIOGRAPHY, AUTOBIOGRAPHY

How should subjects' stories be told? A traditional way would be for the sociologist to aid in the construction of a life-history. This runs the danger of the sociologist's voice dominating the subject's in the analysis and writing up, and this has generally become unacceptable (Clifford, 1988; Geertz, 1988). On the other hand, many hard-pressed teachers would not record their tales without a 'listener' and 'rapporteur'. My solution to this is to assist in biographies only where they emerge from the research, and to encourage in their construction and presentation multiple voices and 'dispersed authority' (Clifford, 1988). I call this 'grounded life-history'. Life-history, biography and narrative in general have been shown to be a powerful technique in ethnographic research (Sikes et al., 1985; Middleton, 1987; Thomas, 1995; Hatch and Wisniewski, 1995). 'Grounded life-history' arises both from the imperatives of other research and from the teacher's own felt need. In consequence, it contributes both to the strength and validity of the research in which it is embedded, and to the teacher's own development. Thus, in one of the 'critical events' discussed in Woods (1993a), a teacher felt it necessary to go deep into his own background in order to explain the emergence and significance of the event. Eventually this burgeoned into a research project in its own right. The biography was constructed through conversations and through the subject's writing over a period of three years, with a good deal of co-analysis and co-writing. I wrote up this life-history in an educational journal, explaining how the teacher had wrestled with and managed marginality throughout his life, and pointing to the strength of the links between a teacher's beliefs, outlook and practices and childhood experiences (Woods, 1993c). In some ways this appeared to be a traditional approach, with the sociologist writing up the account of someone else's life. But it was a collaborative effort, and a joint product, painstakingly built up over three years and involving many visits, and much checking and cross-checking of accounts. There were also large sections of the teacher's own voice in the article. I considered it in many ways a co-authored text (Kincheloe and McLaren, 1994).

D. Thomas (1995), however, raised some interesting questions about this article concerning alternative tales that might have been told, involving 'empirical' authors and texts (the total final life-history); 'liminal' authors and texts (other possible texts); the 'interpreter' (the guide to the text); and the 'over-reader' (the reader of the interpreter's account). One problem was that

Between the empirical author and his empirical text are the shadowy shapes of an infinite number of liminal authors, making textual decisions before a final (?) text version is created. Between the empirical author and his produced text (the empirical text) are those other 'texts' which could have been written on the basis of other intentions, through the exercise of other choices, under differing sets of motivation and within other relationships .... The empirical author is credited with an apparent command of authorial intent. He knows what he is about and is rational in his choice of events, personalities and language. What is then produced becomes the empirical text. Except, of course, like all writers, there is something else at work. An unsettled, itchy, mischievous imp from the compost of discarded memories, or from some inaccessible interiority, pushes the pen to write this word and not another.

(Thomas, 1995, pp. 165–166)

Further, the 'poetic form of the narrative may be a literary device through which the teller of tales seeks to move the interpreter and reader into accepting the legitimacy and plausibility of their stories' (p. 472). This point, of course, has been forcefully made about ethnographic accounts in general – so the interpreter may add a poetic gloss of his or her own to the author's account (Clifford and Marcus, 1986; Atkinson, 1990).

These essential points about validity were then answered, in the same journal, by the 'empirical author', that is, the teacher, P.J. Woods. He pointed out that there had indeed been other liminal authors seeking to tell their tales, but he had brought old-fashioned scientific methods to checking and verifying the empirical text. He had consulted documentary evidence, records, diaries, letters; spoken to significant others; checked and rechecked facts; and closely monitored the expression of his thoughts, ideas and feelings. He was determined to 'get it right', and some of his prepared notes went to five or six drafts. Thomas had also overlooked the close interaction between the empirical author and the interpreter (the researcher), and the dialectical mode in which the analysis was undertaken. The teacher called this a form of 'mutual catalysis' (P.J. Woods, 1993, p. 482; the debate is reproduced in Thomas, 1995).

P.J. Woods (1993) also makes an important point about the 'romantic' context of his story, which also holds for other kinds of research prioritizing the emotions:

The definition [of 'romanticism'] which I would offer is 'that which fosters heightened awareness through increased sensibility'. I am thus concerned with those responses which stimulate the imaginative spirit and elevate the claims of passion and emotion over the critical, classical and intellectual. In philosophical terms this involves a preference for responses resulting from the sensory organs rather than those deriving from cognition or will.

(ibid., p. 483)

As for the 'poetic form of the narrative', this was not a 'contrivance to win over an audience', but a language that best expressed his innermost thoughts and feelings.

Peter's reflections on his life have some of the properties of a 'narrative of the self', as described by Richardson (1994b, p. 521):

a highly personalized, revealing text in which an author tells stories about his or her lived experience. Using dramatic recall, strong metaphors, images, characters, unusual phrasings, puns, sub-texts, and allusions, the writer constructs a sequence of events, a 'plot', holding back on interpretation, asking the reader to 're-live' the events emotionally with the writer.

Though with Richardson 'accuracy is not the issue', rather 'coherence, verisimilitude and interest', accuracy for Peter was very important, involving him in painstaking research on his early childhood (see P.J. Woods, 1993).

Reflecting later on the significance and usefulness of his autobiographical researches for his teaching, he makes these four main points:

1. The embarking on autobiographical research is not only satisfying in itself, but through the attempt to search out the writer's true identity and the meaning of certain 'critical events' in his/her life, there can result a better understanding of the needs and motivation of the children with whom the teacher works, and of those strategies best suited to that individual and which are most likely to support a truly educative environment.

2. That education is (or should be) a two-way process, and that there are not two distinctly separate categories of teachers and learners. There needs to be a realization among all those concerned with the educative process that every learner has the capacity to be a teacher and every teacher needs to have the capacity to be a learner.

3. Educational influences should be accepted from whatever source they come and in whatever context they occur. The most valid of these may not always come from (there is an opinion which would argue that they are more unlikely to originate from) traditionally trained individuals or conventional locations.

4. There appears to be, in my case, a positive link between my early childhood experiences and the kind of teacher I subsequently became. If this finding has a wider application . . . , this would seem to be a strong argument for teachers and academics to become more involved with this aspect of educational research.

(P.J. Woods, 1995, p. 5)

THE EVOCATIVE TEXT

P.J. Woods in his observations reminds us of the arguments in favour of aesthetic language as a valuable form of presentation in qualitative enquiry. Blumenfeld-Jones (1995, p. 33) argues that

Narrative art often features a great evocative beauty of language and image (a beauty which draws us in as it transforms our imagination). Focusing upon highly particularized images enables us to imagine the situatedness of the lives being experienced. Art is exemplary of such re-imagining by finding new languages through which to think.

In British education, some of the works of Charles Dickens, Thomas

Hughes, Somerset Maugham and D.H. Lawrence are all examples of fictitious work based on fact that have that evocative effect, and of raising 'empathetic understanding' (Eisner, 1995b; see also Walsh, 1959). Eisner (1995b, p. 3) claims that such works 'help us to understand because their creators have understood, and had the skills and imagination to transform their understanding into forms that help us to notice what we have learned not to see'. Rose (1990, p. 56), in fact, claims that

> the novel has invaded the scientific monograph and transformed it – not through the use of fiction particularly, but through the descriptive setting of the scene, the narration of the people's own stories, the use of dialogue, the privileging of the objects of inquiry along with the subject or author who writes, and the notation by the author of emotions, subjective reactions, and involvement in ongoing activities.... The future of ethnography lies in a more sophisticated and self-conscious relationship with the novel, that is, with the possibilities of social inquiry that the novel (itself an experimental form) has opened up to us.

An illustration of the influence of the fictitious text emerged during the 'critical events' research and is provided by the impact a particular author – Leo Walmsley – had on P.J. Woods; a far greater impact than any standard piece of research or academic writing. Peter was especially fond of Walmsley's book *Foreigners* (1935). This book is not so much a novel as a cross-section of the life of a young boy, seen through the eyes of that boy, but with the accumulated wisdom, powers of expression, descriptive and organizational skills of an adult, redrawing and reliving his own childhood with precision and affection, but without sentimentality. Walmsley has a crisp and direct style, but he is more than a 'literary photographer' (as some of his critics described him). The description gets below surface features and feelings, and by seeing things 'in the round', holistically, a pattern is constructed. We understand the parts better by seeing them as pieces of a whole. Peter commented that one of the reasons why he can relate so readily to Walmsley's writing is that 'he has demonstrated that the gap between fact and fiction, between reality and the literary creation, is less real than imagined. His was a very holistic approach to life and experience.' The precision and sensitivity of the account arouses empathetic feelings that aid readers' understanding both of *Foreigners* and of their own childhood experiences.

Here is one of Peter's favourite passages in *Foreigners*, with his own commentary following:

> At the best of times I hated school. The room itself, which was under the chapel gallery, was small and dark, and its windows were heavily barred, for the narrow playground that separated it from the edge of the cliff was actually above the level of the floor, so that really we were half underground, and it was gloomy as a prison. Through the bars you

could see patches of sky, so that you always knew whether the sun was shining or not, but the sun itself, even in summer, never entered the room, and while you could hear the sea breaking on the cliff foot, or on the scaur ends if the tide was down, it was not visible. I could always think of a hundred places where I'd rather be than in this gloomy room. I hated having to sit still. I hated writing, and doing sums, and learning poetry off by heart, and learning about nouns and pronouns, and history. I liked looking at maps, and imagining I was seeing the places marked on them, but I hated having to learn off by heart the names of capes and rivers and mountains. I liked reading, but you only got one reader a year for the standard you were in, and you could read it through by yourself in one lesson (skipping the poetry) so that even the interesting bits became dull when you had to go through them word by word, spelling the difficult words out aloud, or writing them on your slate. And while you sat in school you heard all the time the sound of the sea, and the cries of the gulls which often would alight on the playground railings, and stay there, making a queer laughing sound, just as though they were laughing at you, and mocking you because you had to stay in. No matter what time of the year, there was always something exciting to do at Bramblewick.

(Walmsley, 1935, pp. 24–25)

Peter comments:

Whilst Walmsley's works contain numerous passages which have made a lasting impression on me, this is one of the most meaningful. I think that it beautifully conveys the manner in which so-called educational experiences can exclude the real world (and hence relevance). All the boys in that Edwardian classroom knew that the sun was shining outside, but inside gloom and darkness prevailed – through the exclusion of the light of practical experience and relevance. They could hear (but not fully appreciate until they escaped from that environment) the cry of the gulls and the sound of the sea – the living and the elemental worlds. Walmsley also manages to capture the manner in which that drabness is transferred to such learning as takes place. Throughout this short passage we see the dichotomy of thoughtless repression on the one hand and untapped enthusiasm on the other – note how the passage begins in a negative way: 'At the best of times I hated school' and how it ends with a note of affirmation: 'there was always something exciting to do at Bramblewick.'

Against those things he did not like doing – arithmetic, grammar, history, learning poetry and the names of geographical features by rote – he sets down those things which he did enjoy – reading and studying maps. Here is another example of someone searching out those elements in an adverse experience which could provide the foundations for an alternative personal development. Here we see a determination to survive against all the odds. Here we have a child who, whilst at Primary School and Secondary School, loathed poetry and grammar and history, and probably writing too, who – through *real-life* experiences – was to develop into a fine novelist with a deeply rooted interest in archaeology and things historical. This poses an important question, 'How did Walmsley acquire his literary talents and his lasting fascination with the ancient world?' It was certainly not through the conventional education which he received in the Bay Wesleyan or the Scarborough Municipal Schools. (Like D.H. Lawrence Walmsley was to undergo a brief, and deeply unsatisfying, spell as a teacher. Yet what Lawrence and Walmsley were subjected to at the turn of the century is not all that far removed from the ideas of those 'educationalists' and politicians who are advocating a return to 'real learning' today.) This was the question which I decided I had to resolve for myself those many years ago. If Walmsley had not acquired his education in a typical classroom context was there not some other alternative, and much more relevant, approach that we ought to be considering? This was really the starting point of the educational journey which I have made in my post-formal schooling years and which has gradually given rise to that educational philosophy which I hold today (and which is still evolving). My point of departure was not one without hope of successful resolution. Although I did not articulate it at the time, I probably received some kind of inner encouragement from the unexpressed belief that if Lawrence and Walmsley could survive – *so could I*!

(Woods, 1995a, pp. 147–149)

Walmsley's work comes under the category of 'biographical novel'. While fiction, it is based on the author's own experiences. A related genre is 'literary journalism' (Wolfe, 1973) – true stories, but written with some literary freedom. Eisner (1991, p. 30) notes that in these, 'the writer sets a stage that allows the reader to get a sense of the scene and mood'.

Evocative writing has for long been a feature of ethnographic presentation (see Willis, 1977; Beynon, 1985, for examples). The aim is to conjure up the very feel of people's experiences, to recreate atmospheres, and convey ethos. (For other accounts of the use of stories, novels and narratives, see Kreiger, 1984; Denzin, 1989a; McCall, 1990; Seidman, 1991; Fisher, 1992.)

Though I have focused here on the novel as evocative text, there are, of course, other media through which the same effect can be achieved – film, photographs, exhibitions, museums, works of art, drama, diaries, memos and poetry, the last four of which I discuss below and in Chapter 4.

Performance

Paget (1990) has explained why she felt the need to 'perform' her text, rather than present it in written form. She remarks on how standard presentations produce a 'conceptual and abstract science . . . do not intend to invoke or produce experience, but suppress involvement, emotion, and imagination' (p. 143).

> In performing the text, I am not privileging the analytic report, separating it from the experience of life as it is lived . . . . I am privileging the *experience* of knowledge, the communicative act of showing and telling how it happened that, on three separate occasions, a physician diagnosed depression on a woman who was a cancer patient. Performance . . . reawakens and recovers the audience's capacities to participate and feel too. In performing the text, the audience's attention is focused on a vast range of signifiers of meaning (make-up, dress, stage-set, the gender of the performers, etc.).
>
> (pp. 150–151)

Performance is a 'concretion' rather than an abstraction of experience (Arp 1885–1966, 1987). It is both the written text and more, for the text is 'realized in new ways . . . . The multiple interpretive acts of performance enhance, rather than diminish, the intelligibility of the text as a scientific account, because [these multiple interpretations] enhance our understanding of the complexity of the reality to which the text and the science of the text alludes' (Paget, 1990, p. 152). Paget concludes that performance is 'native, artful, subtle, imaginative, interpretive, and dialogical. Above all it is alive' (p. 153).

Drama can, of course, be produced more clearly according to a scientific protocol, as in Richardson's (1993) narrative poem on 'Louisa May'. She points out that standard ethnographic procedures were followed here – real actors and words used, a story, respondent validation, similar setting – though the format was different. Becker, McCall and Morris (1988) have also experimented in 'performance science'. Acting out situations studied by ethnographers, they believe, encourages viewing from multiple perspectives, which in turn can enhance the researcher's understanding of those situations. Ellis and Bochner (1992, p. 80), in their personal story of their lived experience of abortion, aim to recreate an 'experiential sense' for their audience of what it was like to live through it, using 'systematic introspection'. They wrote up the text with the express purpose that it would be performed, so that

> nuances of feeling, expression, and interpretation could be communicated more clearly . . . . An audience that witnesses a performance of this text thus is subjected to much more than words: they see facial expressions, movements and gestures; they hear the tones, intonations, and inflections of the actors' voices; and they can feel the passion of the performers.

Drama can have a similar effect to that of data; that is, it can bring the researcher new insights. Two examples from my research conveyed more to me as researcher than any other method, though the information still had to be worked for beneath and beyond the text of the play. The first occurred in a primary school. I wanted to understand the pupils' feelings and experiences about transferring from the primary to a secondary school. This is known to be a traumatic event (Measor and Woods, 1984), but the pupil experience has been under-researched. I had gained a certain amount of data through the usual ethnographic methods, none of it of any great depth. Then one morning in assembly, a group of senior girls acted out for the rest of the school their notional first day at the secondary. The curious thing was that I could understand little of what was happening in the play, though the audience was spellbound, and burst out in spontaneous loud applause at the end. Clearly, I was not attuned to their culture. But the play gave me access to it. Having noted what appeared to me key signs, symbols, actions and reactions in the play, I was able to discuss these both with the players and with some members of the audience afterwards; and then to relate what they told me back to the play. This was much more illuminatory than the interviews, discussions and study of documents had been. The play provided a link between our two discourses.

The second example concerns a drama that was the actual subject of research. I had been alerted to a school production of *Godspell* as a possible contender for a series of 'critical events' I was studying. I found that two huge gains made by students and staff throughout a year-long career of this outstanding production were, first, the discovery of a range and depth of emotional experience and expression; and secondly, experience in searching for a meaningful truth. Stanislavski (in Hodgson, 1972, p. 94) writes, 'Truth on the stage is whatever we can believe in with sincerity, whether in ourselves or in our colleagues.... Each and every moment must be saturated with a belief in the truthfulness of the emotion felt.' Such belief is promoted by depth and lucidity. Bolton (1984, p. 119) argues that participants are concerned with 'tapping their own reservoirs of emotional memories to find within themselves a sophistication, subtlety or depth of emotional engagement so that in concentrating on the character's actions, a wider, deeper range of emotions may be released'. Lucidity, Collingwood (1966) argues, comes as actors explore their own emotions by means of gesture, speech and other forms of expression, thus discovering emotions of which they were previously unaware, and 'by permitting the audience to witness the discovery, enable them to make a similar discovery about themselves' (p. 47). Drama can do this equally for the presentation of research. (For other explorations in dramatization and characterization as representational techniques, see McCall and Becker, 1990; Schnieder, 1991; Richardson and Lockridge, 1991.)

DIARIES, MEMOS

The recording of an event, and one's relationship to it, as and when it happens, or shortly after, is another way of facilitating the inclusion of the aesthetic and the emotional. The immediate impact upon the researcher might be profound, and something which she or he needs to write about without delay as a means of exploring her or his own feelings. Often, these are suppressed in formal academic writing, or allowed to wane during what can be a lengthy period between data collection and writing up. But the researcher's feelings are important, not only as context for the message of the research, but as part of the message itself.

There is a shift here, from the 'observing' of traditional ethnography towards expressive speech (Clifford, 1986). It does not necessarily privilege discourse over observation (Snow and Morrill, 1995), but rather brings the two elements more into parity. In these devices, the researcher places himself or herself, feelings and all, within the research. As noted earlier, the recognition of one's own feelings helps one understand the meaning of interactions. I give some examples of expressive memos from our current research, together with further commentary, in Chapter 4.

POETRY

> The poet's eye, in a fine frenzy rolling,
> Doth glance from heaven to earth, from earth to heaven,
> And, as imagination bodies forth
> The forms of things unknown, the poet's pen
> Turns them to shapes, and gives to airy nothing
> A local habitation and a name.
>
> (Shakespeare, *A Midsummer Night's Dream*)

The poet,

> will have ... an imagination that he will be able to throw his own soul into any object he sees or imagines, so as to see, feel, be sensible of, and express all that the object itself would see, or be sensible of, or express.
>
> (Woodhouse, in Wu, 1994, p. 713)

Poetry is powerful either as data or as a form of representation. It says a great deal in a short space and, by its choice and juxtaposition of words, phrases, imagery, metre, rhythm, rhyme and layout, conjures thoughts and feelings in a particularly vibrant form. Richardson (1994a, p. 9) argues that 'lyric poems concretize emotions, feelings and moods – the most private kind of feelings – so as to re-create experience itself to another person. A lyric poem "shows" another person how it is to feel something.' Hewitt (1994, p. 202) notes that poets have 'strategies' for arranging familiar elements in an unfamiliar way. Thus, 'by disrupting readers' usual views of the elements under scrutiny, poets make it possible for readers to develop an alternative understanding of them'. Moreover, they lead them to participate in the experience in an interactive way (p. 204).

Richardson (1993, p. 696) explains how she combines the literary and the sociological in her approach to the writing of her poem on 'Louisa May':

> Louisa May is the speaker in the poem, but I crafted it, using both scientific and poetic criteria. I used only her words, repetitions, phrases ... and narrative strategies, such as multi-syllabic words, embedded dialogues, and conversational asides. My intent was for the poem to stand aesthetically and emotionally, for it to be, as Robert Frost would define a poem, 'the shortest emotional distance between two points' – the speaker and the listener/reader, but I also wanted it to be faithful to my sociological understanding of Louisa May's story of her life.

Her aim was to create a 'vivid, immediate, emotional experience for the reader/listener' using the person's own words, and 'to integrate the sociological and the poetic at the professional, political and personal levels'. The purpose of the poem is to evoke, to startle, to stimulate thought, to move, to give expression to the essence of the person's experience, to help the reader understand how the person feels, to induce fellow-feeling.

In commenting on nine short poems she presents elsewhere, Richardson (1994a) notes that the overall narrative is implied, but spaces between the poems invite greater readerly participation than do traditional forms of presentation. As with a number of Wordsworth's poems, 'to the reader is left the creative mental process of arranging the component parts into a satisfying intellectual, or imaginative whole' (Lefebure, 1992, p. 90). Each poem in Richardson's selection is a 'mini-narrative', an episode, representing 'an emotionally and morally charged experience' (p. 8); the poems could be reordered, focusing on different plots or story-lines; they retell 'lived experience'; each poem is a 'candid photo', or 'critical moment'. One could argue that lives are structured on such moments.

We do not know the origin of the poems, or who wrote them, or whether they all refer to one and the same life. Richardson (1994a) asks 'does it matter?' They can fit into traditional ethnography if the poems are representative of a particular life, or, if it is she who has written them, into the sociology of subjectivity (Ellis and Flaherty, 1992). The important point is that the distance between author and reader is minimal, and the 'reader is not simply "told" but *feels* the experience'. The lyric poem's task is

> to represent actual experience – episodes, epiphanies (Denzin, 1989b), misfortunes, pleasures – to capture those experiences in such a way that others can experience and *feel* them. Lyric poems, therefore, have the

possibility of doing for ethnographic understanding what normative ethnographic writing cannot.

(Richardson, 1994a, p. 12)

Elsewhere, Richardson (1993) takes a postmodernist feminist view, claiming that

> In sociological research, the findings have been safely staged within the language of the father, the domain of science writing. 'Louisa May' challenges the language, tropes, emotional suppressions and presumptive validity claims of masculinist social science . . . . Poetics strips these methodological bogeymen of their power to control and constrain . . . . In feminist writings of poets and social scientists, the position of the author is linked aesthetically, politically, emotionally, with those about whom they write. Knowledge is not appropriated and controlled, but shared; authors recognize a multiplicity of selves within themselves as well as interdependence with others, shadows and doubles. Alternate selves are interwoven by common threads of lived experiences. It is this feminist process of 'knowing/telling' which led women listening to Louisa May's poem to feel that I was talking about my own life – or theirs. It is this potential for relating, merging, being a primary presence to ourselves and each other which makes possible the validation of transgressive writing, not for the sake of sinning or thumbing one's nose at authority, nor for the sake of only and just writing poetry – which may be ill suited for many topics, audiences and writers – but for the sake of knowing about lived experiences which are unspeakable in the 'father's voice', the voice of objectivity; flattened worlds.

(p. 705)

It may be disputed, however, whether 'social science writing' is the essential domain of patriarchy. It is not all 'cold-eyed scientism' (see Chapter 1). There is no reason why patriarchy, or any other form of oppression, may not operate through poetry or any other means. Also, social scientific research and writing has made its own contribution to such causes as anti-sexism and anti-racism, as illustrated in Chapter 2. There is a tendency here, as in several writers inspired by postmodernist ideas, to overstate the case. That said, poetry does seem to offer distinctive chances for data collection, and for representation of accounts.

In a similar way, it can expand our teaching repertoire. Harris (1976), for example, acknowledges that the curriculum has some external influences, but that it is enriched by the creativity and imagination of the finest teachers, who are capable of feats of pedagogy which could never have been the outcome of curriculum theory or external educational policy. Harris was interested in 'intuition' and 'artistry' in teachers – 'elusive concepts, easy enough to recognize in practice but hard to explain or categorize' (p. 70). For this reason, his written teaching text took a literary form, and was interwoven with poems by Robert Graves. The poems quoted are not ostensibly about education. But they convey the sentiment, capture the moment, apply *le mot juste*, arouse the emotion, recall the fleeting – but critical – moment, convey the epiphany, summon up in the readers' minds a host of related images concerning their own lives and work, and perhaps cause them to see these in a different way.

Several of the authors experimenting in poetical presentation have found inspiration in the English Romantics. Jackson (1990) ascribes the Romantics' view of art to qualitative research:

> its abandonment of the preaching role, its absorption in the world as given us by our senses, even its surprise and delight in the unexpected beauty that so often breaks ground and sweeps into view before our very eyes.
>
> (Jackson, 1990, p. 166)

The Romantics 'did more than look affectionately at the world around them':

> They constantly sought to look past that world or through it, to see beyond the surface meaning of things. They strove to 'read' their surroundings much as one might read a complicated text or a piece of scripture. Lovers of nature they certainly were, but they also worshipped the human imagination, whose power to envision more than the eye alone could behold was looked upon as the ultimate source of artistic achievement.
>
> (1992, p. 85)

Egan (1992, p. 23) writes that the Romantics' conception of the imagination

> was involved in perception, creating particular kinds of order and making sense of experience for us; it was a conjuror of images of what we had in the past perceived or of images made by combining elements from past perception into new forms; and it was tied into our emotions, evoking responses to what was not present as though it was present. The Romantics added, with much emphasis, that creative insight or intuition most evident in the work of the artist.

The Romantics were no 'naive realists', but brought 'operations of the mind' to bear upon external objects, using their imagination as a 'constantly active and creative faculty that shapes the world we perceive and that uses our hopes, fears and other emotions in that shaping' (ibid., p. 24). The beauty that such imagining produced is truth, according to Keats. Wordsworth also feels that the object of poetry is truth, 'not individual and local, but general and operative; not standing upon external testimony, but carried alive into the heart by passion' (Preface to Lyrical Ballads, in Wu, 1994, p. 258). Hewitt (1994, p. 206) points out that the Romantic poets did not just, or even in the main, commune with nature, but were sociologists in their own way. Their concern was with social situations:

> Even when addressing political topics, they foregrounded the more abstract concerns of sociology – how and why people come together into groups, how aggregate and individual behaviour affect each other, how and why social structures change.

Wordsworth speaks of 'seeing into the life of things'. The ethnographer, also, tries to 'see into the life of things'. Richardson (1994b) complains of the countless number of boring qualitative texts she has tried to read. For thirty years, she has 'yawned her way through numerous supposedly exemplary qualitative studies' (p. 516). They have no 'life' in them. Paget (1990, p. 143) makes a similar comment about conference presentations, claiming for her brand of 'ethnoperformance' that 'above all it is alive' (p. 153). Richardson (1994b) argues that traditional texts have been guided by a 'static writing model [which] coheres with mechanistic scientism and quantitative research' (p. 517). There are opportunities in current experimentation to break out of this static model.

However, before we all rush off to our rhyming dictionaries, a note of caution is necessary. Denzin (1994, p. 504) agrees that many qualitative research texts are boring, but does point out that the interest level of a text has more to do with the writer than the paradigm. Some may even be bored (or worse!) by attempts at 'poetic texts'! Besides, level of interest in itself is not a sufficient guide to the absolute worth of a text. Intellectual coherence, originality, quality of argument and insight, appropriateness of presentation and organization are what matter. Any singular manifestation of these might interest one person, and bore another, depending as much on the reader's predilections, knowledge and understanding as on the text, whether poetry or prose.

Many of us may have difficulty, too, in constructing a quality product in this form. Richardson herself (1994b, p. 521) remarks that 'competing with "real" fiction writers is chancy' – the same might be said of poets! Writing poetry is a hard-earned, rule-governed discipline in its own right, as well as requiring a considerable amount of creative artistry. Can ethnographers master this craft as well as their own? Snow and Morrill (1995, p. 361) make a similar point about 'dramatic performances': 'Do not playwrights and screenwriters have a better eye and feel for that possibility than we do? And why not leave the enactment of our texts to those who are skilled in the arts of the theatre and dramatic presentation?' As Schwalbe (1995, p. 411) points out, rule breaking and boundary crossing are fun, and the 'turn to poetry and other forms of experimental writing may be a way to keep ourselves awake and amused before retirement'. This, perhaps, is too cynical a view, but the point about the need for caution is well made. There is a danger of engaging in transgressive writing purely as a form of self-indulgence, or in the mistaken belief that it resolves many of the problems of social scientific research. Either way, the methodological gains that have been made in previous 'moments' of qualitative research (see Introduction) could be put at risk.

A poem can leave somebody completely cold. It needs a shared frame of reference for it to be understood and appreciated. Yet it operates by terseness and suggestion. A reader has a great deal of indexing to do – that is the point: if the index is provided by the author, the point is lost. A traditional, analytical text, by contrast, provides a wealth of data and explanation, together with commentary on how it was acquired and derived. As Schwalbe (1995, p. 406) notes, 'whereas poetry is coy, prose is exhibitionist'. Even where a poem, or collection of poems, 'works', is it sufficient within itself to stand as sociological analysis? Will it answer all the questions one will want to ask about the material, or about the issues that it raises? More probably it will be a sensitizing device, tuning the reader in to a particular aspect of the research, or aiming to spark a particular response, to evoke, to startle or to stimulate. For these reasons, I prefer to see it as one of a whole armoury of techniques that one may use, depending on the point one wishes to make, or reaction to stimulate.

CONCLUSION

Artistic qualities are an important feature of social research. Through use of the imagination, they stimulate the imagination. They enable 'empathetic understanding', provide new insights, cause us to see things as not seen before, identify patterns that fit together in holistic ways, suggest general truths from particular situations. Methods are being devised and tested to serve these qualities. Enthusiasm, however, has to be tempered with caution. There is the abiding problem of validity, or, if that is felt to be an unhelpful concept, a question of quality, and how we judge it. There are at least two answers to this, one more scientific, the other more artistic. Regarding the first, Hammersley (1993, p. 32) finds nothing wrong with new techniques like evocative narratives or even fictional texts, indeed holds that they may be of considerable value, as long as they are subsumed under a 'subtle realist' model of research involving clear statements of claims made, presentation of evidence on which they are made, and details of the research process, such as to enable readers to assess their plausibility and credibility. Thus, a poem, on this model, would need an accompanying text clarifying the main points and saying how the information behind the poem was obtained. Better if the research that produced it observed standard ethnographic practice as discussed in Chapter 2, and had a controlled sample, triangulation of methods, and clear mode of analysis. The poem would then be presented as one of a range of illustrative materials.

If this is too scientistic for some advocates of artistic experimentation (mainly, perhaps, because it offends what Schwalbe, 1995, p. 407, calls 'sacred inarticulatedness'), there has to be something in place of 'validity', such as 'quality' that is fairly universally recognized as such. This entails criteria like depth of insight and understanding, such as comes from traditional ethnographic methods involving long-term participation in an institution or with a group, and close knowledge of its members. A related criterion is then the appositeness of representation to reflect faithfully the understanding that has been acquired, that is, how the insight and understanding were revealed and conveyed.

There is a third aspect of quality, which can only be affirmed by the audience, and that is the power of the presentation to 'move'. Does it bring catalytic insights, increase understanding, arouse feeling, touch a nerve that starts new chains of thought or feeling, in ways that no other presentational form would? The 'aesthetic, political, emotional link with those about whom they write' is the key. What would be useful here, therefore, is some old-fashioned respondent validation (as there was with the 'Louisa May' poem). We need to know whether people have been moved, and how.

Further, not all research accounts take the form of making claims and advancing evidence to support them, important though that is for some research. This would not be appropriate, for example, in the case of Wolcott's (1994) experiences with 'Brad'; or some of Richardson's and Johnson's poems; in representing atmospheres or moods or feelings. In these areas the search is for understanding and expression rather than proof. It is a matter of truth, like beauty, being in the eye of the beholder, and the beholder's ability to convey that to others. There is something here of the potential for relating to others, of 'being at one with others', and in Richardson's terms 'knowing about lived experiences'. The validity here is in the group recognition, awareness and identification. Since one of the main means at our disposal in this quest is our own feelings, these should be represented in the account – as they are in Wolcott's and Richardson's cases. These considerations lead to a further point, about audiences. Scientific research speaks mainly to the academic community. The new genres spread the net a little more widely. They increase accessibility, speaking directly to the reader's experiences.

I personally favour a 'multidimensional epistemology' (Collins, 1989, p. 132) and 'combination genres' (Richardson and Lockridge, 1991, p. 339). In our current work on teachers' experiences of school inspections, we are experimenting with alternative forms of presentation. We shall use some of the methods discussed in this chapter, together with some of those covered in Chapter 2, in an attempt to convey as faithful a picture of teachers' experience as possible. To this end, we are encouraging teachers to express themselves in whatever mode they find suitable; while we shall experiment with diaries, memos, narrative, evocative description, polyvocal text, etc. – even poetry. Inspections induce profound emotions among teachers, for their whole identities are at stake. They are, in a real sense, 'laid bare' by this process, for the whole of their teaching, and of their selves within the school, are open to the gaze of the inspectors. The teachers' disturbed emotions stand in stark contrast to the strictly institutionalized, almost dehumanized, role adopted by the inspectors (see Jeffrey and Woods, 1996). The teachers' accounts of their experiences provide a rich harvest for transgressive writing. Where and how, however, will this fit into the final account?

If we take poetry as an example, we are experimenting where the opportunity arises (for example, with a particularly lyrical or emotional interview), and where it seems that poetry might aid in conveying the sense and feeling required. We use the teachers' own words, but cut out a lot of elaboration, aiming to present the essence of responses, and, through the stark contrasts, to reveal the cruel ironies in the situation. How might we use such a poem? There are at least three ways. First, it could be presented to audiences 'live', being read, or performed, or shown by overhead projector, as one item in a varied number. Secondly, it could stand in teachers' journals on its own, since the teacher readers could provide all the necessary context from their own experiences. The poem then might help them identify similar feelings within themselves, and thus help towards objectification of any tensions they might be experiencing in relation to these events – a move from private troubles to public issues; or it might aid the survival of agency in its continuing struggle with structure.

In the main, however, thirdly, we would see such an offering being presented together with other material as an addition to, rather than a replacement of, more traditional analysis. It would offer another dimension, another form of insight. At the end of this research, we shall present a view that will be one of a number that might have been given of these events. There is no one single truth to be told. But it will contain a number of truths as far as we can divine and tell them. It will be true to the data collected, true to teachers' experiences, and true to our own research values. There will be plenty of teacher voice and testimony, including some respondent validation. And it will contain the researcher's own account of how he lived these experiences with the teachers, both to contextualize the material and to objectivize oneself, to place oneself within the material. This is not just an indulgence to allow unreflective analysis of the data, but in the interests of addressing the rigour of the research. We give examples of how we are attempting to do this in Chapter 4.

Denzin (1994, p. 501) refers to the researcher as writer as a 'bricoleur', who 'fashions meaning and interpretation out of ongoing experience', and 'uses any tool or method that is readily to hand'. It is a question of fitness for purpose. The purposes of the research community have been too limited. The new approaches offer us an opportunity to explore some of the social areas of life that have hitherto been inaccessible to educational and social scientific research. Karl Popper (1968, p. 226) compares the status of truth 'to that of a mountain peak which is permanently wrapped in clouds'. We might not be able to see it, we might have difficulty getting to it, and we might not even know we are there when we arrive, but we know that it is there. The new methods provide us with some navigation instruments that might enhance our view, and enable us to see a little way through the mist.

> Read me a lesson, Muse, and speak it loud
> Upon the top of Nevis, blind in mist!
> I look into the chasms, and a shroud
> Vaporous doth hide them, – just so much I wist
> Mankind do know of hell; I look o'erhead,
> And there is sullen mist, – even so much
> Mankind can tell of heaven; mist is spread
> Before the earth, beneath me, – even such,
> Even so vague is man's sight of himself!
> Here are the craggy stones beneath my feet, –
> Thus much I know that, a poor witless elf,
> I tread on them, – that all my eye doth meet
> Is mist and crag, not only on this height,
> But in the world of thought and mental might!
>
> (John Keats, 'Ben Nevis')

4 Living and researching a school inspection*

INTRODUCTION

We are exploring our own feelings about, and their impact upon, the current research we are doing, as well as the insights they yield. The study is located within the current radical educational changes in England, and particularly their impact on teachers' work. There have been vast changes in labour conditions generally throughout the world in recent years, giving rise to theories of deprofessionalization and deskilling. There is more contract labour, less scope for creativity, more pressure on time and energies, more 'top-down' prescription. There is plenty of evidence to show that the educational reforms of the late 1980s and early 1990s have impacted hard on teachers. On the other hand, research has shown many teachers to be highly creative in adapting to the new requirements. They have managed to preserve, and in some instances promote, their beliefs and values in their implementation of government policies; and these adaptations have, in turn, acted back upon policy-making in a circular process. These teachers can, therefore, be said to 'own' the knowledge that informs their teaching, and to control the pedagogical process. This is a conclusion we have reached from our research over the past six years into 'creative teaching in primary schools' (see Woods, 1993a, 1995a; Woods and Jeffrey, 1996).

This situation might change radically in the second half of the 1990s. The 1992 Education Act instituted new national arrangements for school inspections overseen by the Office for Standards in Education (OFSTED). The Act requires all schools to have a full inspection by an independent team of inspectors at regular intervals. These inspections are intended to have a marked effect. They represent the government's strongest drive to date for control of the implementation of the National Curriculum process, and for seeing its reforms implemented, and it seems likely that they will have a profound, and possibly traumatic, impact on teachers and their

---

* This chapter was written with Bob Jeffrey.

work, with widespread influence – as yet unknown – over their policies, practices and cultures. This influence is likely to be long-lasting. Schools opt for a lengthy preparatory period, of up to a year, with 'preliminary' inspections. The week-long process of the inspection proper is followed by a report from the inspectors, and a required action-plan from the school with a schedule for implementation. OFSTED inspections are set to pervade the whole of teacher culture, and anxiety levels among teachers are high.

We are investigating the effects of these inspections on primary school-teachers and their work, throughout the whole period of the process. Questions that concern us are: what kind of social and political event is an OFSTED inspection? How are we to conceptualize it as a process? In what ways is it affecting power and control within the system? Is it making the implementation of policy more linear and directive, less circular and negotiative? If so, what are the implications for teacher professionalism, and for education? What new tensions and dilemmas are created for teachers, and how are they resolved? How is the introduction of this mode of inspection affecting teachers' perceptions of their whole selves being integrated within the teacher role, and what are the implications of that for teaching and learning?

We are using qualitative methods – mostly interviews, diaries, documents, film, life-histories, and observation in classrooms, meetings and elsewhere – in six main schools, studying inspections from first announcement to six months beyond the inspection itself, over a three-year period. A feature is the use of free-writing memos, one aim of which is to explore our own feelings in relation to what we are discovering. The aims behind this are to maximize the insight into the teachers' thoughts and feelings, and into our own, and to make evident any biases that may be affecting that insight. What follows is an exchange between Bob Jeffrey, who was doing the fieldwork, and myself, acting as director of the research. Bob was in the middle of coverage of one inspection, which, as forecast, was proving very traumatic for the teachers concerned. Bob was not unmoved by their experience. He was, in a real sense, 'living' the inspection with them. What are the consequences for the research of this kind of engagement?

MEMO FROM BOB JEFFREY – THE OFSTEDED SWANS' PLIGHT IN THE WEEK BEFORE INSPECTION: SUBJECTIVE REACTIONS TO AN OFSTED INSPECTION

Background

Trafflon primary school (a pseudonym, as are all other names here), which is having its inspection this week, is a Victorian three-decker school with what could be at least four classrooms on each floor. However, their small roll means they have a nursery and six classes and many of these have mixed age groups. It is located less than a mile from four of London's main bridges that span the River Thames, and is surrounded by 1970s concrete estates, some new low-rise houses, lots of main roads and run-down businesses. Its intake is mainly Afro-Caribbean and white working-class, with a few Asian pupils. It has one nursery teacher, Vincent, a nursery assistant and six female class teachers, one part-time teacher and a head teacher, Victor. They also have a retired teacher, Carl, who once worked at the school and comes in voluntarily four days a week to do odd jobs and share in some curriculum activities.

I went into the school twice during the week prior to the inspection, the Monday and the Friday. On the Monday I found one teacher in tears, one teacher confused, one teacher emotionally and physically drained, one teacher ill and the deputy head, Toni, just returned from three days' illness, which was a hangover from a virus she had the previous week. She had more time off in the last two weeks than in the whole of the past five years.

On the Friday, I found the head teacher, Victor, depressed, Vicky angry at having, in her words, made two people cry, and Carol, the reception teacher, who had been in tears on Monday, panicking about being interviewed by OFSTED and trying to get her head around literacy statistics to show the school in the best light. Tania, the year 1 teacher, due to retire next year, was waiting for her husband to arrive at 5.30 to give her a hand in the classroom. Toni, the year 3 and 4 teacher, was still in school at 5.30 trying to get her room straight and catch up on her paper work, and worrying as she had done for some weeks about how she was going to give her two children, for whom she was solely responsible, some time this weekend. Chloe, the year 5 and 6 teacher, was still suffering from a bladder infection and on a course of antibiotics. I left that Friday at 5.30 to go to *Swan Lake* at Covent Garden. I found out later that Chloe was the last to leave school at 9.45, with Veronica, the year 4 teacher, leaving at 9.30. As I enjoyed the invigorating and joyous music of the first act of *Swan Lake*, with its party atmosphere, I began to feel quite close to the Trafflon teachers and felt angry that they were not part of this very jolly and uplifting environment.

Emotional reactions

Later, over the weekend and on the first day of the inspection I put together some thoughts about why I really liked these people. The main reasons were:

Commitment

I was impressed with their commitment. These teachers loved the school and the children. They were very proud of children who were part of Trafflon's history, such as a famous comedian who had appeared on television the previous week, and had mentioned Trafflon school; and one particular footballer who had scored his debut goal in the premier division that week. They had displays featuring other famous people who had been pupils at the school. Many talked about how ex-pupils often returned to say how much they had enjoyed their time at Trafflon school. Two of the teachers had spent over twenty years of their teaching career at the school. The atmosphere in the school was a quiet one and a caring one, and the children behaved very well both in the classes and around the school. The teachers all liked and respected the head teacher, Victor, and they all talked about how well they all got on with one another, in spite of some serious altercations in the past. They worked to manage their conflicts and differences.

Their commitment is related to their personal lives. Some had personal tragedies in their lives, personal responsibilities with which they struggled, and in spite of all these they put in many hours for the school because they liked and wanted to be at the school. Carol, the reception teacher who had worked in the school for more than twenty years, lived on her own. She valued this independence and resisted family pressure to return to the Midlands to live nearer her family. They couldn't understand why she wanted to work in an inner city and she had to keep reminding them that this was what she loved about her work. She had never married and after some terrible times with difficult and noisy neighbours had moved last spring, and spent the summer doing her house so she could be ready to give the time to OFSTED in the autumn term. She was the one who was crying on Monday morning because she had been given more paper work to do when she thought she had finished it late on Sunday night. She revealed later that this particular weekend coincided with the anniversary of her mother's death, and the death of two prominent actors that weekend had reminded her of her mother. At the same time she talked about how the paperwork was dominating her practice and marginalizing her natural inclinations to focus on her children, to act intuitively for their development. She made connections with her personal life and talked of grieving for her mother and for her loss of creativity.

Toni, the deputy head, who also lived alone, was keen to address this issue with me early on in my research. She liked and valued her independence but was becoming concerned that with the increase in work her home was becoming her prison. She had no one to share the burden of her increasing work load. She was turning down more invitations and was worrying that she had no other conversation apart from school, in spite of a previous thriving interest in the arts. She is the driving force behind many of the school's planning and monitoring policies, and yet also felt responsible for what she said were her actions in reducing two people to tears. She debated with me whether she had to be tough for the school's sake and how the OFSTED inspection process had politicized her, for she had become aware of the contradictions between what was asked for by

OFSTED and what was important to her in terms of teaching and school development. She was rapidly becoming disillusioned, reflective and in this particular week angry at what it had done to her in terms of illness, for she was rigorous in terms of sustaining her own health, taking many vitamins daily.

Veronica was in her mid-forties with children and a second partner. Her story is more unusual than most in that she suffered tremendously from a brutal father and left home at 17 to get away from him. She worked mainly to get her qualifications, for she always wanted to be a teacher and therefore was a late starter to the profession. In the weeks prior to the inspection her brother, who suffered along with her as a child, returned from Australia and they had an emotional reunion for the first time for over thirty years. During the weekend of the last week prior to the inspection, they had a family reunion involving all their relations from around the country, and her brother visited their father's grave. One of her cats also died that weekend, aged 15, and this added to her distress. One of the incidents in her childhood involved her father not speaking to her for six months and making her eat her meals in the kitchen because she had failed her eleven plus. She has hated examinations since then, finds the paper work frustrating and the thought of the inspection frightening. She is a dedicated teacher whom the head has described as getting two years out of every year she has with a child. She describes her love of teaching in graphic terms, with many examples of what appears to be her exemplary practice, one in which, according to her, each child is given a great deal of her energy and one in which children frequently cry if they have to miss her classes. She does music clubs voluntarily just because she likes music and now has responsibility for it, with, as she puts it, no formal training.

Vicky grew up in Nigeria and taught many levels there. She has been teaching for a couple of years here in primary and has two children to bring up on her own. She is very worried by the overload of work and worried that she is not satisfying her own children's needs. She has to drop them at the childminder's before 7.30 a.m. and travel for a further forty-five minutes on public transport.

Chloe has taught in this school for more than twenty years. She looks after an ageing parent recovering from alcoholism at home, with many demands made upon her. She can't talk to her mother about her work, for 'she doesn't understand the long hours and commitment', and she is frightened of her whole life being trampled on by the OFSTED inspection. Everybody tells her she is a good teacher, she is meticulous with her records, runs a well-controlled class and is usually enthusiastic and confident. She has had some serious infections this week. Her friends tell her she is obsessed with school and she worries about her mother managing on her own when she is at work. She has given up church responsibilities for the two weekends prior to OFSTED and also may have given up some support into the bargain. Some large coloured photographs of all the staff have appeared in the foyer of the school, and she is dismayed because she feels these are exposing even more of what she conceives of as her blemishes and faults, as well as looking into her soul through the way the eyes are portrayed. She travels by public transport for over an hour, changing to main-line services to get to this school, where she has taught all her career.

Clare is the part-timer who was given responsibility in September for ensuring that those children in the special needs register get extra time. She has taught for over twenty years, considers herself a good teacher and a disciplinarian. She was very concerned about her accountability in this area and found it difficult to tie teachers down to sharing curriculum plans. She has let her concern about being examined in this way be known to all the staff and had earlier in the term been in tears for over an hour. She has left other schools because she didn't like either the style of teaching in the school or the autocratic style of the head; she has been at this school for over eight years and speaks in effusive terms about the staff, the children and the head.

Tania was about to retire and had taught in England for many years after arriving from Cyprus during the 1950s. When I first talked to her some two months ago she was worried about the inspection, wondering whether it would ruin her retirement. After one chat, she told me the next day she had talked it out with her husband and she had decided to resist at all costs the possibility that the inspection might harm her, and therefore she didn't need to talk to me formally.

Carl is the volunteer ex-teacher who loves the school and the staff. He is forever singing their praises and tells the story of how he had a nervous breakdown while teaching and how a previous head had helped him through it. He is an ex-RAF man who knows he is the clown of the staff, the butt of their warm jokes, and is very committed to them and the school.

Working-class teachers

Most of these teachers are what I would call working-class teachers. I have not gathered all the statistics yet, but it has become clear that many of them have had a struggle to find themselves in the position in which they want to be. Carol, the reception teacher, went to secondary modern school after failing her eleven plus, gained one A-level, and went straight to college and then to this school, where she enjoys her language post and never has wanted a managerial role, for class teaching is her main interest. Clare, the part-timer, did have a middle-class father who was a French fashion designer, but he died when she was 20 and left only debts. She went to grammar school and then college. Tania trained in Cyprus and began teaching here in the 1950s, and has used this job to support her family, who as immigrants haven't had it at all easy. Toni, the deputy head, came from a family interested in education, but she failed her eleven plus, has a couple of A-levels and went straight from college into teaching, which she feels she enjoys and makes a valuable contribution to as deputy head. Veronica, as mentioned earlier, left home at 17 and worked in between getting qualifications for entry into college. All she ever wanted to be was a teacher, and she loved school. She eventually qualified and though she downplays her academic potential she waxes lyrical about her teaching and her children. Vicky, the Nigerian teacher, was concerned when she arrived here in England that she didn't understand the primary system that her children were to enter, so she decided to get a job in a primary school to find out about it. She has grown to enjoy the enthusiastic children and the close relationships a primary teacher develops, in contrast to her second-ary experience. Again the immigrant status has meant she stays within a working-class frame. Chloe also failed her eleven plus, but she gained her A-levels and a teacher's certificate. She has taught at this school for over twenty years, travelling long distances to get here. Victor, the head, began his working life as a hospital porter, gained his qualifications late and has committed himself to teaching and working in one London borough.

The rise of these teachers, from working-class backgrounds in the main to respected professionals in an inner-city school, is firstly to be celebrated and not demeaned as is hinted at in government rhetoric about ill-qualified teachers. Secondly, in the main, they have all committed themselves to the working-class pupils of this particular area, with some of them, like Clare, specifically rejecting the teaching of more middle-class pupils. I'm aware that these classifications are problematic but their use is initially limited to this memo.

The pain of it all

I am moved by the pain of it all, by the stress, by the plummeting of self-esteem, by seeing how their cherished values in terms of pedagogy are being marginalized, by the fear of failure, and by the tensions created. I am particularly moved by the way in which these people who have committed themselves to their pupils and their work, and gained over the years some measure of confidence about what they do and can contribute to society, find themselves as no more than units to be examined and observed, scrutinized and assessed. This particular week was the lowest time for them as they entered into the fringes of the central spotlight of power – the OFSTED inspection.

The attention to detail

It was during this week that the teachers finally polished up the detail of their lessons for the inspection week, polished up the labelling of the displays, polished their rooms, hiding any blemishes such as old resources, and polished their plans and records and marked their books up to the present day. This public attention to detail in the written form of over-whelming paper work is the opening up of each teacher to those who will inspect them. Teachers always pay attention to detail or they could not do their job, particularly in inner-city schools, but the ownership of that detail stays with them as part of their professional role. The public focus on detail not only opens teachers to the possibility of scrutiny but marginalizes their opportunity to talk and express themselves in wider, broader teaching philosophies and political values. The attention is on the detail of management of the curriculum, the classroom and the school, not on the principles and values of teaching and learning. In this week principles are swamped by detail. Toni, the deputy, found herself on the Friday repeating to herself a mantra about the inspectors: 'I'm better than any of you on your best day.'

The media intervention

On the Monday of this last week prior to the inspection a Panorama programme was shown on BBC 1 focusing on failing schools and failing teachers. It polarized two schools with good and bad inspection reports, and quoted Chris Woodhead, the Chief HMI [Her Majesty's Inspector], frequently talking about 15,000 'poor' teachers. This was poor documen-tary, according to the *TES* [*Times Educational Supplement*], one which makes no contribution to the development of schools. Some in the public arena of education suggested the Chief HMI was acting for the government. On Friday, OFSTED launched another report claiming that small classes did not affect the quality of education except in the first two years of schooling. It was further claimed that the quality of the teaching was the prime factor in high achievement levels, and comments were again made about failing teachers. Both these reports added to the teachers' feelings of being besieged with only a few friends around them – the parents and volunteer workers in the school. Again, my feelings were moved by how these two particular media items added to their general depression.

Teachers as people

These teachers have been very open with me about their feelings, their lives and their work. They are able to criticize each other, to me, in a way in which I also feel that they understand, support and respect each other. They know each other well and they are able to express frustration with each other while at the same time maintaining very close relations with each other. I would in most cases put this kind of action down to multiple discourses or a coping strategy. However, I believe, this is a single discourse in which they are able to criticize one another because they know that it is only the action that is being criticized and not the person, for they show in many other ways their constant support and warmth towards the object of their criticism. These are people who value each other as people.

Conclusion

The week prior to OFSTED is traditionally known as the worst week. I suggest that through this focus and the holistic method employed we are able to see these teachers as people as did the BBC 2 *Modern Times* programme on an OFSTED inspection of 15 November. More and more primary teachers are being expected to perform a teaching role, not as artist or scientist or a mixture but as a technician. In performing a role teachers are then defined by the 'role-giving institution', and their own control of their work is further diminished. Teachers as people are obscured and, as we and others have argued [Jeffrey and Woods, 1995; Nias, 1989], primary teachers' personal commitment plays a large part in generating feelings about teachers' work and their pupils.

The swan maidens in *Swan Lake* are forced to play the role of swans during the day as a result of becoming victims of an evil spirit. The spell can only be broken if one who has never loved before swears to love Odette forever. Her lover Siegfried is tricked by the evil spirit into swearing love to another, but when he realizes his mistake he is reunited with Odette. They have only two options; he can marry the 'other' Odile and the evil spirit will release Odette from her role as a swan, or they can both die together by drowning themselves in the lake of her mother's tears, and destroy the evil spirit in the process. It's not difficult to guess which option the lovers take. Let's hope there is another solution for the teachers affected by OFSTED inspections. Marriage to the OFSTED values of managerialism and constant examination is generally not acceptable to most primary teachers, and the unity in death of the spirit and the self of the person, however harmonious, will cause a loss of commitment to their work.

It might be the case that my strong connection to these teachers is an empathetic one based on my own history. I failed the eleven plus, taught in the same area for twenty years, though I did not know this school or any of the teachers prior to my research involvement, and I am of the same educational generation as many of them. However, there is bound to be some form of relationship between any researcher and the researched, no matter how distanced, and the reflexive account has to include some details concerning the position of the researcher, for it illuminates the perspective and analysis as well as explicating the power relations [Bourdieu and Passeron, 1977].

COMMENTS FROM PETER WOODS ON BOB'S MEMO 'THE OFSTEDED SWANS...'

Sharing the experience of a social drama

The essence of this is that this event, of which the memo comments on merely the preliminaries, is a highly traumatic experience for the teachers – and for the researcher. This is clear from the extreme emotions reported involving tensions, breakdown, grieving, pain. It is a social drama, with characters shown in sharp relief, a gripping plot enveloped in suspense, building up to a denouement, as yet unknown, with some neatly drawn cameos along the way, good guys and bad guys, and above all a feeling at the end that you have been wrung through this experience with them. As in the 'performance science' and 'dramatic presentations' reported in Chapter 3, this 'natural drama' can produce a new form of truth for the participants and the researcher as their emotions are tested, and through the researcher, the audience can make similar discoveries for themselves.

I mentioned in the Introduction Gouldner's two sources of sociologists' perceptions: (1) empirical studies and theorizing, and (2) 'personal realities', derived from the sociologist's own experiences, and often disguised or hidden, or not fully consciously realized (Gusfield, 1990, p. 104). Bob is concerned here with his own 'personal realities' and how they are affecting his research outlooks. He does not want to contribute to 'the hegemony that the rhetoric of impersonality exercises' (Berger, 1990, p. xix); a hegemony which still largely prevails, leaving a central part of the story – the sociologist's own involvement – out of account. Like Kreiger (1984), Bob is asking 'Why did certain things move me?' He is not content to allow these feelings to affect the analysis in some significant but unstated way. He is not keen to move straight into 'persuasive rhetoric' (Atkinson, 1990), or to simulate a rigorously scientific account. He is saying, 'Here is the researcher, this was how he felt, and these are the reasons.' Readers can identify Bob in the account, and judge accordingly. They know how he was feeling, and they can see how he was thinking – an 'ethnography of the mind' in LeCompte's (1987) terms, or an 'autoethnographic text' in Denzin and Lincoln's (1995, p. 355). The aim in the memo, therefore, is for the author to explore his own strong feelings aroused in the research with the teachers, and the reasons for them; but ultimately, it will be to present an account that will evoke in readers similar feelings to both his and the teachers', such that readers will have a sense of having experienced the event (Denzin, 1989b).

Bob feels a strong identity with these teachers. He sees them as whole people with lives of their own, which none the less affect, and are affected by, their teaching roles and performance. He not only empathizes but sympathizes with them in a number of unequal power struggles – between teachers and the government (in the form of the inspectors), between teachers and the media; and with some of them as victims of a class society and a selective educational system. There is a marked theme of injustice here. As well as this sympathy, he has deep admiration for them. Several of them have won through in life by their own efforts against the odds, and their dedication and commitment to the task of teaching and to their young pupils are of a high order. They have also been putting up a good fight against what are seen as the more unreasonable elements in recent legislation. In common with many another sociologist, Bob is aligning himself here with the 'underdog' (Becker, 1967). However, unlike some other sociologists, he wants to explore the bases of this alignment, and to consider the implications for the validity of the account. Thus the 'authorial voice' itself speaks, and is part of the meanings it constructs.

The aim in this particular memo is understanding rather than validity (cf. Wolcott, 1994), relevance rather than rigour (Stake, 1981), pursuing the idea that research 'should rely more on personal experience and personal meaning as its data, and more on participant observation and introspection in its method' (ibid., p. 1). Bob is concerned therefore with the teachers' lived experience. He does not rely simply on their accounts for this – data he collects by recognized methods and then analyses. He lives the teachers' experiences with them. He is profoundly moved by his interaction with them. He is thinking of them even on his night out at the ballet, relating that to what he has observed and what he has been told at the school during the day. Allowing free rein to his own feelings allows him to engage with them, to develop rapport with them (would they have been so 'very open' otherwise?), and to heighten his own understanding (Smith, 1980).

Swan Lake provided more chances for understanding. The teachers' plight has stayed with him into the evening and becomes caught up in the ballet. It is thrown into vivid relief by the grace, beauty, art, fun, harmony, great accomplishment and sheer pleasure of the performance. Behind the enjoyment he derives from this experience, worries generated in the research and why he should feel such worries nag away at him. He feels constrained to get them out of his system by writing this memo over the weekend. The research week and the ballet were both cathartic episodes or critical events, sparking off feelings and lines of thought that bore on each other, and heightened receptivity to each. Moved by each, he was more moved by both in conjunction. The researcher's holism here matches that of the teachers' – no relaxing at the end of a hard and stressful week, no switching off at an appointed hour; the mind, the feelings continue to stir.

His feelings are a source of sociological insight, and enable him to fill out the idea with empirical detail. For example, what we seem to have here in the teachers' reactions is trauma deriving from a clash between role and person, and between two opposing views of how the two should relate with respect to teachers. Nias (1989), for example, has shown how, for primary teachers, self and role are fused into one; and that certainly seems to be the case for these teachers. The effect of the government's reforms is to encourage a more utilitarian approach to the teacher role, causing crises of conscience among teachers. There are also issues of power and control, the inspectors appearing to act for an increasingly centralizing government. Their forthcoming visit presages another possible 'nail in the coffin' of teacher professionalism. We can see all the personal suffering this entails, but behind this are social issues of general concern.

Methods

This seems a good example of what I have termed a 'warm-hearted' approach (Woods, 1990c), in contrast to the 'cold-eyed' alternative view discussed in Chapter 1. Under the influence of qualitative, humanistic and feminist approaches, an alternative approach has developed, laying emphasis upon subjectivities and the self, seeing the self as situated in a particular labour market, and bringing a whole-life view to bear, both in the sense of how the teacher role is tied up with other roles in society and of how a teacher's own biography underpins current beliefs and attitudes.

Of course a warm-hearted approach may be viewed as self-indulgent or exhibitionist through a cold-eyed view. One reason is the different research approach in itself. Ellis and Flaherty (1992, p. 4) suggest that another is that researchers typically 'have been males from upper middle class, Anglo-American, professional backgrounds where emotions are suppressed or, at most, viewed as private experiences'. We need both the scientific and the subjective view. The underlying discipline, sociology, needs to take its place as 'quasi-science, quasi-humanities. As such, the goal is to arrive at an understanding of lived experience that is both rigorous – based on systematic observation – and imaginative – based on expressive insight' (Ellis and Flaherty, 1992, p. 5). Moreover, they are not separate, unrelated lines of attack – they feed into each other. It is a small but key step from here to include the researcher's subjectivity.

In this particular application of the warm-hearted approach, consider-able heat is generated. But, as noted in Chapter 3, if we can trace the sources of our anger, worry, sadness, etc., these extreme emotions take our understanding to new levels. That is exactly what Bob is trying to do here. Smith (1980) advises researchers to engage in self-examination when they find themselves in a 'heightened state of emotion' (p. 10), 'the better to distinguish between emotions that are generated from the situation and those that may be self-generated and irrational' (Jansen and Peshkin, 1992, p. 705). Bob does this. He certainly 'goes native', but not in the counter-productive way in which this is usually represented in the methodological literature (though see 'Dangers' below). He is 'humanly involved', not completely taken over. The analysis will derive from this involvement. By exploring his own feelings, he allows the reader to see his account of the teachers through those feelings, not presenting them as from some mythical, distanced, scientific, objective observer, completely absent from the text. In this way, readers can establish the 'trustworthiness' of the text (Lincoln and Guba, 1985).

It is also an interesting example of participant observation. Bob does not find direct access to teachers' experiences, thoughts and feelings through actually taking on a recognized role within the institution, and engaging in self-analysis through the role. He does it through merging the self with the other in a whole-life sense, abandoning the role of detached, scientific observer, and crossing the 'self–other border' (Fine, 1994). He is able to do this to a large extent because there were aspects of his own career that gave him insights into the teachers' experience and feelings (Rubin, 1981). He had himself taught in primary schools, mainly in the same kind of area, for some eighteen years. His own working-class origins similarly gave him insights into the struggles involved in upward mobility, in contesting class barriers, and in the feelings of solidarity against the odds among the teachers in the school. Consequently, the empathy is such that he has lived the week with them. He has made a role for himself that the teachers, in the circumstances, embrace within their own culture. He is thus privy to that culture from the inside, appreciating their cognitive perspectives and their feelings through his own. An interesting question is: did Bob have any influence himself upon the culture, as participants often do? (This is partly answered by Bob's second memo, below.)

In presentation, Bob rejects objective, distanced rhetoric in favour of expressive speech (Clifford, 1986). He is not just presenting the teachers' views and experiences as some kind of 'naive reality'. This is what he and they made of them – the construction of knowledge is a joint affair between researcher and teachers. The memo's style is also interesting. As Jansen and Peshkin (1992, p. 715) note, 'The textual strategies authors use in engaging their subjectivities is [sic] an integral part of the meaning they convey':

1 It starts with a bang on a list of casualties. It is dramatic, but not melodramatic, being based on fact. It then steadily builds up a picture of individual and collective trauma.
2 The *Swan Lake* experience is skilfully used. It envelops the account, providing a beginning and an end to the 'ethnography of the mind'. It gives the appearance of a story-line, and contains a moral. But it is the antithesis with the teachers' experience that furnishes its main force, setting that experience in finely etched relief.
3 The choice of words and phrases highlights the antithesis, and stimu-lates the reader's feelings. The 'invigorating and delightful music' of *Swan Lake*, its 'party atmosphere' and the 'very jolly and uplifting environment' are a stark and sudden contrast to the 'depression', 'anger', 'tears', 'panic', 'worry' and 'suffering' that preceded and followed it.

4 Similarly, sympathy for the players – the teachers – is aroused by the portrayal of their hardships in their private lives: 'terrible times', 'anniversary of her mother's death', 'home becoming prison', 'suffered tremendously from a brutal father', 'one of her cats had died', 'ageing parent recovering from alcoholism', 'nervous breakdown'.

On the one hand, we might say that these teachers are professionals, and that their professional duties are there to be discharged whatever the background. This, presumably, would be the inspectors' approach, involving an ascetic application of their formulae. On the other is the recognition that for these teachers, teaching is a whole-life enterprise. As such, their personal backgrounds and life-histories cannot be left out of account. They will tell us a great deal about the emotional charge that is summoned up at times of crisis.

Part of the argument is that teaching is an emotional business for these teachers, and their emotions can have very positive effects for their teaching, as we have attempted to show elsewhere (Woods and Jeffrey, 1996); but they can also have very deleterious effects if aroused in circumstances and for reasons that seem to them to run counter to their heartfelt convictions. The presentational task here is to convey that emotion, its strength and depth – and incorporating aspects of life-history helps to achieve this – within an academic framework (since we are declaredly still working within a scientific frame), involving analysis, categories and systematic organization. Such research requires the ability to move freely between an 'insider's passionate perspective and an outsider's dispassionate one' (Van Maanen, 1988, p. 77). There is a combination of art and science in the memo. There is a strong aesthetic element there, most notably in the sense of beauty conjured up by the description of the ballet, contrasting with the ugliness of the teachers' predicament. This, too, is deeply felt. The ballet (and on other occasions, for Bob, opera) is not just a convenient source of metaphor, and this was not just an occasional night out for him at Covent Garden. He is an habitual attendant. He has explained that, for him, 'dance and music represent an opportunity to explore emotional experiences in a formal context. The productions nourish my emotional desires as well as representing the traumas of life through emotions, leaving me feeling both satisfied and more aware of the humanity involved in social and political settings.'

Dangers

There may be problems of bias (see Jansen and Peshkin, 1992, p. 706). Bob is clearly aware of this, otherwise he would not have written this reflective memo. In it, he is getting his feelings out of his system, and beginning an analysis of them. He is not presenting his view of the teachers in a final report as some kind of objective truth. This, therefore, is a way of having both 'passionate involvement' and 'dispassionate distance'. But is the distance dispassionate enough? It seems worth raising a few questions. How far has the researcher 'gone over to the other side', that is, accepted the norms of the teachers' culture and given up on the researcher's persona (Thomas, 1995)? Does his admiration for them blind him to other possibilities? How far are the teachers 'playing up' to the researcher, giving him what they think he wants, and possibly thereby exaggerating their reactions and selecting only dramatic incidents from their backgrounds to recount? After all, it does make for a 'good story'. If not exactly 'fiction', how much exaggerated or concealed truth is there? How much is sympathy for the teachers a little overdrawn – for example, is 'She had no one to share the burden of her increasing work load' the teacher's or the researcher's sentiment? How far are some claims a little extravagant (perhaps 'teachers always pay attention to detail or they could not do their job')? How far, also, might the teachers be using the opportunity to release some pent-up emotions in what is undoubtedly a trying situation for them, but not necessarily an unjust one? After all, we are not seeing the full picture here. This is the week *before* the inspection, the most unsettling, worrying, alienating time, the kind of liminal stage that takes us back to first principles, makes us ask why we joined, reminds us of all previous horrors, appears to mortgage the whole future. I wonder if their feelings about this actual week were different *after* the inspection, and whether they would cast their worries recounted here in a different light.

The above is a 'triangulation of time' point. One may also ask how far undue sympathy is aroused for the teachers in a political sense. The whole thrust of the memo is towards creating a sense of injustice. The teachers are the heroes and heroines; the inspectors, and behind them the government and the media, are the villains. How far is the portrayal of the teachers a romanticized one? Would our view of them and our feelings about them be any different if this account were accompanied by the inspectors' viewpoint? To what extent might the researcher have been carried away by his own feelings, values and background, 'filling in the ambiguities...not with what was truly there, but with nostalgia and fantasized memories of my own...past experience' (Smith, 1980, p. 5)?

The researcher is also 'positioned' (Rosaldo, 1989), because of age, gender, experience, etc. The feelings being teased out in the memo are a product of the conjunction between the event being researched and the researcher's own biography. If the memo were to be developed into an article, therefore, there would need to be something more explicit on the researcher's biography.

The memo is highly successful as a work of art. The question is what frame we are to put around it, and where we hang it in our gallery.

MEMO FROM BOB JEFFREY – 'CONFESSION TIME': ADDITIONAL COMMENTS TO PW'S 'COMMENTS ON BOB'S MEMO "THE OFSTEDED SWANS"'

I didn't mention in the memo how far I had become involved. There were three occasions when I offered some advice or help to people who were somewhat distressed or worried. I've been worrying myself about how to explain these incidents to you and now seems the right time.

The case of the marginalized part-timer

A part-time member of staff, who others had told me was pretty disturbed by the idea of OFSTED early in the term, was still in a state when I eventually talked to her. Her extreme reactions were also contributing to anxiety in the staff room, according to some teachers. To cut a long story short, she was finding it difficult to plan her work because class teachers were too busy to give her information she needed to carry out her programme, which she had been given only a few weeks before by the head teacher related to SEN [Special Educational Needs] work. After some discussion about her worries I suggested that she put down on paper what arrangements she had up till now, present it to the head and staff for approval, and basically establish her position clearly so there was no ambiguity, should the inspectors question anyone about her work. She did this and was extremely grateful for my help, gave me a Christmas card and has been extremely complimentary about my involvement with the school.

The case of the dodgy inspector

The head teacher had become gradually more stressed as the process proceeded, and this was noted by many staff; and in conversations with me whom he sought out regularly for chats. We discussed many of his problems and sometimes I did offer some advice as to strategies I had seen adopted elsewhere. However, during the inspection week, after talking to a number of staff, it became clear that one of the inspectors was not acting according to the standards laid down in the handbook. I collected these anecdotes and in discussions with the head teacher a strategy was developed to make the most of this aberrant behaviour. Because the inspectorate team were also inspectors in the school's LEA [local education authority] there already was a sympathetic relationship between the school and the team. The Registered Inspector was approached by the head with his complaints, and the outcome was that no complaint would be submitted but the Registered Inspector assured the head that every effort would be made to ensure that this particular inspector's findings were scrutinized. I am unaware if any other considerations were taken into account. [A little cryptic but possibly wisely so.]

The case of the worried postholder

One of the experienced members of staff with responsibility for a particular curriculum area was worried about her lesson on the penultimate day of the inspection. She knew the lesson would be seen as representative of the quality of her curriculum area and her as postholder. We had already talked a little about the differing power relations between teachers and inspectors and what strategies other teachers in other schools had used to address the issue. As she gathered her equipment together, during the lunch time, I could tell she was worried. I had got to know her and her background quite well, and I could not leave her to go in to the lesson without a helpful word. I suggested that it would help her if she took the initiative in terms of the power relationship in the classroom, and suggested some small ways in which she could establish her self as less of a victim and more in control of the situation. She was grateful for the advice, used it, and said clearly to others afterwards that I had helped a great deal.

These confessions highlight a general sympathy I felt for these teachers, and my tone in conversations is evidence of that, though the transcripts will also show counter-arguments, devil's advocate questions, and a sprinkling of 'why do you let it worry you? Why do it?' I trust my actions don't compromise you or the research, but perhaps we ought to discuss my actions in the light of future inspections.

As to your comments, I think all the analysis you have constructed is relevant and reflects my position accurately.

REPLY TO 'CONFESSIONS' FROM PETER WOODS

Many thanks for the 'Confessions' – very interesting, and a sharp contrast to the dehumanized behaviour of the inspectors we saw on television. I'm sure you were right to help in the ways you describe – it seems a continuation of living the experience through with them. If you feel the pain with them, it makes sense to help alleviate it if a clear opportunity arises, especially if asked to do so. You can hardly stand idly by when somebody is in difficulties and there is something you can do to assist. It also helps alleviate one's own concerns that nag away at you in those out-of-school hours. We are not in the 'fly-on-the-wall', non-participant observer business anyway, as in King (1978). Nor are we in the kind of participant observation study which holds something back, as in Hargreaves (1967) and Pollard (1985a). You are playing for higher stakes, and your association with these teachers runs higher. It seems you have to follow this through in a fairly full-blooded way. This is surely good for trust and rapport, and for insights into innermost thoughts and feelings, though your help is not given with this calculatedly in mind.

It raises further interesting questions about your role and your relationship with the teachers. Zajano and Edelsberg (1993) discuss how Zajano, in a research relationship with a teacher, graduated through phases from suspect stranger and then cordial acquaintance, to welcome guest, followed by expert resource, valued colleague and confidante. Your role certainly seems to comprise the last four. You are carrying your empathy on from the appreciation of feelings within the situation as you found it, to proactive advice and help, that is, making a direct intervention in the action and influencing the situation in some way. You are the researcher, but also a potential counsellor, adviser and friend. This latter is an aspect of the collaboration which is a general feature of our work and one of the declared aims of the research: 'To develop collaborative research methods with teachers. The aim is to explore the possibilities of democratic evaluation in this area, both to enrich the quality of the research and to contribute to teacher development.' We go on to say that

> we are particularly interested in the idea of the school as a 'research park' (Davies, 1994). We aim to assist teachers in their own evaluations of inspections and their reactions to them, and thus developing their own research models. We feel this to be especially important given the subject under study. All inspections are potentially stressful, inducing self-doubt, confusion and strong emotional reactions. OFSTED is even more threatening in this respect. Our research may help teachers view these processes objectively and analytically, and to 'come to professional terms' with them.

The research will thus be 'open'. Regular feedback will help increase the school's identification with the research process, and feed into in-service training (INSET). The research, therefore, cannot be considered non-interventionist. In some respects it is partisan, with a conception of research as *praxis* (Lather, 1986). We are interested, like the inspectors, in educational improvement, though our conception of what that constitutes and how it is to be achieved differs in some key respects, as does the teachers'. There are other issues related to those differences, to do with aiding people in their struggle against domination, revealing practices, particularly hidden practices, that operate against commonly held values of fairness and justice, portraying the needless misery that is caused by such practices, and providing insights that might help alleviate the situation. Teachers are an oppressed group of people at the moment. Those in our sample are also working-class – and most of them (all the full-time classroom teachers) female. Some of them are also members of ethnic minorities. There is a lot of oppression and injustice here, with a long history, that goes way beyond the classrooms of the research! Not surprisingly, there are elements of a critical sociology in your approach. But the partisanship is balanced in two ways. One is through attention to the traditional rules of ethnographic research as set out in Chapter 2. The other is through researcher reflexivity, such as you are showing in these memos. Your presentation thus does not masquerade as some kind of objective truth independent of researcher involvement, but appears with you, your values and identity, your ways of seeing and feeling and thinking, openly incorporated into the research.

Lofland (1995, p. 43) might term this 'fettered' research, since that done in 'a spirit of unfettered enquiry counsels a dispassionate and disinterested attitude... [involving] an emotional attitude of judiciousness and calm concern, with patient and careful examination and continual reexamination of all data and concepts'. However, whereas Lofland presents 'fettered' and 'unfettered' research as polarized approaches, I believe it is quite possible to bring the qualities of calmness, patience, etc., to bear on partisan research. It is quite possible to feel passionately about the research one is doing, and to reflect on that passion calmly, at length, and repeatedly, until some resolutions are found that bring harmony to the data one has found and the feelings one has about it. The passion in this case seems to me a positive advantage.

There is something, too, of Denzin and Lincoln's (1995, p. 354) point about qualitative research being a 'moral, allegorical, and therapeutic project'. We subscribe to the view of teaching as a moral craft (Tom, 1984; Elbaz, 1992), and the interventionist stance of the research is necessarily imbued with similar principles. Your memos make interesting use of allegory. And I'm sure that teachers will attest to the therapy that the research in general has provided for them – not just through instances where you have rendered assistance, but in listening to them and being prepared to 'give them voice'.

MEMO FROM BOB JEFFREY: APPRECIATING 'THE ART OF THE PRIMARY TEACHER'

The inspection at Trafflon school happened three weeks ago and a verbal report has been heard. There is, as with all inspection reports, a large gulf between the feelings the teachers have about their practice and the language used to describe that practice in the reports. This was on my mind as I once again found myself reading the reviews of a new ballet I watched a few days ago.

The critic's review and the inspectors' report

Twyla Tharp's new ballet *Mr Worldly Wise* had its premier at the Royal Opera House in December 1995. It is the simple story of a man weighed down with a Bunyanesque sack representing Rossini's 'cultural baggage' (Parry, 1995: all further unreferenced quotations in this memo are from this review), a man, like Rossini and by implication the audience, spiritually depleted by his own 'vitality, speed and grandiosity' (Gossett, 1996). The music is a selection of Rossini's work, mainly focusing on a solemn mass he wrote in a late period in his life. His capabilities are compared in dance to a younger, creative character who outshines him every time. However, he is transported to another land by a 'veiled vision' and is entertained by performances of grace and beauty representing undispersed souls. In the final act, invigorated by these visions, he 'regains his dignity' and reclaims the world from his younger competitor, who takes up the baggage.

As I watched this ballet I thought of many of the experienced primary teachers I had encountered in this OFSTED research. Characters who, like Rossini, were admired for their art and craft, by parents, colleagues, head teachers and pupils. Characters who had become somewhat burdened by the trappings of increasing bureaucracy [Jeffrey and Woods, 1995] and managerialism, and who, like Rossini, still struggled to be creative and, as they lived out the last era of their teaching career, wished to feel creative and fulfilled in a world that appreciated their art. I resolved to explore the idea of appreciation through, firstly, comparing a critical review of the ballet and an OFSTED report. The former is written by Jann Parry of the *Observer*, 17 December 1995, and the latter was written about Flately School (another school in the OFSTED research) by an OFSTED team.

There are a few similarities between the review and the report. Both comment on the factual plot or context, and both describe the performance of the characters, though the report does not single anyone out except the head teacher. Both refer to the quality of presentation and levels of achievement. However, there is one significant difference, and that is in the language that is used to paint the picture and draw up the report. The ballet critic 'came down on the rapturous side of the fence', she was 'exhilarated', and while she observed that 'the work has not cohered into the sum of its parts ... the company is sparkling' and the whole ballet is 'a grab bag of delectable goodies'; whereas 'the school provides good value for money'. The report has, of course, no overtly subjective indicators, but it says 'there is a welcoming ethos ... enhanced by attractive displays [depersonalizing phrase] .... It is a happy school where pupils' backgrounds and cultures are valued ... [and] assemblies have a positive effect on pupils' all round development.' These are the only qualitative comments in the report. The review interprets scenes, 'the image is a metaphor', whereas the report appears to present scientific truth. Performances in the ballet are danced 'with heartbreaking grace' whereas the 'quality of teaching is sound or better in most lessons', 'the cutting edge choreography is both goofy and rhapsodic' whereas 'where teaching is good it is characterised by effective organisation and management, good subject expertise and clear planning'. There is an air of appreciation in the review, as one of the principal dancers 'while dancing with crystal clarity was concentrating too hard on the opening night to enjoy herself'. There is no attempt in the report to acknowledge the humanity of an inspections situation, only the criticism 'some teachers fail to use an appropriate range of teaching approaches'.

I am not suggesting that one genre – that of the ballet critic – can be applied to a different context – that of a school inspection. The former is expected to use a more subjective approach, though even this genre or discourse has a body of knowledge that applies to the art, and the use of superlatives is designed to excite the reader by painting the more vivid picture. The report has a more distanced approach, is determined by set criteria, is constructed by a team, and has a limited vocabulary with which to express the inspectors' observations. The report is intended to appear more scientific and detached. [In fact the actual evaluations in the inspection process are subjective judgements, though this process is hidden from the reader by the quantitative method used to make a final evaluation.]

However, what the contrast does show is that the review is more appreciative of what the writer is experiencing. The review is able therefore to appreciate qualities, i.e. what is germane to the situation [Eisner, 1991], whereas the inspection focuses on a list of components and is only able to report literally by evaluating each part in turn. Eisner argues that to appreciate a scene one needs to be a connoisseur. Like a wine connoisseur, the educational connoisseur needs to consider everything: intention, structure, curriculum, and pedagogy. An OFSTED inspection does have a comprehensiveness to it, but the inspectors are limited in the form that they use to evaluate the scene. The language is prescribed and the foci are single components. Eisner argues that educational criticism should have four dimensions – description, interpretation, evaluation and thematics – all of which are present in the review; the report only has description and evaluation.

The main question here is: why should a more appreciative approach be taken to the inspection of schools? There are two reasons. First, OFSTED argue that they are interested in 'improvement through inspection'. The form that they use is given credibility because of the legitimacy bestowed by the state and other civil institutions, e.g. the *Guardian*, *TES* and the main political parties. This power may well then influence teachers and schools to adapt their working approaches to mimic that particular form. However, it will not encourage teachers to become educational connoisseurs, whereas an appreciative form might encourage teachers to develop their sensitivity to classroom climates and to evaluate improvement through adopting all four dimensions that Eisner suggests.

Secondly, primary teachers' work is an art to be 'appreciated', and the form of an OFSTED inspection is such a contrast to that art. The tension between those two different forms is traumatic for many primary teachers, and any improvement advocated by policy makers or local inspectors will be seen as not improvement but a take-over. 'You must now teach not facilitate' was said to one school's staff in a pre-OFSTED check-up, and the reaction was hostile.

Lastly, it was not lost on me that Mr Worldly Wise in the ballet, who was suffering 'at the edge of madness', was shown 'a realm of order and proportion and community and grace, in which activity never conquers dignity'. This is not the world post-OFSTED that primary teachers are being shown by the way in which the OFSTED inspectors carry out their role and by the nature of the role they perform. Theirs is a realm of authoritarianism, based on technicism, generating community conflict between teachers and parents and a total lack of grace and dignity. Mr Worldly Wise was shown through the dancers a world of undispersed souls, and he learnt from that. Dispersing teachers' souls from their work will create dispersed souls. This is what Twyla Tharp thought Rossini was seeking in the hard times of old age, and it appears to us that our experienced teachers would value more appreciation and less dispersal.

COMMENT FROM PETER WOODS

I am interested again in how you continue to live the inspection in your most precious 'off-duty' moments – indeed how certain aspects are highlighted at those times. Here we have an event outside the school, and standing in some contrast to the subject of your study, providing insights into that subject, particularly, in this case, the inspectors' report. There are a number of interesting comparisons and contrasts. The ballet has affinities with what the teachers are trying to do. It is a creative, artistic, aesthetic project, and there are important aspects of teachers' work, we argue, that are similar. These are overlooked in the inspectors' report, working within the confines of a contrasting discourse. The memo illustrates the power of metaphor and of the comparative method in vividly depicting the conflict between two opposing discourses. Questions one always asks are: how far are the comparisons accurate? How far does the analogy overstate the case? These are scientific questions that we need to bring to the artistic, humanistic cast of your memos. The two in conjunction – science and art – make for considerable strength, as indeed they do in teaching (see Chapter 1).

5 Collaborating in historical ethnography

Researching critical events in education

INTRODUCTION: CRITICAL EVENTS

I have described and analysed elsewhere the phenomenon of critical events in education (Woods, 1993a). In this chapter, I shall discuss the methodology of the research. 'Critical events' are exceptional kinds of activity that occur from time to time in schools and that bring radical change in pupils and sometimes teachers. Some children achieve standards their teachers hardly thought possible (cf. Nias et al., 1992). There are 'great moments of teachability' (McLaren, 1986, p. 236), when teachers transcend the contradictions of the job and achieve the 'peak experience' of which Maslow (1973, p. 77) writes, and in which they 'become aware of their full identity' (Nias, 1989, p. 200). Some teachers say that the experience has 'changed their lives', and that 'they will never be the same again'. Others feel their dearest beliefs and values have, for once in their lives, found a combination of circumstances where they could be shown to work, and work uncommonly well. There can, of course, be *negative* critical events, that is, those that have educationally retrogressive consequences. I have described some of these in Woods (1990a). They have somewhat different methodological implications, but they were not my concern in this research, nor are they in this chapter.

The events chosen for study came to my attention through the media, my existing relationships with schools, or colleagues in other institutions. They were all judged outstanding by a range of people, including pupils, teachers, parents, advisers and academics. Several of the events had won an award. Reviewing the data and comparing cases produced a core category ('critical event'). I then sought to specify its main features, its structure, the conditions which give rise to it, the context in which it is embedded, the strategies by which it is handled, and the consequences of those strategies (see Strauss and Corbin, 1990, for this mode of analysis). This then threw up a number of related subjects for study, notably the roles of the critical agent (the central initiator and co-ordinator) and of critical others (people who were crucially involved but had no formal role within the institution: see Woods, 1993c), the nature of pupil and teacher development, the distinctive generation of 'communitas' (Turner, 1974; McLaren, 1986), the learning theory, and how change was accomplished.

I chose four critical events to analyse in this way:

1 the making of a children's book, *Rushavenn Time*, written by a well-known children's author, Theresa Whistler, with children and teachers from Brixworth primary school in Northamptonshire;
2 the making of a film of community life in the village of Laxfield, Suffolk, by children at the local primary school;
3 the planning and design of a heritage centre on an actual site in Winchester by groups of children from Western primary school and All Saints Community primary school (the 'Chippindale Venture');
4 the production of the musical *Godspell* at Roade comprehensive school, Northamptonshire.

These were the ones that illustrated most completely and vividly the nature and significance of critical events. They also represent major media of expression. Eisner (1985, p. 211) argues that teachers should seek to 'provide the conditions that enable students to secure deep and diverse forms of meaning in their lives', and in order to do this, we 'must develop multiple forms of literacy'. These four events provide a range of such 'forms of literacy', and offer opportunities to substantiate some of those 'deep and diverse forms of meaning'.

One of the problems in researching these activities was in employing ethnographic methods, which I judged to be the most suitable in this kind of research, for matters that had happened in the past. The long-term engagement in the situation as things actually happen and observing things at first hand which are the most prominent features of the approach were not possible here. Another problem was in identifying and characterizing the criticality. It was possible to explore pupil and teacher gains fairly systematically, but I also hoped to capture the emotional and aesthetic import of the experience and to represent it as felt by the participants. A third concern was how to maximize any benefits from the research for teacher, pupil and educational development. In what follows, I explore some approaches to addressing these questions.

HISTORICAL ETHNOGRAPHY

Teachers cannot plan for criticality so that it inevitably occurs. All they can do is to construct an appropriate context and assemble as many relevant factors as possible. Whether the event sparks into that kind of life depends on other elements largely unforeseen. What this means, methodologically, is that it is difficult to study critical events as they are happening. It would be useful to do so, since not only would the process be observed at first hand, but comparative studies could be undertaken of events that worked to differing degrees of success. Invariably, however, the subject for study cannot be identified until it has occurred. As Kelchtermans (1991, p. 7) has observed, with regard to critical incidents, 'The "critical" character of an event is defined by the respondent...events can only become "critical incidents" afterwards, retrospectively.' Therefore it is not possible to make a general list of potential, critical incidents. Hence the need for historical ethnography. This is the exploration of events that have occurred in the past, using qualitative, naturalistic methods that aim to explore meanings and understandings, and to recreate cultures and contexts in the evocative manner typical of ethnography. The chief methods are extensive interviewing; use of documentary evidence made at the time of the event; and visiting scenes. A measure of observation can be involved, especially in witnessing celebratory functions which signal the successful end of the event (by which time the criticality is becoming evident). By comparing a number of such events, it is possible to see what they have in common.

Among the advantages of historical ethnography in relation to critical events is that it is labour-intensive. From the historical point of view, it allows for what Hexter (1971, quoted in Smith et al., 1987, p. 18) calls 'processive explanation', a way of capitalizing on knowing how things turned out. The ethnographer could claim that the 'progressive focusing' (Hammersley and Atkinson, 1995) has to some extent already been done in the sampling of exceptional events. Once, within these, critical events have been identified, one can go ahead immediately to 'saturate' (Glaser and Strauss, 1967) knowledge of particular aspects of the event. The event is clearly demarcated, integrated and developed, and participants are able to reflect on the event in its entirety and in more general educational context. Because these are such notable events, there tends to be a great deal of evidence available, though it might not be collected together and organized. I saw the Rushavenn informant, for example, many times over a three-year period, and at a number of these meetings he produced new evidence he had discovered, and that he had forgotten existed. Lots of people know about these events, and are eager to share their experiences. There were none of the traditional difficulties that occur when negotiating access (Burgess, 1991; Troman, 1996). Indeed I had a sense that my enquiry was seen as integral to the event. The event seems to me to have a clear structure with stages of conceptualization, preparation and planning, divergence, convergence, consolidation and celebration. My activity seemed in some ways to be part of the celebration, but leading mainly to a new evaluation/recording phase.

Historical ethnography is not to be confused with what Rist (1980) has termed 'blitzkrieg ethnography', involving just two or three days of fieldwork, or with those studies which isolate outcomes from processes or a small subdivision from a larger whole. Nor, clearly, is it the 'condensed fieldwork' that Walker (1986) recommends, since the rationale for that was more or less immediate feedback to the teachers concerned in order to inform their teaching. While I saw feedback as important, I never conceived of it as anything close to 'immediate'. For while this may lack the classical ethnographic character of studying processes as they occur over a lengthy period, compensatory salient features are in place which take a similar amount of time to work through. These reflect the similarity of concerns of both history and ethnography for context, naturalism, holism and interpretation (Edson, 1988). Thus historical ethnography retains the focus on natural settings with film, tape, witness and visit; and it employs time, people and place sampling (Ball, 1990a) to enrich the description, fill out the picture, and enhance the validity. There is the same employment of multimethods in the attempt to build up the story as it was experienced by participants. There is the same emphasis on trust and rapport, and in seeking understanding of people's perspectives. While in traditional ethnography this rapport takes time to develop, it was quickly established in these cases. The critical event embraced us all. Having been granted entrance, I was a member of the club, membership then being consolidated by the lengthy conversations that took place.

The initial burst of interviews took place over two or three days. All were followed up in some form or other, both extending the range of interviews, and intensifying the discussion with the major participants. In the case of the head teacher involved in the Rushavenn project, the detailed discussions have led in the three years of our association to a full-scale life-history (see Chapter 3). This further illustrates the earlier point about the importance of these events within these teachers' lives. In general, they drew on their biographies extensively to explain the meaning of the event to them (see also Goodson, 1991). Life-history techniques were used here, building on previous work in Woods (1987a, 1990a) and Sikes, Measor and Woods (1985). The schools, teachers and some of the pupils involved in the other events have all been revisited, and their current opinions and perspectives on the event sought – another form of triangulation. This was of particular interest in the Rushavenn and Laxfield projects. Here, pupils, now several years older, were able to look back and reassess the event more dispassionately and in the fuller context of their educational careers. They were able to bring qualitative analysis to bear, comparing different styles of teaching that they had experienced over the years. Stephen, for example, now a 17-year-old sixth former, reflected on what he called the 'number-crunching' character of much secondary school teaching in contrast to what he saw as the truer educational experience of the Rushavenn project, which occurred at primary school when he was 10 years old. He commented on the traumatic nature of his transfer from primary to secondary school, making the important point that the more successful the primary school in creative encouragement, the more the experience of culture clash at secondary school, where more instrumentalist policies prevailed. The Laxfield pupils also compared their experience on a wider basis. At their secondary school, 'creative work' was 'more the teacher, and not so much of you' (Woods, 1993a, p. 71).

The interview, therefore, is seen as a process involving pre- and post-interview strategies and reflection, and several and varied interviews among a range of people connected with the event as they, together, progressively over time *construct* an account of the event. Between them they recreate and analyse the event in three respects bearing on (1) information gathering, (2) evoking the past, conveying feelings associated with the event, and (3) testing out various explanations, which then become grounded in the data. A succession of interviews, talks or conversations (Woods, 1985) took place, therefore, generally until no new material or thoughts were being generated (Glaser and Strauss, 1967).

The research suggests some interesting possibilities for this kind of historical ethnography. It combined 'narrative' and 'structural' history (Stone, 1981), that is, it sought to make each event intelligible in its own terms – to tell the story, or stories, of the event, in their full richness, producing 'artistic verisimilitude' (Tuchman, 1981, p. 33); and to set up an explanatory model which showed that they have related properties. This model was grounded in the narratives. Secondly, it facilitated a focused, holistic view. As noted earlier, though they involve a considerable amount of planning, one cannot predict how these events will turn out. The 'divergent' phases may allow too much licence, their 'convergent' phases may unduly constrain, so as to render the event uncritical. When they have come to fruition, one can see them as a whole from beginning to end, and the typical structure from initial conceptualization to final celebration is more evident. The story is there for the telling. Subjects' accounts in large part take the form of oral history. These are supported by a battery of documentation – including taped, photographed or filmed recordings of teaching episodes, reports, children's work, teachers' notes and evaluations, teachers' field notes that log the structure and processes of the event, school records, artifacts, diaries, newspaper reports, articles, reviews, letters, and records of discussions with pupils and 'critical others'. This kind of evidence performs a number of functions, including:

1 contextualizing – providing a range of views which helps situate the event;
2 chronicling – contributing to the story;
3 triangulating – providing cross-checking of objective data and general claims;
4 validating – presenting proof and/or illustration of claims;
5 giving primary data – for example, where teachers had kept records of phases of the event, planning, teaching methods, and pupils' work;
6 allowing participation by proxy – for example, one could study the videos of the stage performance and rehearsals of *Godspell* at leisure. They contain detail impossible to take in at one, or even two, viewings. The mother of one of the cast, for example, had 'seen it loads of times, and she says, even when she watches the video now, she still sees things

she hasn't seen before, and that's the strength of it' (Woods, 1993a, p. 132);

7 enculturating – personal and private materials such as letters, diaries and poems afforded access to the innermost thoughts and feelings of the person and to the group culture of which they were a part, and offered a kind of honorary membership;

8 stimulating – raising questions, intimating themes, prompting hunches and creative thought (see Smith et al., 1988).

Historical ethnography may take a number of forms. Smith and colleagues studied the history of an institution and its district and the life-histories of its members, following a qualitative study at the school fifteen years before (Smith and Keith, 1971). Their research was therefore conducted at individual, institutional and district level (Smith et al., 1985). Critical ethnographers would argue for the need for wider referencing in broader social and historical movements, as opposed to the 'presentism' and emphasis on observation of traditional ethnography (see, for example, Quantz, 1992). It would certainly be interesting to study critical events in this way. For example, from the point of view of teaching as work, how do critical events compare with other experiences over the years? How far, for instance, do they represent counteraction to alienation, 'penetrations' of more usual routine conditions of existence (Willis, 1977)? How far are they a product of the 'progressive' era of the 1960s and 1970s? Comparative study combined with history might also be instructive. Do such kinds of activity feature elsewhere? If so, in what kinds of system?

Such broad questions were not the subject of this study. I was more concerned with what might be considered micro-historical ethnography, seeking to retain some of the benefits of 'presentism', while giving it a degree of historical perspective, and being mainly concerned with processes within and structure of the events and their effects on partici-pants. An essential feature was the recency of the events. Identification of them came largely through hearing about the 'celebration', which typically concluded the event, and which in some instances I was able to join. There was continuity, therefore, between the event and its study. The aura remained, excitement and sense of thrill were still at a high pitch, communitas maintained, fine detail remembered. The study retained, therefore, some of the benefits of 'presentism'. It was able to combine traditional historical sources with oral accounts from involved partici-pants. The slight distance between event and study allowed for more considered appraisal of results (what exactly had been learnt) and teacher reflection (for example, on own self-development), and helped situate the event within individual careers, and the ongoing life and work of the school. One of the major differences from traditional ethnography is the researcher's dependence on others' testimony and other secondary data. An ethnographer is his or her own primary source of data, being an eye-witness to the event (Smith et al., 1988). Not being present at the event as it happened means that one does not experience the emergent, unfolding process as it occurs, and the research misses the triangulating force (on others' accounts) of one's own observations. On the other hand, ethnographers have to some extent to select what they see, and to construct accounts of their own (Atkinson, 1990). Also, in this research, the comparative lack of first-hand involvement was less of a concern than it might otherwise have been, since another major feature was that of collaboration.

COLLABORATION

There has been considerable interest in collaborative research between teachers and researchers recently (Argyris and Schön, 1976; Carr and Kemmis, 1986; Hustler et al., 1986; Day, 1991; Louden, 1991; Biott and Nias, 1992). This research was in this broad tradition. Just as the teacher as critical agent co-ordinated the event, I co-ordinated the research. Like the events, it is a joint product. I have collected, selected and organized the material and written the accounts, but I have tried to remain faithful to teachers' and pupils' perceptions. The events are not written up as by an outsider looking in, with the traditional analytical distance, but from the inside, combining my own 'researcher-mode' form of appraisal with the 'reflective practitioner' mode of the teachers. The liaison will not work with teachers who are more 'technical rationalist' (Schön, 1983) in their approach.

'Critical-agent' teachers were something more in this case than the traditional 'key informants'. They were providing not only a vast range of information, but their own considered evaluation. They have a number of qualifications as evaluators. First, they are highly credible people, concerned to get accounts right. They want proof for claims made, and are not content with first impressions. The teacher at the centre of Rushavenn, for example, was one of these (see Chapter 3). Students, incidentally, were also rigorous in their pursuit of the truth. Stephen, for example, succeeded in conveying to me how he and others felt about Rushavenn, rejecting some of my attempts to assist – 'No, it wasn't that' – and searching for the closest definition of what he wanted to say.

Secondly, critical agent teachers were centrally involved and possess detailed and wide knowledge and experience. As Egan (1992, pp. 149–150) has observed, in judging how successful we have been in engaging students' imaginations, extending the range of their emotional sensitivity and human understanding, 'the finest instrument we have for evaluating degrees of success in such a unit is the teachers' sensitive observation'. They have experienced it as participant observers, seeing, thinking, feeling, discussing at first hand.

Thirdly, they have been detached, and reflected on the event at a distance as it were, in discussion with others, in writing reports, or in considering the implications for the improvement of their own teaching. As 'reflective practitioners' they cast a critical eye over their work. If it is not being productive they want to know why. They are able to confront (Smyth, 1991) normal processes and ask 'why' questions as well as 'how' ones. Some teachers might make false claims about their work, for career purposes, for self-esteem, or as a necessary kind of therapy, using persuasive rhetoric to convince others of their worth. While few (in any sphere) might be entirely free from such considerations, reflective practitioners do bring a certain rigour to their self-appraisal. Besides, their claims have to be supported and put to the test, just like the researcher's.

This leads to the fourth point, for they have already collected a considerable amount of evidence in the form of the documentation mentioned earlier. This forms part of the corpus of evidence together with that collected independently by the researchers, and with the testimony and judgements of others.

Fifthly, their evaluation can be compared to that of others, some of whom might have been involved in the project, some not – such as pupils, parents, members of the community, inspectors, education officers, other professionals with a particular interest, education correspondents and academics.

The collaboration, therefore, was not consensual in the sense of accounts from either side being accepted beyond question. When I began the study of each event, certain analytical frameworks were already in place. I provided a means of testing these, by comparing them with the views of others, and with an assessment of the evidence. I could also bring to bear comparative elements from my work on the other, related events, and my research experience generally. My description and analysis were then tested against their, and others', understandings. I wrote a draft, and sent copies to critical agents and critical others for comment. Some factual inaccuracies were corrected and some missing information provided. In some cases, further interviews were held. In this manner the event was reconstructed by the participants in the research.

Considerable attention has been paid in recent years to giving teachers 'voice' (Elbaz, 1991; Goodson, 1991). A. Hargreaves (1991), summing up this line of argument, states, 'Failure to understand the teacher's voice is failure to understand the teacher's teaching. For this reason, our priority should be not merely to listen to the teacher's voice, but also to sponsor it as priority' (p. 11). To this might be added the need for that voice to be given the opportunity to speak of processes, of what actually happens, and not just characteristics of teaching style, and job satisfaction. In research terms, this means seeing teachers less as objects and subjects of research, and more as people who have something to say of worth in its own right. They are, in a sense, co-research workers, with equal rights, and subject to the same strictures, concerning, for example, the burden of proof, as researchers. This is empowering for teachers in at least two senses.

First, they share in the construction of the account. Critical theorists have pointed to the power enjoyed by researchers and authors in setting agendas and writing the report (Smyth, 1991). Teachers are often seen as 'material to be used'. While independent research into their public practice is a legitimate pursuit, there are occasions when joint enquiry is indicated. These occasions will be more often rather than less if one's aims include educational improvement, since this has to be done through teachers.

Secondly, in researching the event in collaboration with an external researcher they have deepened, integrated and codified the account, and added to the legitimation of the practice. Schön (1984, p. 43) argues that, for professionals, 'a crucially important dimension [of their work] ... tends to remain private and inaccessible to others'. Smyth (1991, p. 28) points out that 'because awareness of our own thinking usually grows out of the process of articulating it to others, as practitioners we often have little access to our own reflection-in-action'. In encouraging articulation and externalization, the research, one might claim, promoted identification and ownership of that particular kind of knowledge. It enabled them also, in Clark's (1992, p. 93) terms, to 'blow their own trumpet,' not in a 'showing off' way, but in confronting and answering difficult questions like 'What have I been doing lately that is worthwhile and interesting? What ideas and insights have I had that might be useful to others? How do I want to frame and remember the positive side of this year?' It means 'making coherent and public the ways in which your professional development is developing'. The research, in other words, contributed to the criticality. In some ways it is part of the celebration, but requiring a new form and process, offering the experience to a wider audience.

In their work on teacher narrative, Connelly and Clandinin (1990) claim that,

> in our story telling, the stories of our participants merged with our own to create new stories, ones that we have labelled *collaborative stories*. The thing finally written on paper [is] ... a mutually constructed story created out of the lives of both researcher and participant.
>
> (p. 12)

Similarly, they both take part in the process: 'the narratives of participant and researcher become, in part, a shared narrative construction and reconstruction through the enquiry' (p. 205). To this collaboration in process and product might be added an initial affinity in values. In this respect I might be considered a late entrant to the group communitas which was such a strong feature of these critical events. I sympathize with the education philosophy, teaching approach and style of management espoused by these teachers. No doubt this was a factor in the selection of events, and in the rapport that was established. There was a communality of aim, therefore, and of spirit. I was almost as excited by these events as they were. In a way they were critical events for me also. They were all providing evidence in their different ways of the efficacy of an approach with which I identified, but which had recently come under attack; and they illustrate the possibilities that exist within the system if only certain conditions applied (on the difficulties of collaborative teacher–researcher work between people of differing values, see Troyna and Foster, 1988). I played a dual role, therefore, of involvement – trying to get as close to people's understandings and feelings about their experience as possible, by almost becoming one of them (a kind of historical participant observer!) – and of detachment, in trying to gain a view of the whole, and introducing some forms of analysis.

EVALUATION

Evaluation, as well as research and teacher development, was also a prominent aspect of the enquiry. I was concerned to generate theory from the case studies, being intrigued by the nature and functions of critical events; to aid teachers in their reflectivity; and to evaluate the events as educational activities. These modes of enquiry are often separated in the literature as discrete activities. I find it difficult to separate them. Understanding their nature enhances one's appreciation of the effects of critical events. Being concerned with a number of them permitted generalization, and the development of the concept beyond the particular instance of it. Particular cases could then be compared to the general model. Its properties provided a hypothetical framework for the analysis.

Yet though the events had common properties, they were also unique – a prominent feature of their criticality. There will be other critical events in these teachers' lives, but not quite like this one. It is necessary, therefore, to bring out the special quality of each event, to try to capture its spirit. This, however, is not easy, since it is to do with emotionally charged aesthetic appreciation which is difficult to express in words (Hargreaves, 1983). Yet the highly articulate teachers and pupils involved in these events did their best to capture or recapture the essential quality of each of them.

It will be seen that this is an artistic pursuit. The enquiry had certain scientific properties in its concern for a range of sampling among the participants, the use of multimethods, exhaustive interviewing, cross-checking of accounts, continuous comparative analysis at various levels, and theory generation. These largely apply to the sociological product. As an educational activity, however, one has to focus on what Eisner (1985) calls the 'expressive objective'. This is

> an outcome of an activity planned by the teacher or the student which is designed not to lead the student to a particular goal or form of behaviour but, rather, to forms of thinking-feeling-acting that are his own making. The expressive curriculum activity is evocative rather than prescriptive,

and is intended to yield outcomes which, although educationally valuable, are not prescribed or defined beforehand.

(p. 77)

Eisner identifies a third kind of objective, one that lies between instrumental and expressive, and that provides a clearly specified brief, but leaves the range of possible solutions open. The teacher is encouraged to provide 'high degrees of structure in setting the problem' but leaves 'the avenues for potential solutions wide open' (p. 79). Evaluation here takes the form of an appraisal after the enquiry of 'the relative merit of solution to the objective formulated'.

Both these types involve artistic activity. Eisner believes that educational evaluators should not 'seek recipes to control and measure practice, but rather to enhance whatever artistry the teacher can achieve' (p. 91). Diagnostic (not prescriptive) theory can help in the cultivation of what Eisner calls 'educational connoisseurship', basically 'the art of appreciation', and 'educational criticism', which is 'the art of disclosure' (see Chapter 1). This research is within this artistic mould. As it was a collaborative activity, the teacher and pupils were involved in 'connoisseurship' and 'criticism'. The enquiry aimed to round up and draw out a range of views and materials on the event. It sought to aid teachers in their own reflection and criticism. It gave voice to pupils as well as to teachers. Who are better qualified to speak of their own learning? As Nias (1989, p. 205) says, 'teachers rely in the last resort for recognition upon their pupils, for no one else knows, or can know, how effectively they have taught' (see also Guba and Lincoln, 1981; Riseborough, 1985; Sikes et al., 1985). On the political front also there is a case to be made for collaboration with pupils. As Qvortrup (1990, p. 94) argues,

If we seriously mean to improve life conditions for children we must, as a minimum precondition, establish reporting systems in which they are heard themselves as well as reported on by others. This is a very modest demand of, or on behalf of, a population group which at a societal level is mute, and is being kept mute by adults, the dominant group.

The voices of the pupils are heard here, therefore, quite strongly (see also Rowland, 1987).

The research aimed to be a creative activity in itself. First, in collating the responses an integrated whole was externalized. Secondly, in seeking to 'articulate the ineffable' and pursuing this as far as possible, meanings and understandings were enhanced. It was not a matter, simply, of collecting information and opinions. The participants were encouraged to plumb the depths of their subconsciousness and to experiment with words and phraseology to find the formula to embody and convey their experience and feelings. In this process, one is trying to 'exploit the potential of language as an artistic medium, not merely as a descriptive one' (Eisner,

1985, p. 141). The evaluator acts as a sounding board here, and in following the usual interviewing techniques as recommended, for example, by Dean and Whyte (1958), and responding to the interviewee, prompting, summarizing, putting a point into other words, tries to help elucidate and sharpen the teacher's own mind. 'I never even thought of it like that', said the *Godspell* director, 'but that's probably exactly what happened.' In this way, the evaluator hopes to be able to give a 'vivid rendering of how that game is played' (Eisner, 1985, p. 131), and 'to capture the richness of the consequences of wide forms of knowing' (p. 132). The idea is to do this so that 'the reader will be able to empathetically participate in the events described' (p. 138), and to experience with those involved their feelings, understandings, hopes, fears, triumphs and failures. With this in view, a large part of the story is told by the people who made it. This keeps faith also with the collaborative principle, seeking to present the account in their terms, and to ensure that their 'voice is heard to speak throughout the construction of the story' (Day, 1991, p. 545).

RESPONDENT VALIDATION

As argued in Chapter 2, where reconstruction of events and perspectives is the aim, respondent categories should figure prominently in the account, and there should be some form of respondent validation. I was interested to find out, therefore, from the participants whether I had represented their views correctly and whether I had 'captured' the event as they knew it. The account had to be accurate, but the task also involved putting material together in such a way as to construct an integrated and coherent whole, and to convey the feel and excitement participants associated with it (Van Maanen, 1988). Since 'feel' is not a matter of words, this presented some difficulty, both for participants and for me. It is easy both to understate and overstate the case. Again, they could judge how closely I had represented their experience. What were my participants' responses?

Theresa Whistler, the author of *Rushavenn Time*, who worked with the children on its construction, wrote,

It is a most interesting and living memento of what was such a happy and absorbing experience – it brings back the very feel of it ... what strikes me most is the great interest of having so many articulate and extended quotes from the children's own reflections looking back. I am astonished at the vividness and fullness of their memories ... [the group] became very attracted by the chance to take this long reflective look at what they already know their lives would not have again ... the project helped them to know themselves.

The teacher in the community video project 'found it most exhilarating to have our work compared to the model of critical events', and hoped the book 'will have some influence in the current trend away from projects'.

Whilst she had done some interesting work with her pupils since the research,

> the video project still rates as tops for creative excitement and relation-ships with the children....I have enjoyed reading your very able analysis of our project. It is interesting to see how, what seemed to be my own ideas of how to go about things, tally with certain educational theorists.... [I am] delighted with the overall structure, and feel very rewarded by your interest, and supported by the links with educational theory.

One of the 'Chippindale' teachers read the draft 'with great interest', and was 'very happy with what you have written from Western's point of view and feel it reflects accurately our experience of the venture'. The other teacher 'really enjoyed' reading the draft. One of the planners thought it 'an excellent draft and an enjoyable read, contributing a great deal to their understanding of our environmental education project'. He was particu-larly intrigued with 'the comments of other contributors'.

The Rushavenn teacher discussed his reaction at greater length. He was 'impressed by the authenticity' of the account. He referred, first, to the factual evidence, and the way this was 'carefully recorded and re-assembled in the script'. He noted 'the many and sometimes lengthy consultations we had had, the drafting and re-drafting, the gradual accumulation of evidence, the memory search over a lengthy period'. At another level, he thought that the text had

> as far as it is humanly possible, recaptured the ethos of the event, and the feelings, the emotions, all of the exhilaration, excitement, wonder, occasional frustrations and set-backs and how they were overcome, the pushing into new frontiers, the way in which we felt so different in this situation compared to school, all part and parcel of discovering and rediscovering our essential selves.

He had gained some new insights, particularly from what the students had said. They had been 'extremely enlightening', and this would have been 'essential reading' had he been going on with the project. This endorses the point made earlier about the benefits of pupil evaluation. He summarized his view on the text:

> You can re-live it intermittently over time, but what you've required me to do is to sit down, and over a period of time recall as many aspects of our experiences as I possibly could. You've put all this together and re-created almost in total in fact what actually happened. It's as if I was in possession of the pieces of a jigsaw which a long time ago had been complete but over a period of time had got scattered. As I found them again I gave them to you, and you've re-created the picture I originally had.

Research does not always go as well as this, as I shall illustrate in Chapter 7! However, as far as these comments are concerned, several points are being conveyed. First, the accounts contain a certain truth in the perspectives of the participants. Then, their understanding of the event is heightened, particularly by the input of others and by the analysis using educational theory. They are pleased that something special in their teaching, and an unrepeatable experience, has received attention and been recorded. And they have derived reassurance and a sense of reward from my interest. This last point might be considered by some a further aid to validity – if, in fact, the participants were left stronger and better equipped to do their job in the ways they thought best. The Rushavenn teacher, for one, said he welcomed being involved in the research as 'it helped give him a sense of proportion and balance at a time of confusion and uncertainty in schools.'

As discussed earlier, the articulation of 'tacit knowledge' (Polanyi, 1958) leads to more definite ownership. The knowledge has been given shape and substance. However confident in one's own intuition, one must be more open to criticism from others and to moments of self-doubt without the benefit of articulation. Such work, therefore, serves to stimulate and focus teachers' awareness of what they know, and enables them to develop their knowledge.

Others can benefit from this process also. As Tyler (in Hosford, 1984) notes, 'the professional practice of teaching, as well as that of law, medicine and theology, is largely a product of the experience of practitioners, particularly those who are more creative, inventive and observant than the average' (p. 9). It might be claimed that this applies to the participants in this research, and that their 'putting it into words' helps others both in providing examples of exceptional professional activity, and in aiding their own self-reflection and efforts to articulate key, but hitherto unexpressed, aspects of their practice. This might be an example of what Fullan (1992, p. 120) terms 'interactive professionalism', operating not in a face-to-face situation, but in a more general sense of a profession keeping itself informed and marking new developments for general advancement. It is one way in which teachers would be 'continuous learners in a community of interactive professionals' (ibid.).

The 'critical events' teachers' testimony was subject to the same kinds of test of validity as my own report would be. Thus, I have not included everything that I was told. Points, for example, that were relayed at second or third hand, or that seemed otherwise to require substantiation that was not forthcoming, were omitted. I was able to press for clarification and for documentation, and to challenge things that did not ring true. I had both an insider and outsider role, the one taking me close to their experiences, the other distancing me from them and putting claims to critical test. This, I would argue, counters any suggestions of undue romanticism that might be made about these accounts, a point often made about the kind of teacher thinking involved when it is not put into action. Definitions of 'romantic' include 'pertaining to an imaginative lie', 'talking extravagantly or with an infusion of fiction', 'extravagant, wild, fantastic'. These events are some of these, certainly. They are fantastic, magical in the sense of amazing, as I have defined it; they do involve imagination, a great deal of it, and sentiment. They are extravagant in the sense that they go beyond normal bounds. But they are not lies, or fiction, or wild. They are carefully controlled, they deal in real education, and, for those involved, strike an uncommon truth (see also Goodman and Goodman, 1990). The onus is on the researcher and writer to represent this extravagance accurately, neither more nor less than that experienced. This accuracy will derive from the validating techniques discussed above, but will also reflect, hopefully, some of the sensitivities associated with the 'Romantic' intellectual tradition, as discussed in Chapter 3.

There is a sense, too, in which these evaluations are offered to the teaching community as providing some benchmarks for their own experiences. The validation, in part, is done by them as they assess the credibility of these cases through their own experience, their personal, practical knowledge and their private theories, and put them into practice in their own teaching with renewed confidence and vigour. This view of validity places emphasis on 'the insider's perspective', and follows logically from the principles of collaboration on which the research was based (Lather, 1986; Erickson, 1986; Lincoln and Guba, 1985). In identifying such cases in their own work, they may find something of value here in aiding their own reflectivity, and possibly bring something further to bear on the phenomenon. If it brings a measure of reassurance at a time of depression and sustains hope for an educational approach seen by many as currently under siege, then the research will have achieved its aim.

6 Tools of the trade
Extensions of the ethnographer's self

INTRODUCTION

The presentational task of ethnography is sometimes held to be 'painting pictures in words', 'capturing a likeness', recreating the 'very feel' of an event, evoking an image, awakening a spirit, or reconstructing a mood or atmosphere. I have discussed some of the methods used for these essentially artistic tasks. But what tools do we use in applying these methods? Are they as important to the ethnographer as they are, say, to the artist, musician or sculptor? What effect do they have on the process and on the finished product?

The advent of the word processor has revolutionized the writing process for many people. There a number of excellent texts that describe its accomplishments and potential in the analysis and presentation of qualitative work (for example, Tesch, 1990; Becker, 1986; LeCompte and Preissle, 1993; Snyder, 1993). This book is being composed on one – though using a sheaf of handwritten notes. Is there much more to be said? Well, yes, if only because different people have different preferences. The pen (or pencil) is in danger of becoming outmoded, superseded in all respects by the new technology. We may lose sight of its advantages, so well are they concealed. It can still play its part, indeed for some it is still the chief piece of equipment, surprising as this may seem. Some students who find difficulty with machines should not feel stampeded into their use. Pens and pencils have served many fine writers in the past. William Faulkner said that the only tools he needed were pen, paper, tobacco, food and whisky. Have the pen and pencil now become outdated? In one respect, clearly not, for the ethnographer carries a pen or pencil at all times. It is an indispensable piece of equipment in data gathering – though the lap-top or notebook computer is increasingly used even here.

Before, therefore, the pen becomes consigned to academic archaeology, I want to raise some points about its usage. In some respects, this may seem rather a trivial matter. But I argue the opposite. Writing is not a mechanical, linear, technical exercise simply of placing what is in one's mind on paper, the writing tool – whether pen, typewriter, word processor or whatever –

merely being the recording device. It is a much more complicated activity in which the whole writer's self is engaged. Writing is an expression of the self. The writing tool, as an extension of self, is central to the psychological processes involved. This then – the psychology of writing – is the main point of this chapter, rather than the means itself.

THE ETHNOGRAPHER'S SELF AND THE PEN

> Writing is nothing less than 'the enlargement of the soul of the writer'.
>
> (Ueland, in Cook, 1992, p. 13)

In the painting by Michelangelo, *The Creation of Adam*, an energetic and busy God is portrayed in the heavens sustained by cherubs and angels with finger pointing down, giving the languid but beautiful Adam a charge of life-energy by touching Adam's lazily raised hand. On a much more humble note, for sure, and one requiring more effort than that depicted by the painter, the ethnographer comes to life, plugging in to the 'life of things', at every turn jotting down notes, fashioning aides-memoire, scribbling memos, experimenting with analysis, constructing drafts, making corrections, recording ideas. The researcher is never without pen/pencil. Data press and crowd the memory, ideas form and float in the mind, playing games like 'catch me if you can'. The pen concentrates the mind wonderfully.

The pen makes both a material and symbolic link between writer and written. The latter is neatly illustrated by newscasters, who, pen in hand, end the news by screwing the top back on the pen and putting it in their pocket, while talking to their colleague. The pen gives the newscaster a sense of connection of self with the news. Sitting in a TV studio reading from a teleprompter under the glare of bright lights is an unnatural situation. The pen is a lifeline that makes it seem real. The symbolism is that the newscasters are writing the news that appears on the screen. It gives them more of a sense of control, and of self-identification with the viewer.

It is not uncommon for artifacts to become extensions of the self. Willis (1975, 1978), for example, gives a graphic description of the motor bike and its meaning to the 'motor-bike boys':

> Not only is the ontological security of the motor-bike boys demonstrated in their mastery of the motor bike, but the qualities and function of the machine itself express their sense of concrete identity within an unarguable reality.... The solidity, responsiveness, inevitableness, the *strength* of the motor bike matched the concrete, secure nature of the bikeboys' world. It underwrote in a dramatic and important way their belief in the commonsense world of tangible things, and the secureness of personal identity. The roughness and intimidation of the motor bike, the surprise of its fierce acceleration, the aggressive thumping of the unbaffled exhaust, matches and symbolizes the masculine assertive-

ness, the rough camaraderie, the muscularity of language, of their style of social interaction . . . . The ensemble of bike, noise, rider, clothes *on the move* gave a formidable expression of identity to the culture, and powerfully developed many of its central values.

(1978, pp. 16, 53, 57)

In another analogy, an art form more allied to writing,

> The potter working at his wheel is not merely forcing clay into shape through exercise of will and fingers; rather he is creating a symbol of the very essence of the earth and its eternally changing history. For a few moments, he becomes an extension of the clay, experiencing its plasticity, feeling its willingness to go in certain directions, sensing how far and how long it can be worked without collapsing . . . . It is hands and mind and spirit concentrated on extracting from the clay its most poetic possibilities.

(Bevlin, 1970, p. 125)

Similarly, Herbert Read portrays sculpture as 'not a reduplication of form and feature; it is rather the translation of meaning from one material into another material' (1931, p. 185).

Can the same be said of the pen? Compared to a motor bike, it is an uncomplicated, almost insignificant piece of equipment. But that is part of its beauty. It can be secreted in a pocket, or in a hand, or behind an ear. It sits in the hand naturally, like an extension of it, an extra digit.

> Between my finger and my thumb
> The squat pen rests; snug as a gun.

(Seamus Heaney)

But what an explosion of riches can emerge from it! It has affinities with the ethnographer, therefore. In the field it is unobtrusive, mostly hidden from view, in fact. Yet it is to hand, ready to act. It channels thoughts in an uninterrupted flow from mind to paper. It may be a simple object, but it can be aesthetically pleasing in itself, a pleasure to hold and to look at – as might be said of its product, which undoubtedly bears the individual hallmark of the writer. It is also amazingly multifunctional. It can do words, shorthand, notes, sketches, diagrams, figures. In this way it offers a kind of instrumental triangulation.

Writing, let alone ethnography, is a very individual matter. We build up a whole plethora of processes and materials, some of which may be trivial to others but central to us, to aid in this hardest of tasks. It is a question, therefore, of what tools suit the individual and the most productive relationship that can be set up between them. One may need a 'Mont Blanc Solitaire', with ribbed German silver stem and 18-carat gold nib. Or perhaps a 'Tomboy Zoom', a cigar-shaped Japanese pen; or an 'Elysée en Vogue'. It might be that a 'Platignum Man from Uncle Special' does the trick. Much of Harry Wolcott's (1990a, p. 14) writing 'has been done with Bic pens on lined yellow pads'. Philip Larkin is reported to have used 'a succession of Royal Sovereign 2B pencils' with which to write his poems (Motion, 1993, p. 344). The composer Robert Simpson uses the gold pencil which belonged to Carl Nielsen to work on his symphonic scores. Solzhenitsyn selected from a range of pencils to suit the mood of a paragraph. Pat Sikes likes to use a particular type of red biro, a Staedtler fine. She had a box of twelve of these at a particularly productive time of her career, and uses them for luck. She has two left (personal communication)! I personally prefer a Parker III B biro. It is comfortable, reliable, with a good flow, and it suits my style of handwriting. I have a number of these situated in strategic places. Nick Hubbard, a colleague, uses a Parker 51 which his wife bought him in 1972. It is both an 'aesthetic object' and 'a central means by which I record my ideas on paper'. He comments 'I have always used black ink because it looks bold and permanent. Somehow using the same pen with the same coloured ink for all these years has given the act of writing a sense of status and personal identity, perhaps an expression of the self' (personal communication). Nick agrees that there is a symbolic link between writer and pen, and notes the cultural significance:

> Most important is the notion that a pen is an emblem of cultural identity drawing one closer to an interaction with the text one is creating and indeed reading. The 'material and symbolic link between writer and written' as an act of personal culture is very strong. It creates a personal engagement with a text which is physical as well as mental. There are opportunities for a direct interaction involving underlining, inserting and recording ideas and impressions alongside the text. In this way the read text and the written response create a bond which the word processor cannot maintain because of the transfer of ideas mechanically to a screen. Another aspect of this is represented by my response to learning another language. I go to a French class once a week. I quite consciously handwrite my homework. For me to be able to 'write' another language is not only to engage with it from a technical point of view, but also to provide a means of re-creating and imbibing, through one's own developed skills, a culture which one wants to understand and identify with. The relationship becomes that much closer. In writing, one is using a skill which is ancient, which has been handed down and again is culturally significant. It is how many of our forbears recorded their lives and somehow it is one of the few personal skills left to us, enabling us to maintain our autonomous self.

SOME USES OF THE PEN

As therapy

> Assist me some extemporal god of rime, for I am sure I shall turn sonneter.
> Devise, wit; write, pen; for I am for whole volumes in folio.

A pen can become highly personalized, a tried and trusted friend, a companion countering the loneliness of writing. In my wishful, adolescent days, like Shakespeare's Armado in *Love's Labours Lost* above, I used fondly to imagine a magic pen that answered all my examination questions perfectly. All I had to do was lay it on the paper and it was away! One of the hard lessons of life is that there is no such magic other than what you accomplish through your own efforts. However, a pen that has been through those efforts with you has acquired some of those 'magic' properties. Words have flowed from it before. It has experienced pauses, some of them lengthy; it has gone on false trails, doodled, been chewed and sucked, used as a chin- or back-scratcher, but it has always, in the end, delivered the goods. There is something very reassuring about, at the beginning of a writing session, just picking up a proved, successful pen.

There are other ways in which the pen can be an excellent conductor of feelings, such as when a young pupil, involved in a creative group activity designing a building, used to jam her pencil down hard into the paper and screw it round, because she could not get her own way in a team discussion; or when the leader of one side in a debate, whilst the other side were preparing their case, suddenly seized on a point and scribbled ferociously on paper, the pen rasping on the bare top of the desk, sealing the point with a triumphant and emphatic full stop, thus undermining the opposition without saying anything before his turn.

It has to be recognized, however, that the pen does not act as liberator for everybody. It can, in fact, be quite the reverse. In Boswell's *Life of Johnson*, Tom Birch is described as being 'as brisk as a bee in conversation; but no sooner does he take a pen in his hand, than it becomes a torpedo to him, and benumbs all his faculties' (Boswell, 1791, p. 40).

As gleaner

> When I have fears that I may cease to be
> Before my pen has glean'd my teeming brain,
> Before high-piled books, in charact'ry,
> Hold like full garners the full-ripen'd grain.
>
> (John Keats, 'When I have fears')

To 'glean', I gather, is 'to collect what is thinly scattered, neglected or overlooked' (*Chambers Twentieth Century Dictionary*). Granting Keats the customary poetic licence, the pen is useful whether the mind is alive with activity or faintly twitching. In the latter case, 'doodling', experimenting with words, new formulations, sketching figures and diagrams, annotating transcripts and other documents, the pen helps to stir into life, to formulate and to collect, an idea here, one there, a shape here, a possible connection there. Writing can be very untidy in the early stages – arguably, the more creative, the more untidy and chaotic. We may have internalized more formalized models of writing, like the teachers in a design project who only wanted their children to produce 'neat' work, consigning their experimental scribblings on odd pieces of paper to the waste-basket before anybody could see them. However, these scruffy sketches were the items the architects, who were assisting in the project, were most interested in. They were the most creative products.

Where the mind is 'teeming', the pen serves as a means of selection, discipline, sifting and refining, putting a brake on excesses, encouraging the more likely ideas, concentrating the mind. Thoughts have to come through a communications channel. They have to be intelligible and coherent, to oneself as well as to others. The pen represents a way in which the writer can have a conversation with self. Perhaps it is well, at times, that it can only move so fast – it reins in the galloping, potentially stampeding horse to a more viable pace. Where there is need to register a suspected valuable thought while the pen is already engaged on externalizing others, there are strategies available, such as a scribbled noted word in the margin. This 'gleaning' is an artistic, creative process. Eric Newton (1962), speaking of art itself, though his words apply to all forms of art, states that

> Every artist knows from experience, but few laymen ever realize, the constant inter-play between mind and hand as a work of art progresses .... The original imagined image is actually far from complete, and as soon as the artist sets to work his medium begins to modify and clarify it; unless he is a bad artist, he will accept and take advantage of these modifications.

Such a view is consistent with a view of ethnography, in part at least, as an artistic activity.

As facilitator

There are many ways in which the pen facilitates the research process at every stage. This is clear enough in writing, note taking, jotting down ideas (wherever you may be), composing aides-memoire, making sketches, and recording future prompts during naturalistic interviewing. There are some less obvious ways.

As a listening aid

Some researchers are nervous about using tape recorders, or even taking notes, during an interview. In some instances, however, a researcher taking notes is seen as a compliment to the interviewee. One aims in ethnographic interviewing for naturalism, rapport, unobtrusiveness, as in participant observation; but too much concession to informality and relaxation can be counter-productive, affecting the interviewees' motivation to tell the tale, raising doubts in their minds about the quality of and interest in what they are saying, devaluing the discussion to the plane of casual and passing conversation (though there are times in ethnographic research when those kinds of conversation are indicated). Note taking in interviews therefore is not just a matter of recording information, but of anchoring the discussion through the communicatory outlet of the pen, and of motivating the interviewee. It thus aids the quality of the ethnographer's listening as well as the interviewee's talking. Nick Hubbard marries this point to another function of the doodle:

> The word processor precludes an alternative, more fundamental function of the doodle. I am an inveterate doodler as I talk with people, listen to them or have conversations with them on the telephone. These doodles usually take the form of interconnected triangles which can end by enveloping the page in front of me depending on the length of the conversation or telephone call. Doodling for me represents a link between what a person is saying and what sense I make of it. It helps me to listen, to think and interpret and I can lose concentration without it.
>
> (personal communication)

As a promoter of ideas

Examples are making mind-maps (drawing branches, tracing interconnections, identifying patterns in the data); brainstorming (noting down free flow of ideas, free-writing or speedwriting to overcome 'writer's block'); bubble outlining; 'brick-laying' (Cook, 1992); and so forth.

As a stage in drafting

Cox (1986) has noted that the idea of drafting has changed with the word processor, there being no real first draft; and Chandler (1987) opines that writing produced with a word processor can obscure its own evolution. Does this matter in ethnography? I think it does for a number of reasons:

1 I find it useful to track back over previous drafts. Often, material rejected or altered previously may be brought back, or notes and references made around the page in margins come back into the reckoning. In some drafts, it helps to see the written comments on

printed drafts. The whole process is recorded from beginning to end. Apart from aiding the researcher's progress towards completion, one might claim that, rather like the bulk of the substantive research material that cannot be got into a report, this record of progress through drafting stands as a kind of commentary on procedural validity. Replying to the D. Thomas critique reported in Chapter 3, P.J. Woods (1995, p. 180) commented on the importance of the pen:

> During the course of his reading of the text which he [the 'empirical author'] has written he may find himself saying, 'This is not me. This is not what I wanted to say.' To regain control over his material he has, through reading and interpretation, to suppress any liminal texts which do not accord with his precise authorial intention ... ... I still have the Waterman pen with which I used to compose texts in large, outdated diaries.... The crossings-out on the handwritten page represented either a failure of literary intent on my part, arising perhaps from fatigue or lack of inspiration, or – and more comforting for the truly creative artist – a denial of the alternative expressions welling up from the competing liminal authors.... When using a word-processor the denial may be more permanent, but the penned corrections were useful reminders of the presence of 'ghost-writers'. This is why I still prefer to write in pen and ink rather than seated before a word-processing screen. Regrettably, convenience and lack of time mostly dictate that I adopt the latter modus operandi.

2 Clive Bell (1956), in an essay on Virginia Woolf, tells how he discovered 'a dirty manuscript ... a longish piece of 5000 words or so, but was, I dare say, cut down for publication. I should be amused to see how it looks in print, though I cannot say that in manuscript it reads particularly well' (p. 92). Bell's observation draws attention to an important difference between written script and print. The same words can have a different impact, may convey different meanings, may read differently. As teachers, we can appreciate this point with regard to the badly handwritten essays we have to deal with, but even with well-written manuscripts there is a difference. This is because there is a finality about print which gives it superior legitimacy. Until recently (the convenience of the word processor has caught up with even me), I preferred to do the first two or three drafts in longhand, rewriting, deleting, inserting, rearranging and, most importantly, reorganizing. What one is actually doing in these drafts is carrying the analysis along, seeing new opportunities for classifying and categorizing, and perhaps gaining new insights. Widdowson (1983) notes that 'In writing one so frequently arrives at a destination not originally envisaged, by a route not yet planned for in the original itinerary' (quoted in Hedge, 1991, p. 22). The handwritten draft is open to this kind of radical revision. The typed one is more closed, more final. Writing is a recursive activity, with drafting,

revising, replanning (Hedge, 1991), which Shaughnessy (1977) describes as a 'messy process that leads to clarity' (quoted in Hedge, 1991, p. 21). My messy, handwritten drafts with their convoluted alterations reflect this process. Word processor experts might not have this problem, but I find it a useful method in demarcating stages of the analysis/writing-up process.

I discovered this by chance. I used to like to get my handwritten drafts typed up as soon as possible. A number of pressures combine to promote this haste – exhaustion, a feeling that you have got as far as you can go, wanting to see something for one's efforts, wanting to see it recorded in case of a fire, or sudden death, or some other mishap, pressures from others, deadlines. On 'handover' days, I used to drive in to work taking especial care that I did not have an accident on the way. It was a relief, as well as a sense of achievement, to receive back the typed-up copy. On one occasion, my secretary was away for a longish period on compassionate leave, and so the well-oiled chain of operation was broken. I had a number of choices, but I chose to press ahead with revisions to the draft before she returned. I did this several times, in fact, and the revisions were quite radical; more radical, I believe, than they would have been had I been revising from print. I was working on a paper that I eventually called 'The charisma of the critical other: enhancing the role of the teacher' (Woods, 1993d). Originally, there were two main separate, almost unconnected, sections. I then realized that these were subsumable under one main concept, that of charisma. Then, looking at the data again from the point of view of charisma, I could see three main categories, and a number of subcategories of those. The whole had a much stronger conceptual unity than the original draft, and I was much happier with it when it finally went for typing. Further alterations were more cosmetic. Of course, the paper might have developed in that way had the early draft been typed as it stood, or had I word processed it myself – but I have had no comparable experience from my use of the word processor as yet.

3 Using longhand or word processor may have an effect on quality. There has been research on this, but the results are inconclusive (see Snyder, 1993, pp. 58–59). Many no doubt find the quality of their writing improved by the use of word processors. I count myself among them. Some, who may feel compelled to use them, may not be best served by them. I have at times detected in some papers or theses produced entirely by word processor a tendency to list, to itemize, to represent research data wholesale, unedited, so that there is little sense of process – an essential feature of ethnographic work. These papers are disjointed, mechanistic. They record data end to end. They make points staccato fashion. They do not seem to have much of the writers' selves in them.

Are their ideas and selves flowing out through the machine, or is the machine exerting a reactive influence on those ideas and selves?

Of course, this last point may not be the fault of the machine, and the experience of others presents a contrary view. Snyder (1993, p. 55) for example, reports that

> Robinson (1985) believes that the word processor facilitates both the formulation of thoughts and their expression at all levels, from the juxtaposition of words and ideas to the logical development of para-graphs and cohesion of argument or narrative. Because word proces-sing takes over much of the mechanical operation involved in the writing process, the student is released to concentrate on the logic, organization and clarity of the piece.

Many excellent texts are no doubt produced solely through word processors. But equally, some will, like Nick Hubbard, 'sometimes become so tied up with the process of learning the ins and outs of the technology that it tends to interfere with the ideas I want to get down' (personal communication). More, therefore, might be written if some authors varied their means of production. We need to find out what works best for us.

Some writers have certainly found the word processor a constraint on creativity. Iris Murdoch (in Hammond, 1984), puts the case:

> I do not go near a word processor, or even typewriter. I cannot imagine how thinking can take place on those awkward machines. For real thinking, as in philosophy or writing a poem or novel, one must use a notebook or paper which can be turned over, a pen which scratches out, opposite pages on which variants can be placed and so on. It must be apt and ready for the eye; easily accessible. The word processor is, of course, tidy, but what is the equivalent of turning back to correct a section ten pages back in the notebook? A word processor needs 'clues' to turn back. One would have to spend time programming it so as to make it even more simple. Why not use one's whole mind in the old way, with pens, paper, notebooks, etc. instead of dazzling one's eyes staring at a glass square which separates one from one's thoughts and gives them a premature air of completeness? People can no doubt become very skilled with these machines, but I think it's all going in the wrong direction.
>
> (pp. 15–16)

Joanna Trollope (1994, p. 46) recalls the point about self and its extension:

> I'm useless at machines. I like the silence and the act of writing. It feels as if there is an artery from my brain to my right hand that the ideas run straight down. It's more intimate to write by hand, and my books are intimate so it sort of fits.

John Updike finds aesthetic value, and more, in the handwritten page:

> It seems to me that the book has not just aesthetic values – the charming little clothy box of the thing, the smell of the glue, even the print, which has its own beauty. But there's something about the sensation of ink on paper that is in some sense a thing, a phenomenon rather than an epiphenomenon. I can't break the association of electric trash with the computer screen. Words on the screen give the sense of being just another passing electronic wriggle.
>
> (in Max, 1995, p. 13)

The combination of factors needed to bring writing off is so subtle that some have invested in it a spiritual quality. Kingsley Amis'

> experience with the word processor turned out to be entirely negative, and straight away, too. So far, I have found my mind, my typewriter and the Oxford Dictionary to be entirely adequate for my needs. The only thing which will improve my writing is more talent, which we know comes only from God.
>
> (in Hammond, 1984, p. 16)

Peter Porter found that

> unless you can bash a typewriter with your fingers, unless some of the aggression which is part of the mode of creation can be discharged through your fingers, I think it will get into the work and fuck it up. So an electric typewriter to me – let alone a word processor – is an abomination and an offence against the Holy Spirit.
>
> (in Baker, 1989, p. 267)

In similar vein, Jessie Bernard (1990) insists on using her *old* typewriter:

> Typing is more than transferring thought to paper. It is for me an act of aggression. I pound the keys to get rid of my aggressions. I owe my reputation for non-aggression to the keys. I batter mercilessly.... Now I am fighting all my friends who insist I must have at least a word processor. Again, no way. Writing is not for me a matter of processing words. Words are very real entities for me, not of course human, but certainly having personalities.
>
> (p. 342)

Some people seem allergic to any kind of machine. Antony Sher (*Guardian*, 24 April 1993) records that 'machines smell his fear' and 'turn on' him. A student of mine said that she could not relate to a word processor. It kept telling her 'error' and 'wrong password', and ruffled her confidence. Marshall Cook never thought he would get used to his electric typewriter humming at him the whole time: 'Whenever I'd stop to think, it seemed to be saying, "What's the matter, hmmmm?"' (1992, p. 98). Cook, like many others, has found these machines wonderful aids to his creativity and productivity, though he cautions, 'never lose your ability to create with blunt Craola on paper sack while riding the bus to work' (p. 99).

Such comments recall the point about self. Some writers feel liberated by word processors. Some need the typewriter to bash. Some prefer to write longhand. The pace of writing is closely geared to one's thought processes. For some, the word processor has speeded this up, enabling faster, more productive thought. Gabriel Garcia Marquez has found writing easier 'since I made the greatest discovery of my life: the word processor.... If I'd had this machine 20 years ago, I'd have published two to three times as many books' (in Hamill, 1988, p. 51). For others, the flow of the ink, the scratch of the pen, the contact with paper, the handwriting (a personal signature), the way the pen shapes a particular word, may all be important. The overall effect of a longhand draft, even with corrections, may be aesthetically pleasing. There is only one of these, and it records the pain as well as the joy of creation. It is a distinctive expression of self, like a signature. Lawrence Stenhouse once produced a beautifully handwritten draft for a conference (later published in Burgess, 1984b) – the only time I have experienced this happening. It seemed particularly meaningful, being more of a personal statement, and appropriate to the content of the paper, which was 'an autobiographical account'. There is a closeness, almost an intimacy, in such a presentation, as there is in private letters that we write and that we wish to imprint with something of our selves, as contrasted with business letters that we type or send by electronic mail. Eisner (1991, p. 36) talks of 'the presence of voice in text.... We display our signatures. Our signature makes it clear that a person, not a machine, was behind the words.' For this reason, and because of their scarcity, some handwritten manuscripts acquire great value. John Osborne sold the original manuscript of *Look Back in Anger* to pay for 'some expensive dental work'. Harold Pinter has given sixty boxes of his (handwritten) papers to the British Library, after rejecting offers from the United States for the literary archive. Since I read about this, I am carefully preserving my own original manuscripts in a file duly marked as such in bold letters!

In the rhythm of production

Writers develop a certain rhythm aligned to their own personalities, abilities, resources and social situation. For many years I worked closely with secretaries, with them typing successive drafts. This was more than simply a technical exercise. I felt there was a special creative relationship between us. One, whose speed, accuracy and general work rate were the wonder of the faculty, I am certain was a factor in a period of higher productivity I experienced during the 1980s. She would look forward to the next chapter or article with great eagerness and would be very disappointed if it did not appear on the promised day. Many a time I found myself working through most of the night to honour a promise I had somewhat rashly made. We both had a personal investment in each other as members of a team, and I, certainly, found that an important factor in pressing on with drafts to completion. I have had fruitful discussions with secretaries about content, organization and layout. They therefore do not just 'type', but engage with the text, and more importantly with the process of production. They inject a personal note, help to humanize proceedings and to take things on to a new stage, provide the writer with a useful breather while she or he has the assurance that things are moving along, and eventually present the draft in a new form, which consequently may be seen in a new light. Similarly, the author does not just 'correct' the word processed draft, but sees new possibilities and revises accordingly. I also found useful the time-lag between submitting drafts for typing and receiving it back. Writing, for me, consists of a series of peaks. I get so far with a draft and can go no further – time for pause, rest, reflection and a regathering of thought.

Some might see such 'peaks' more as 'writers' block'. One antidote to the latter is to try to persuade ourselves that it does not exist. Philip Larkin, for example, rejected the culture that talks of 'writers' block'. He produced poems at the rate of four a year, of which one 'was no good'. But he did not consider himself 'blocked', simply unprolific – 'that's all there is'.

> When I did write, it was in the evenings, after work, after washing-up. It was a routine like any other. And it worked very well. I don't think you can write a poem for more than two hours. After that, you're going round in circles and it's much better to leave it for 24 hours, by which time your sub-conscious or whatever has solved the block and you're ready to go on.
>
> (in Leader, 1991, p. 7)

Those of us who have lived through the technological revolution have had to adjust our work practices and roles. I was a comparatively late convert to the word processor. I was reluctant to change what I saw as a reasonably successful formula. Also, it would have an effect on others. One secretary defined her own role largely through the activity of typing my papers. When everybody else seemed to be deserting her for word processors, she relied on me to provide meaning for her work. Role development might seem the ideal answer for both of us, but that would have taken years that neither of us had. It was only on her retirement that I took the time for the 'pause' and 're-equipping' that Becker (1986) found necessary to make the transition. My 'rhythm of production' has now changed. But while the word processor has undoubted advantages and what still seem to me unlimited possibilities, it cannot, for me, engage in a close personal relationship with the author.

Having a personal secretary, or even a share of one, is a luxury not enjoyed by everyone. Students in particular are often advised to equip themselves with word processors – apart from other advantages, it works out cheaper in the long run than having to pay a typist. But they should consider whether it is worth the time and energy they have to put into learning how to use them; especially when they need, in the end product, to emulate the high standards of accuracy and presentation that professional typists achieve. I have seen PhDs strewn with errors (one had an extraordinary variety of dash and hyphen), badly spaced, inconsistently laid out, poorly printed. Wolcott (1990a, p. 94), also, himself a convert to the 'genius of computers' and 'word processing as an indispensable tool in writing up research', notes that

> A drawback of the amazing new word processing programs however has become evident in my reading of student papers (and occasionally colleagues' papers as well). The ease of production often results in faster rather than better writing. Capabilities for easy revision often are ignored. Hastily written and hastily proofed first drafts are tendered as final copy, printout is equated with 'in print', the sketch proffered in lieu of the careful rendering.

The skills of word processing and presentation are not gained in a day. Some may find them difficult, and be better occupied on the main task – constructing an original, quality script by whatever means they find easiest. In many cases, this *will* be a computer. In some, it will be other means.

IN PRAISE OF THE WORD PROCESSOR

Lest my argument be seen as an example of 'Luddite postmodernism' (a comment from a colleague on an early draft), I wish to emphasize my support for the word processor. Computers can have the same liberating effect on some and association with self as the pen has on others. Consider this testimony from somebody who used to find writing his 'worst nightmare':

> I did not learn how to write until I learned how to use a computer.... The computer helped me to discover that there was more to writing than just spelling. First of all, the computer was something new and different and was a relief from pencil and paper. All my life pencil and paper had been a nightmare. When I picked up a pencil and paper to write, my stomach would automatically tighten, and my nightmare would begin. The computer helped me view writing in a different way. It helped me to shed my fear of the pencil and paper. Sitting down in front of a computer was not nearly as frightening to me as sitting down with a pencil and paper. For this reason, I immediately saw the computer as a sign of hope. I had never been able to put down the right words with a pencil, but sitting at a keyboard seemed to free my mind. A pencil was like a piece of dead wood in my hands, and trying to make this stick form letters

always seemed awkward and difficult. When using a keyboard, however, the letters seemed to come out through my fingertips. The writing seemed to be closer to my brain .... The computer allows me to be inventive, to go beyond the simple words I know.

(Lee and Jackson, 1993, pp. 23–28)

This sounds remarkably like the close connections between thought and product that some found, as discussed earlier, through use of the pen. The computer, for some, has catalytic qualities. Through its use they discover skills they did not know they possessed. They find a way to do things that have been obstructed to them for years, not through any complete personal deficiency, but because they have not found or been presented with a method that works for them. The same may well be true for some researchers, brilliant data gatherers and analysts, but stuck on the writing, who have found new chances with the word processor.

Snyder (1993, pp. 62–63) concludes from his extensive research on the matter that 'most writers, regardless of age, enjoy writing with word processors, and believe that their use enhances composing and revising strategies, as well as the quality of their writing'. The word processor is a tremendous boon to writers, increasing the range of work practices available and offering more control over the final product. I can type much faster than I can write, and I can change things much more easily. That being so, I make more changes, more often, which *ought* to mean a better product. There are physical limits to the extent that one can cut and paste with pen and paper, but no such limits with the word processor (Collins and Sommers, 1985). There are also those marvellous facilities for compiling tables and diagrams through the use of spreadsheets. So one can work on the integrity of a piece to a higher level. It is also very easy to incorporate and work on other material, transcripts of tapes, for example, that may have been done by somebody else on a compatible machine.

Computers may lack the personal stamp, but there is a strange compulsion about working on these machines, which is at least the equal of the 'therapy' of the pen. This starts with switching the machine on to welcoming noises and faces, through to the thrill of seeing the finished work emerge from the printer. It has something to do with control both of the writing process *and* of the machine. One is practising a dual skill, and the more the computer skills are worked on, the more second nature they become; but also the more further skills come within reach. Nick Hubbard, who used to feel hostile to computers as a 'negation of the mutual reliance central to democratic modernization' (thus requiring human interaction), but 'deep down suspect I really wanted to possess the "knowledge"' because of his fascination with technology, discovered their usefulness almost by accident. He writes,

There is no doubt that having the 'knowledge' helps me to feel that I am not excluded from the modern project, that as a middle aged person on the road to discovering technology I am undergoing a process of renewal which denies the central image of old age and its propensity for a reactionary view of the world.

(personal communication)

Here we have computers assisting in a renovation of self.

We live in a technological age, and through these machines we keep in touch with the developing world, presenting an entrée for any new advantages that may arise. Through the Internet, academics are becoming much more closely linked all over the world. Information is rapidly becoming more readily available. Research teams, and supervisors and students, need to be linked by modem. Through this means they can, very speedily, exchange letters and memos, transfer files, engage in conversations, co-author and co-revise papers through a succession of drafts. Word processing is but a part of this whole ensemble of activity. It would be foolish to turn one's back on these dazzling opportunities. My argument is that it would be equally foolish to turn our backs on lessons from the past and to forget other tools that are available, and that may indeed be more suitable for some. I now find that I use both pen and word processor in writing, in roughly equal proportions. It is not a case of either/or. These tools complement each other; they are a formidable partnership in the most difficult part of the research enterprise – the writing up. Wolcott (1990a, p. 24), whose writing 'sometimes flows easily, sometimes slows to a snail's pace', still finds that 'when the words don't come easily, I leave the computer keyboard and retreat to my Bic pens and yellow pads to push words on to paper one at a time'. It is at such times that one feels one is writing in blood rather than ink, 'bleeding' as opposed to 'free-writing', for which the word processor is so helpful (Becker, 1986).

In this way, I am incorporating the computer into my routines without basically altering them other than improving their quality and speed. Whether computers can do as good a job here as working solely on hard copy is probably a matter of a writer's personal approach. Research – for example, that of Bridwell-Bowles, Johnson and Brehe (1987) – suggests that writers have more success on the computer with editing than with composing, and therefore those who like to do most of their thinking in advance of writing are likely to find more satisfactions than those for whom writing is an act of discovery (see also Sharples and Pemberton, 1992). But in a way this draws too sharp a division between these modes. For editing and revision, arguably, are at the heart of the writing process for most authors. As Yang (1992, p. 188) writes,

Revision is an indispensable way to making writing better. Skilled writers revise constantly, trying to resolve the tensions between what they want to say and what the sentences actually record .... [Revision] is the way they shape prose into meaning for an audience, and the way they discover what they want to say, sometimes to their own surprise.

They know they cannot do it right the first time, and they live with temporary chaos in the meantime. Through revision they move from semi-formed ideas to elaborated texts, create what they believe they want to say and then change their minds, probably more than once.

It is certain that computers will soon have most, if not all, of the facilities afforded by having the full text in front of you (Bridwell-Bowles et al., 1987), and that they will more easily facilitate revision and composition alike. As Sharples and Pemberton (1992, pp. 325–326) conclude, 'There is no single best approach to writing.... Computer systems to support the writing process will be of most help if they fit the writer's perception of the task and assist whichever strategy the writer chooses to adopt.'

One of the postcards on the wall in front of me here as I write (on my word processor for the moment) is of Van Gogh's painting of *Wheatfield with Reaper*. It shows a man with a hand-sickle tackling a huge field of a bounteous crop of wheat. Beyond the field and a lake, a house, presumably his, nestles beneath the hills. The sun, rising or setting, hangs in a clear sky. The man is never going to finish that field, not with that implement. What he needs, perhaps, is a combine harvester. It would get the job done faster – but it would be a different picture!

7 Audiences and the politics of dissemination

A sower went out to sow his seed: and as he sowed, some fell by the wayside; and it was trodden down, and the fowls of the air devoured it.
And some fell upon a rock; and as soon as it was sprung up, it withered away, because it lacked moisture.
And some fell among thorns; and the thorns sprang up with it, and choked it.
And other fell on good ground, and sprang up, and bare fruit an hundredfold.
(Luke 8, 5–8)

INTRODUCTION

Dissemination is usually discussed in terms of intent and activity of the author (for example, Richardson, 1990; Nespor and Barber, 1995). What audience does one have in mind, and how does one approach different audiences? But what about the perceptions and intent of the audience(s)? Audiences are not passive recipients of research messages. They actively make sense of them, interpreting them in their own way, incorporating them into their own frameworks. Sometimes these can be at considerable variance with the intentions of the author. Research for educational use, therefore, needs to follow through to see exactly how such research *is* used.

My dictionary tells me that to disseminate means 'to sow or scatter abroad; to propagate; to diffuse; to distribute'. Distribution, however, can fall on stony ground and fail to germinate, or can get choked by thorns. It is not enough simply to give talks, circulate papers and publish books and articles. These are means. The end product is to make a difference, sow a seed that will grow into something, add to knowledge, change practice for the better, affect policies. Educationists have a good record in the former, but not in the latter, at least with respect to teacher practice (Desforges and McNamara, 1977; Degenhardt, 1984; Schensul and Schensul, 1992; Smithers, 1995). Recent trends in research assessment do not help. Where accountability through performance indicators which favour quantity rather than quality holds sway, it is numbers of publications that count. The emphasis is on the sowing, not the seed, on use of the medium, not the message. This has two unfortunate consequences. One is that it prioritizes streetwise knowledge of dissemination over content. The other is that it ministers to a traditional model of educational research dissemination in that distribution is the end of the process. Publication, for example, is the final product, not the use that is made of it. There is an urgent need, therefore, from an educational viewpoint, to address this issue. Methodologically, also, qualitative researchers need to move into this area. For long, 'analysis' and then 'writing up' were areas of mystery, little studied. Recently, however, both areas have been opened up. Now we need to move still further down the line.

This is even more important given the nature of qualitative research. All its various stages are more or less co-terminous, or at least spiral (Lacey, 1976). Data collection and analysis inform each other, and lead to revised research designs. Writing up starts almost immediately. In many instances, also, dissemination can be a constant. Further, in considering how research is to be used, we need a broad conception of 'use'. Miles and Huberman (1994, p. 304) note that one needs 'to think not just of general audiences such as "practitioners", but also of sub-audiences, such as innovators and gatekeepers'. They also note that there are 'levels of diffusion and use'. They do not include among their examples, however, illustrations of 'misuse'. This takes us into the politics of research. The key lies in a quotation they use of Glaser's (1978, p. 13):

> What a man in the know does not want is to be told what he already knows. What he wants is to be told how to handle what he knows with some increase in control and understanding of his area of action.

The problem here is that 'what a person knows' may be founded on any one or more of a range of bases, such as personal experience, ideology, prejudice, faith or 'common sense', as well as scientific research. We do not play out our lives within the context of research findings. It might be hoped that where these are derived from rigorous research, they have some influence upon choices and decisions. However, there are other powerful influences at work.

I want to consider some attempts at dissemination that lay emphasis on educational improvement and that highlight some of the issues involved. I deal here with some attempts to do this through the medium of teachers. There is a long history in this line of approach, in, for example, action research, teacher–researcher and reflective practitioner enquiry, and various kinds of collaborative research (Stenhouse, 1975; Hustler et al., 1986). Here I shall examine, first, a different kind of attempt to work through teachers in what might be regarded as macro-dissemination. This is the Discussion Paper of Alexander, Rose and Woodhead (1992), which attempted to initiate debate among primary teachers with a view to changing primary practice from the Plowden orthodoxy, with its emphasis on child-centred teaching, to one more geared to the National Curriculum, entailing a mix of methods, including more whole-class teaching. Secondly, I shall look at a collaborative project from my own research, an

attempt at micro-dissemination, which had similar aims to the collaborative research reported in Chapter 5, but which brought a totally different
response from the teachers involved. These cases, though vastly different
in some respects, raise similar questions about the aims and uses of
research, the political context of the research and political interests
involved, and criteria of truth and quality. I discuss these issues in the
final section.

THE DISCUSSION PAPER: AN ATTEMPT AT MACRO-DISSEMINATION

In January, 1992, the DES (Department of Education and Science) pamphlet
'Curriculum organization and classroom practice in primary schools: a
discussion paper' (Alexander et al., 1992) was published. This was a major
initiative, given a great boost by the Conservative government of the day,
heralded by the media, and leading to heated debate among academics
and teachers. It was important for a number of reasons. It indicated a
progression in the government's attention, following the institution of a
prescribed National Curriculum in 1988, to pedagogy, hitherto something
of a sacred teacher preserve. The politicization of the educational process
was taken a stage further. Various groups had strong and keenly felt
interests in the exercise, and made varying interpretations, as did members
of the team that actually produced the paper. The media ensured that the
process from inception to publication was acted out against a backcloth of
social drama and moral panic.

Alexander had for long argued that primary education had been
bedevilled by polarized thinking and by ideologies which constrained
teacher culture and careers. His 1984 book exposed the progressive, child-
centred ideology which pervaded primary schools, and his 1991 Leeds
report (discussed in Alexander, 1992) showed that a heavy investment of
resources by the Leeds authority had not significantly raised expectations
and results in the schools, which remained relatively low. While giving
support for some areas of activity in Leeds schools, which he had been
researching for four years, Alexander was strongly critical of the fixation
with progressive ideology in some schools, and the way it was embedded
within the culture of LEAs (local education authorities) and colleges of
education, thus operating as a constraint within schools. He recommended
radical changes in the teacher's role, with practice based less on ideology
and more on pragmatic enquiry.

The invitation from the Secretary of State to contribute to a discussion
paper with the task of 'reviewing available evidence about the delivery of
education in primary schools, and to make recommendations' must have
seemed a golden opportunity to:

1 raise the status of primary education;

2 feed the results of research into practice;
3 stimulate discussion among teachers;
4 secure more resource for primary education;
5 make use of the media;
6 have research feed into politics.

These may be excellent objectives, but their achievement is anything but straightforward. Politics and the media have their own ideologies. Research is used selectively to support these ideologies, not to interrogate or modify them. This had been demonstrated in 1976 with the reception of Neville Bennett's *Teaching Styles and Pupil Progress* (see Bell, 1981, for an account of this); and, even more ominously, Alexander's own Leeds report of 1991. In his 1992 book, he records that 'a complex and carefully qualified analysis was reduced to a simple pathology', the recurrent themes, 'often reduced to caricature', being 'declining educational standards . . . the pervasiveness of "trendy" teaching methods; the baleful influence of a (Labour) LEA . . . and of an "educational establishment"' (p. 165). Equally ominously, in her 1993 presidential address to the British Educational Research Association (BERA), Caroline Gipps (1993, pp 3–4) observed that

> Research and evaluation is still being funded by central agencies but the work is subject to delay in reporting, or not being reported at all, misreporting in the popular press and a general discourse of derision (Ball, 1990b) which has, effectively I fear, asserted the primacy of common-sense knowledge over specialist, expert knowledge and assigned it (forever?) to the sidelines.

The effects of the Discussion Paper in schools are unclear and indeed would be difficult to measure. In the four schools of our research in one LEA, teachers viewed the paper as endowing retrospective validation of practices in their classrooms rather than initiating new ones (Woods and Wenham, 1994). In this way it was helpful to more formal teachers' sense of self, enabling them to 'come out' after years of suppression in an unfavourable climate. But there were no signs of 'personal adjustment' (Becker, 1964; Lacey, 1977), that is, teachers redefining their selves for closer accord with the recommendations. Rather, where they disagreed with the paper they sharpened their own beliefs through contrastive definition without fear of being legislated against. In this sense they came to own the process of the implementation of the Discussion Paper, and they could exploit it creatively in resolving the new range of dilemmas thrown up by the National Curriculum. This is one example of the appropriation of research by a group, or groups, with particular, and widely varying, interests.

Even so, as far as schools were concerned, the Discussion Paper might be said to have achieved its aims given the nature of the dissemination intended (at least by one of its authors; see below), that is, through discussion among teachers, reflection, legitimation and ownership – though the National Curriculum itself was seen by the teachers as a greater influence. The paper may have helped loosen the grip of constraining versions of the progressive ideology. Equally, however, it may have compromised more liberating versions. However, for the purposes of this chapter, I am more interested in earlier stages when a variety of constructions was put upon the paper by a range of interest groups. There are four major points I would want to draw from the career of the Discussion Paper (see Woods and Wenham, 1994, for a full account).

First is the difficulty, perhaps the impossibility at times, of academic argument combating in the political arena. The paper was initiated by the Conservative government of the day. It had its origins in the thinking of the New Right during the 1980s. The immediate opportunity was presented by a scare about reading standards in 1990 and the Leeds report of 1991. The forthcoming general election of 1992 increased the political urgency. The initiative, in an area of public concern where moral panics (Cohen, 1981) are easily generated, might prove an effective vote-winner in an election year (Bennett, 1992). The Conservatives were in some disarray following the downfall of Margaret Thatcher, and the Labour Party was showing greater unity of purpose. Education featured prominently on the political agenda. 'Educational standards' could be relied upon to stir public concern, and their alleged 'lowness' could be laid at the door of the opposition's championing of progressivism and egalitarianism in the 1960s and 1970s. A highly partisan press would ensure that the government's views were given maximum and headline publicity. The government controlled the timing of the document, including the highly significant matter of its release to the press two weeks before it was sent to the schools; the membership of the drafting group, ensuring that, while they were given a free hand, two were government employees (Jim Rose and Chris Woodhead, at the time Chief HMI and Chief Executive of the National Curriculum Council respectively. The NCC was responsible for the implementation of the government's reforms), and the other (Robin Alexander), while an academic and a member of the vilified educational establishment in government eyes, was on recent record as a critic of progressivism; their terms of reference, which focused on organization and teaching methods, not curriculum content (this latter, and especially the amount of it, being the major concern of teachers); and the climate within which it occurred. Michael Fallon, Under-Secretary of State for Education, for example, announced at a well-publicized DES seminar that there was too much 'play, paint and happiness' in primary schools. Shortly after this, Kenneth Clarke, Secretary of State for Education, commissioned the Discussion Paper. The journal *Education* carried a summary of his speech under the heading, 'The Plowden party is finally over.' The *Sunday Times* announced

'Education's insane bandwagon goes into the ditch.' Such pronouncements were common throughout the period.

The phase following publication was marked by Alexander attempting to put his construction on what he considered to be the real message of the document – a modest discussion paper with carefully qualified conclusions, based on evidence, and for teachers to debate and decide – in the face of government, media and Woodhead claims that it was harder edged and carried more prescription. Alexander's academic protestations about misinterpretations were swamped by political rhetoric and media hype. In the muddled debate about what the paper was about, control of the media was a crucial factor in deciding whose interpretation was to prevail – at least in the short term (see, for example, the debate in the *Guardian* involving Woodhead, Alexander and Phillips, 11–14 February 1992).

Secondly, in the context of immediate reception of the document, myth prevailed over reality. Wallace (1993) has drawn attention to the significance of myths in this regard. He draws on the work of Bailey (1977). For him, myths were 'oversimplified representations of a more complex reality', and politics was 'the art of bringing unacceptable myths into, and preserving one's own myths from, derision' (Wallace, 1993, p. 324). Anthropologists have been intrigued by the power of myths. There seems general agreement that they are connected with change, that they prepare the way for change, and lay down rules for action (Malinowski, 1926; see also Eliade, 1959). They rely on profound emotional impact. Closely reasoned argument is not usually the best resource for that. Myths are artistically shaped, pruned to reveal certain details starkly, to identify people almost stereotypically, and to present action simply, yet dramatically (Lewis, 1980, p. 334). Actual details, thus, are not important. Indeed, some of those presented may be proved incorrect. But this does not matter. It is the inner, symbolic, emotional content that carries most weight. Myths, therefore, are an exceptionally influential tool for the manipulation of consciousness, and for winning political control (Sorel, 1950; Sykes, 1965). Alexander's protestations based on reason and evidence were of no avail in this arena, but were simply incorporated in the mythology and turned against him (see, for example, Phillips, *Guardian*, 14 February 1994).

Thirdly, if academics are to have an effect in the political arena in the manner they intend, it would seem highly advantageous to present something of a united front, as the teachers did in their struggle against assessment in 1993. The Discussion Paper, however, aroused as much opposition as support among academic groups. It was not just a matter, therefore, of myth and ideology. There were plenty of grounds for academic debate, and it was a debate in which feelings ran high. Siraj-Blatchford (1993), for example, saw the report as an attack on the professional identity of early-years' teachers, ministering to Clarke's aim to 'bury progressive education for good'. These teachers were the scapegoat for governmental failure (see also David et al., 1992). Dadds (1992) defended Plowdenism and progressivism. Drummond (1991, p. 120) had previously appealed to her colleagues 'not to see our child-centred principles nibbled away at, corrupted, abandoned . . . and being clear what we will stand for through thick and thin'. Darling (1994, pp. 108–109), in a review of Alexander (1992), remarked that 'The Plowden Report had taken three years to complete: its dismissal was written in seven weeks.' Teaching was 'not to be seen as an activity informed by educational theory, especially not by progressive educational theory', but rather as a 'practical accomplishment which involves acquiring a battery of techniques to be deployed in the delivery of a pre-specified curriculum' which, he went on, suggests 'whole-class didacticism'.

The Discussion Paper was to receive strong criticism in some quarters for its style (see, for example, Dadds, 1992; Hammersley and Scarth, 1993). While few, perhaps, would disagree with the main thrust of the content on classroom organization and teaching methods (see, for example, the response of the National Association of Headteachers, 1992), some felt there to be a superior, hierarchical tone in parts of the paper (see Dadds, 1992; Siraj-Blatchford, 1993). The paper emphasized the 'necessity' of subjects in the 'modern primary curriculum' (Summary para. 3.2), and the fact of statutory orders. It accused many teachers of having been slaves to dogma. Hammersley and Scarth (1993, p. 496), however, found that 'the approach adopted by the authors smacks of an attitude towards professionals in education and other fields that seems to have become all too common over the past decade or so in government circles; and it is an attitude that itself exudes dogmatism'. Hammersley and Scarth see it here as an instrument of deskilling and deprofessionalization (Lawn and Ozga, 1981; Apple, 1986).

Fourthly, the document allowed scope for confusion over its status. How it was perceived in this respect was critical for its interpretation. Alexander and Rose both stressed that they were clear from the outset that they were preparing a discussion paper, that is, something that was not mandatory, but which would stimulate debate. This, in fact, was incorporated in its title. Some academics certainly read it in this way. Campbell (1992), for example, saw it as a 'discussion paper, not an empirical study. . . . It can only "provide a basis for the debate".' It was the 'beginning' not the end of that debate. In similar vein, Richards saw the paper as a cultural intervention. He argued that the culture of primary education does not admit of quick change (see D. Hargreaves, 1980; A. Hargreaves, 1988). The climate has to be prepared, and the execution effective. The paper, despite its faults, helped in this process and provided a basis for teachers to discuss issues.

Woodhead, on the other hand, judging from a *Guardian* article (11 February 1992), seemed to regard it as a report, and one that should form the basis of the specification for the details of curriculum organization and classroom management, which would guide the inspection of school performance. The fact that the authors were asked to make recommendations lent weight to this interpretation. Clearly, a 'report with recommendations' is harder-edged than a 'discussion paper' with, perhaps, 'suggestions'. The press certainly seemed to regard it as a report. A *Guardian* leader (12 February 1992), for example, saw it as a 'seminal document commissioned to provide a definitive view on the present state of primary education'.

Yet another version was to view it as an academic paper, subject to the same tests of adequacy, and making no concessions to the 'need to speak directly to teachers'. Parekh (1992, p. 92) suggests that government reports are not 'scholarly academic compositions', although they are usually 'based on the available, and sometimes specially commissioned, research'. None the less, some stringent tests were applied to the paper by readers. Dadds (1992, p. 131), for example, comments, 'None of the evidence used is referenced in the text, making it difficult to check the reliability, validity and generalizability of the research, that, one is led to believe, underpins many of the assertions and certainties offered.' The authors had explained that this was to 'maintain continuity in the discussion' (para. 5), a not unreasonable policy given the well-known failure of academic texts to seem meaningful to teachers (McNamara, 1976). Hammersley and Scarth (1993), however, take the academic argument further, pointing to conceptual difficulties about things like 'dogmas' and 'progressivism'; problems about evidence for claims such as that teachers' expectations of children are 'too low' (paras 3.8), or that many teachers are prey to 'dogmas'; and about claimed causal links, between, for example, 'progressivism' and 'lower standards'. Having found its academic credentials wanting, Hammersley and Scarth hazard a guess as to its real purpose. They conclude that such interventions 'seem to represent a concerted policy to establish and operate central control over education' (p. 496). The Discussion Paper is seen here as a political document. In similar vein, Siraj-Blatchford (1993, p. 413) offers a view that progressivism and teachers who espouse it 'have become a scapegoat for governmental failure with its national reforms – the Discussion Paper being a major medium for the message' (see also Carr, 1994). Hammersley and Scarth recognize that it is labelled a 'discussion paper', but feel that 'in a crucial respect this document does not facilitate rational discussion about the issues with which it deals' (1993, p. 495).

One of the intriguing features of the paper is that it attracted both virulent opposition and enthusiastic support. Among those subscribing to the latter were some of the most prominent academics in the field, who themselves had produced much of the relevant research. Bennett, for example, writing in the *TES* (1992), talked of the 'sane, competent and balanced' report, and found that the 'available evidence has been faithfully synthesized and evaluated' – research evidence that has been 'consistent for over a decade'. Simon (1992) was also warmly supportive, speaking of a 'thoroughly intelligent, acute analysis of primary practice, drawing mainly on the considerable amount of research carried through over the last ten or fifteen years' (p. 91). 'As a discussion paper', he found it 'first class' (p. 96).

How does one account for these extreme differences among academics? It seems they attributed a different status to the paper, which even caused them to see the business of research differently. For Bennett, Campbell and Simon, the paper was broadly in line with what they saw the generality of research was indicating, and they concentrated on its main message. Some may even feel that a preoccupation with rigour can be counter-productive. Smithers (1994, 1995), for example, argues that 'much educational research suffers from subordinating the picture presented to checks on accuracy, often inappropriately derived from the sciences' (1994, p. 21). Even so, the authors admitted that there were some confused messages in the paper. They said that the evidence was 'not good enough to provide a foundation for conclusions about trends in achievement, one way or another'. Alexander admitted, in interview, that 'unsubstantiated claims were made over standards', and 'there should have been a softer conclusion'; while Woodhead accepted that there was 'no incontrovertible evidence of falling standards'. Yet Section 3 of the paper concluded that there is 'some evidence of downward trends in important aspects of literacy and numeracy'.

I shall discuss the issues involved here further, but first I consider a very different example, which none the less throws up similar problems.

A CASE STUDY IN MICRO-DISSEMINATION: A CRITICAL INCIDENT

The Discussion Paper was an attempt to engage with teachers on a national scale. Academics have for long sought to work with teachers locally in collaborative research on the principle that giving teachers a share of ownership and control empowers them, makes them co-producers of knowledge and feeds directly into their practice (Connell et al., 1982; Smyth, 1991; Schensul and Schensul, 1992). Thus knowledge generation, formulation of policy and implementation are integrated in the teacher. Teachers, however, do not always wish to collaborate, or to be disseminated through. They may be reluctant collaborators, or they may be willing, but prefer working to a model that leaves the academic in control of the research (see Gitlin, 1990). I want to focus on a research project of mine where I had collaboration in mind, laid the ground carefully and successfully, as I thought, yet encountered total and virulent opposition from the collective staff and governors in a critical incident at a crucial juncture in the research, which effectively brought the research to an end.

The incident was disturbing to everybody involved, and directly contrary in its effects to the intentions of the research.

The background

My broad aim was to monitor attempts in primary schools to follow up the recommendations of the Swann Report (1985) and to work with teachers in evaluating their efforts. In practice, this would involve documenting and assessing examples of multicultural education, in the context of helping to promote the general cause through democratic collaboration between researchers and teachers. I needed to do some groundwork for this to learn about primary schools and the issues that concerned them, in the process learning something about that old 'mystery' of primary school teaching, and to lay the basis for a research proposal that would allow me to appoint a research assistant. Negotiating access into a pilot school was painstaking and took over a year. I eventually made contact with the head of Compton Junior School (a pseudonym), a multiethnic school with a large number of Afro-Caribbean pupils. The head himself was keen on the research from the beginning, but his staff, as I gathered later, less so.

My research diary records the strategies employed by me and the head in securing access to the school. When the research began, I spent eighteen months there, at roughly one day a week, starting with observation in two classrooms, but ultimately concentrating on one. I monitored teacher style and pupil progress as a participant observer. But I was to do this not according to the anthropological model of participant observation, but with and through the teacher. She was the first point of reference for data gathering, analysis and writing up, and she was to have a part in designing the later research proposal. Clearly, developing trust and rapport was essential, and my notes contain frequent references to how I felt this was achieved with the head (after our first meeting: 'good talk, sense of rapport, an intelligent, perceptive, humane man. I liked his comments about his staff'); with the classroom teacher, whom I got to know very well ('always co-operating, but also confiding in me about her innermost feelings and concerns'); and with the rest of the staff ('staff room chats, some of their work monitored by request, more confidences, provision of OU material – PW a resource for everybody'). Some of the confidences drew my attention to a management problem in the school: for the head, the recalcitrant nature of his staff; for the staff, the authoritarian and critical approach of the head. For both, feeling and frustration ran high, and at times, both experienced extreme stress, which they both described to me with considerable frankness. I felt that there was some therapy about their confiding in me, but primarily a desire that I should appreciate what they saw as the key factor in their current professional lives – the micro-political context within which they had to work.

My participation did not run to involvement in these politics. As the outsider, I could empathize with all. Further, I had something in common with all, supporting the head in his views on multiculturalism and anti-racism, and the staff on democratic participation. My research within the classroom was on teaching methods and teacher–pupil interaction, and was not affected by the micro-political rift in the school. It was, in consequence, a rewarding and happy eighteen months for me as researcher. The head was very supportive of the research, and I recorded that he was a 'shrewd and powerful pathfinder and trailblazer for me', and 'sensitive, insightful, and keen'. I had excellent relationships with my teacher and her class (I was told they looked forward to my coming each week), and with others. I had contributed to teaching, identified and described some good practice, and written three papers. I had begun to develop the notion of 'creative teaching', which seemed to me to be the key to primary teachers' success, and which was to lead to the research reported in Chapter 5, and beyond. I had contributed to the LEA's recommendation to spread news of good practice. Access had steadily widened and deepened over the period to the extent of being taken into confidences. I had shown that the aims of the research were negotiable. In short, I had fulfilled the aims of this period, laying the basis for the major research which was to follow. I now heard that my application for a research assistant had been accepted, and, given the successful ground-work, I proposed that the main research take place in the same school. To my surprise, this precipitated a major crisis.

I was aware that this represented an important threshold. Previous ones had been entry into the school through the gatekeeping activities of the head, and entry into classrooms with the full consent of the teachers. The new proposal, however, involved an escalation of the research. A research assistant would be in the school on a more regular basis. While continuing the work which I had begun, it would not be the personal, localized activity that I had engaged in, but a whole-school affair. Further, while trust and rapport might have been generated with me, it was a quality that rested on personal negotiation, and was not transferable. In the highly charged conflict situation within the school, an unknown new person operating with a wider brief, and with the enthusiastic support of the head, raised alarms rather than hopes. This is another range of problems associated with what Porter (1994) has called 'second-hand ethnography'.

I had also been aware of tolerance levels beyond which staff were not prepared to go – with the head in their teaching, and with me in my research. My field notes are strewn with warning signs about the critical state of relationships in the school, and of my 'being caught up in the power battle'. There were crisis points, where the carefully negotiated access suddenly seemed threatened, invariably followed, however, by break-throughs, and being taken into further confidence. As in theory, where 'breakdowns' of original plans often turn out to be the most creative moments of the research (Turner, 1994), so in personal relationships, where doubt, suspicion and misunderstanding leading to discord can be catalysts for stronger relationships, once resolved. One of these crisis points had been when I showed the draft research proposal to my teacher. She was cooler towards me on my next day in, with not much conversation and avoiding eye contact. But we had eventually thrashed it out, and I revised the research design to meet her points. She was still not overjoyed to hear the proposal had been accepted. She had confided in me that 'the atmosphere was deteriorating in the school', and they were 'beginning to fight each other'. In this context, the research could be an additional burden, perhaps a weapon to be used against them. She 'faced a summer of worrying about it'. That clearly was not right and had to be resolved. I was confident that it would, as we had such a strong personal rapport, and I was determined that the teaching staff should have a share of ownership and control in the research. In the process, perhaps some of the underlying management issues might also be tackled, the research being a catalyst for bringing some of those into the open. The research was balanced on a razor's edge, but given the difficulty of finding a school in the first place, the enormous potential in this one, plus the fact that I had had a successful period there, including overcoming several crisis points and crossing several thresholds, I judged the risk worth taking. It was the wrong decision.

The meeting

I made it a condition that the research secure the agreement of the whole staff. The head invited me to a combined meeting of staff and governors that was being held the following week. The following are extracts from my notes made immediately afterwards:

> A chastening evening! I was limited to 15 minutes' presentation by the aggressive-looking chairman. He opened the questioning, picked up by other governors, by an inspector, and eventually the staff. Questions about 'how', the 'sample', the issues, the factors outside the school, keeping them informed, better communication channels, ignorance of staff. The note of complaint was taken up by the governors with a certain venom and hostility. The only people who seemed to like the idea of the research were the head and the inspector. The latter asked some reasonable questions in a positive way, including how I was going to get the support of the staff. Wouldn't they feel threatened having me in their classrooms? I referred this one to the staff, hoping naively for a sound of support from the two I had worked with. I got it from neither. One complained vehemently about their ignorance about the research and invited other staff to speak ('There are mumblings around here'), whereupon another declared 'We know nothing about it, who is going to be involved, which teachers, how it's going to be done; my head's

reeling with all the things that have been said . . . ' The other teacher, with whom I had been closely involved, invited by the head to speak, said nothing about what I had seen as our successful collaboration over the past eighteen months, but echoed the same fears for the future as her colleagues. The governors escalated the hostility. Will you cover non-teaching staff, office staff, parents? Will other schools be considered? Will you cover all ethnic groups? Including Greeks? 'There are no Greeks here', said the head, but this governor insisted 'There is a large Greek community in the town, so will the research be looking at Greeks? What samples are involved? Will you look at all the pupils?' (I say we must select, we can't possibly cover all – more frowns and black looks.) 'Will you also be consulting the pupils about this?' asked the Greek woman, and continued to look daggers at my answer . . . 'And parents?' asked another (a good example of not listening or not hearing what I had already said, suggesting that it was perhaps an issue other than the research that was on the agenda). The chairman insisted that I report back to them from time to time so that they could assure themselves that the school was not being 'used'. Conditions, strictures . . . came thick and fast. The killer punch came from dear old Mr Bunyan, a kindly gent, who was a governor and who had always been radiantly pleased to see me in the school, who was 'appalled that the staff had no knowledge that a research assistant was coming into the school next term, that this had been known for nearly two weeks, that we must have had plans for this to happen for some time, it was preposterous that nothing was said . . . '(Of course things were said, but forgotten or overlooked.) The chairman had now given up. There were so many people pressing to ask questions, and his '15 minutes' had long since gone. He threw up his arms in despair, and sank resignedly into his chair. . . . There was an undercurrent of suspicion and hostility, quite nasty on occasions . . . a world of difference between the constructive way the inspector put his questions and the destructive way in which they were taken up. The chairman concluded by asking me to take note of what had been said, and 'to come back to us in words that we can understand (ripple of laughter) with an early and full report'. The research, however, was clearly at an end.

The functions of this meeting have to be seen in the light of the perceptions of the parties present. Perceptions of the research seemed to be influenced by, first, position in the school (head, classroom teacher, researcher; see Hustler and Cuff, 1986), and, secondly, situation (school, classroom, the world at large). The head, rightly or wrongly, was seen by the staff as potentially using the research as a resource in his power struggle with them. Its actual qualities as research were as nothing in this bitter contest, which currently, it seemed, bore on every moment of their working lives. Note should be taken, too, of the sensitivity of the central research issue – that of 'race'. Among a discordant staff there was almost bound to be conflict on this issue, and behind it all loomed the spectre of racism. In this context, I was seen as being in league with the head and received the full force of their opposition. They, for their part, saw the meeting as an opportunity to get a message across to the governors about the lack of consultation, communication and democracy in the school. One told me later that there was 'nothing personal in it. We wanted inspectors and governors to know what we had to put up with, and were sorry you were at the centre of it. We were worried you might have been disturbed at the meeting.' They were able to present a strong and united front, doubtless after much prior staff room discussion, in a situation where they had the ear of a sympathetic and powerful third group, that is, the governors. Some of these, like Mr Bunyan, had had discussions with teachers in advance of the meeting and came with pre-formulated views. Staff and allied governors were able to generate a barnstorming mood of opposition, which others joined and which swamped and enfeebled logical, academic discourse in the same way as Alexander's carefully argued points were eclipsed by the media.

In this very fraught micro-political context, my research proposal and I myself were of little consequence, little more, in fact, than a political football (being 'kicked around' from one to another is a fair analogy for the experience). What I had intended as a collaborative research project (there are many ironies here!), the outcomes of which would directly inform teachers' practice, had been appropriated by them for dissemination of another kind. The research had been subsumed within the power struggle. Only within the localized arena of one teacher's classroom had the research operated as intended, for there the personal could prevail over the political, and public issues become privatized. It was the context of rapport, trust, confidences – and genuine research. When it threatened to break free of these moorings, trust turned to suspicion and fear that it had been a conspiracy all along – converting the whole of it to a political, non-personal frame.

One lesson emerging is that however strong personal relationships seem to be with individual teachers within the context of their classrooms and their own personal agendas, they can be otherwise within the structural context of the school, where other factors, such as staff structure, school management, school policy and school organization, come into play. The teacher is situated within a complex organization and interprets his or her position accordingly. This will influence how the researcher is perceived – variously as bona fide researcher, as personal and professional friend, or as political opponent. All three applied in my research, the last most markedly at the meeting. Yet, as before, in a curious way, it led to a heightening of the personal friendship in the personal sphere. There were several indicators of this; for example, expressions of relief and support from staff when I next went into the school ('My goodness, we're pleased to see you!'); and notably a phone call to me from her home, of one and a half hours' duration, from the teacher with whom I had been most concerned. During this she told me how much she had enjoyed working with me, and wondered if she were missing a great opportunity. She genuinely volunteered to be involved in the research (previously, she told me, she had been constrained by the head), shared in more confidences about her colleagues and the head, and concluded with 'We must meet socially for a drink or a meal either here or there, or half-way.' This entry into the informal world of this teacher, outside the school and the teacher role, where we could put all the problems associated with those at a distance, was a considerable advance, and one I never succeeded in making at the school. It was another one of those 'breakthroughs' that had followed earlier 'crises', but it was a breakthrough limited to the personal and classroom context, and a phase of the research that was over.

There is an irony, therefore, in the final function – that of providing a route out of the school. The problem of 'leaving the field' can be a considerable one (see various articles in Shaffir and Stebbins, 1991). It was not easy here, since the head did not care for my 'unilateral decision' and 'closed mind' on the matter, put a different construction on the meeting, and pointed out that 'it will reflect badly on the school' and that he had thought of resigning. His parting handshake was limp and tepid. He had lost out again to his recalcitrant staff, and from his point of view I must have seemed lacking resolve or, what was worse, on their side. But if his feelings were hurt, he recognized the logic of the situation. As for the staff, the restoration of personal relationships, stronger than before, kept open the prospect of some future appropriate research, and provided for a courteous, rational and, in the end, collegial parting of the ways.

SOME BASIC ISSUES

A number of issues are raised by these examples. I select three overlapping issues for consideration here: use, politics and validity.

Use

Both cases considered here illustrate a variety – and confusion – of uses. They are not untypical of the problems that can arise when more than one use is involved or perceived. For example, Smithers' report on 'Britain's educational revolution' is applauded by Sofer (1994, p. 88), though she reports 'one leading academic' calling it a 'complete and total shambles'. Sofer notes that this is a glossy brochure with many popularizing features. She accepts its message, and acknowledges, by inference, that the report may reach places with its 'central truth' that more formalized presentation would not. Smithers (1995) argues that educational research should be more 'useful', without, however, noting that a number of other questions are involved, such as useful for whom, in what ways, and for how long (see Murphy, 1995). One might compare the efforts of Richardson (1987, 1990) to disseminate her research on single women who have affairs with married men to a popular, as well as to an academic, audience. Richardson's work is generally admired, but the dissemination choices have attracted criticism. As Grant and Fine (1992, p. 428) note,

> Writing for a popular audience involves...a series of compromises, some of which involve the kinds of qualifications that one can make regarding one's 'truth claims', the complexity of the analysis, and the extent and form of fieldnotes included. Some of these popular ethnographies violate norms of academic discourse and read like novelizations of the life of their central characters.

Grant and Fine go on to observe,

> Although these works directed toward lay readers do help persons...they run the danger of dismissal as nonserious scholarship by the professional reader, who must infer theoretical relevance and methodological precision rather than find these laid out in the scholarly mode.

Applying these points to our two examples, as far as the micro-case is concerned, the research might have been more successful had it had more evident, actual focus on 'teacher use' rather than appearing as camouflaging rhetoric for more sinister designs. For this, the research might have been restricted to the personal, classroom context, where trust and rapport had already been established, rather than shifted contexts to the school arena, where the head held authority, which raised doubts among the classroom teachers about the original purposes of the research. The alternative was to seek another school with a more collaborative culture where head and staff worked in closer harmony. A clearer research design, worked out in closer consultation with the staff, over a number of meetings and allowing for their input, would have helped.

Similarly, clearer and more specific terms of reference might have obviated the confusion over the Discussion Paper, though, as noted, a measure of confusion was functional in political terms. Miles and Huberman (1994, p. 300) feel that 'the critical question is *which* effects you are intending for *which* types of reader'. They distinguish among aesthetic, scientific, moral and activist effects. The Discussion Paper would appear to be 'activist' ('enable improved decisions, provide guidance for action'), supported by a scientific base. Some would argue that it was weak at the point of intersection.

Behind all these other questions lurks the one of whom the Discussion Paper was for. The question of audience is critical. Nespor and Barber (1995, p. 50) point out that 'There is force in the arguments of literary theorists that the meanings of texts are constructed in the activities of reading and that readers can appropriate unintended meanings or "read against the grain of the text's dominant voice" [Clifford, 1988, p. 52]'. But Nespor and Barber argue that texts are constructed for specific audiences. So who were the audience for the Discussion Paper? Perhaps it was multiple, various, or different for each member of the team? Was it for Clarke, the Secretary of State for Education, and the Tory party? The New Right faction? The National Curriculum Council? Academics? Teachers? All of these had a stake in proceedings and sought to appropriate the paper for their own interests.

The answer may lie in its form and style rather than in its content. Richardson (1990, p. 32) notes that

> All writing is encoded, serving the rhetorical function of locating it in a particular genre, helping the reader to know what to expect, and thereby, in actuality, helping the writer, who can then draw upon the habits of thought, glosses, and specialized knowledge of the reader. Audiences have expectations regarding 'their' texts. Overall organization, code words, title, authorial designation, metaphors, images, and so on, serve as signposts to potential readers. When the audiences for the same book are diverse or discrete, the writing problem becomes more complex and important, because the text has simultaneously to reach differing readerly sensibilities.

What sorts of encoding are there? Richardson points to trade encoding, academic encoding, and moral/political encoding, and notes that 'Problems with writing books that transcend genres begin with deciding which of the potentially conflicting encoding conventions to deploy when' (p. 33). Further, 'taking the narrative stance of omniscience [raises] the major... question about authority' (p. 38; see also Van Maanen, 1988).

The aims of the research and the audiences to whom it is addressed will determine the nature and content of the dissemination, and how it is to take place – through writing, talks, reports, the media, the teacher, or the research act itself. Both macro- and micro-cases discussed here suggest the need for the researchers, if they are interested in the impact of their research, to take more responsibility for all phases of dissemination, which include, as far as audience is concerned, the consumption and processing as well as receipt of research products.

Politics

Both examples illustrate how dissemination is affected by political considerations. In both cases different and sometimes opposing interest groups sought to appropriate the research for their own purposes. The researcher may wish to convey her or his construction of the research, and to stay neutral as far as these interests are concerned. As we have seen, however, this is difficult to do in the perceptions of others. Alexander, Rose and Woodhead might claim that they attempted to maintain a common front to all, reviewing the evidence on its merits, but this did not prevent the attribution by some of different kinds of motive, however unintended they may have been. Forsaking academic distance and negotiating access into a person's or group's confidences can have a similar effect in certain situations. Success involves, ideally, entry to innermost secrets and desires, a privilege accorded a trusted and potential ally. However, entrance into one group might arouse suspicion in another. Also, as we have seen, access on one set of terms in one situation is not necessarily transferable to another set in another situation, albeit with the same people. Whatever the researcher does, he or she is at risk of being attributed to sides by inmates, and the products of the research used as a resource in their own particular struggles. This seemed to be happening in both of our examples.

This raises the question of the control of dissemination. In both instances this appears to have been lost by the researchers concerned (cf. Bennett, 1976), despite their best efforts. The media, teachers or head teachers can take over and subvert the aims and products of the research. Academic debate and argument – the researcher's main resource – were of little avail in the discourses of derision that ultimately attended the reception of both projects. It is impossible to secure complete control of the use one's work is put to. But perhaps some political work of one's own might yield more control. For example, making alliances, anticipating potential problems and preparing the ground, perhaps by giving the various groups – in the case of the Alexander, Rose and Woodhead paper, early-years' teachers, the supporters of child-centred education, and research methods experts; in the micro-case, the staff as a whole – a chance to comment in advance. In general, academics clearly have to be politically aware, especially so in the aftermath of the radical restructuring of the educational system that has taken place in recent years. Continuous reflexivity on one's own position within the research process is also even more of a requirement.

Validity

The Discussion Paper was attacked on grounds of validity, but clearly different definitions of validity prevailed. Most academics would agree that no concessions should be made as far as rigour is concerned, but they may differ on form of presentation. It would seem appropriate to align presentation to the target audience, but, if this involves summarizing or selecting, having further evidence and argument readily available. This is the only sure defence against erroneous interpretation. It must be tempting to meet media misrepresentations by similar discourse to theirs, marked by an immediate, non-reflective, broad-brush, derisive and conviction-of-certainty approach. In the long term, however, the desertion of the academic ground would open up more radical, and more justified, grounds for criticism. Interpretations of the Discussion Paper were extremely variable, and provide a good example of how, in the last resort, we have no control over how people will interpret our research reports and the use they will make of them. Awareness, anticipation and active briefing might, however, anticipate some interpretations and provide guidance for others.

Some argue that validating is done through the practitioners assessing the credibility of the research through their own knowledge and experience, and putting the research into practice through their own teaching (Lather, 1986; Erickson, 1986; Lincoln and Guba, 1985). This was the stated aim of the Discussion Paper, and was what happened in the schools of our research on the Paper's implementation (Woods and Wenham, 1994). It also happened at Compton Junior, but not in the way anticipated. Both cases show that style is of crucial importance. The Discussion Paper, arguably, roused more resentment over its style of presentation than over its content. My presentation at the governors' meeting was clearly not helped by my 'researcher-speak' tendencies. At the same time, there is a danger of appearing patronizing if one departs too far from the academic mould (Desforges et al., 1986).

Both cases illustrate the problem of criticism of teaching practice. In speaking directly to teachers, do concessions have to be made on this score for fear of the message being counter-productive? If so, what implications would this have for validity? Threadgold (1985, p. 255) attests that 'teachers are extremely defensive about criticism implied or expressed'. Teachers especially do not take kindly to criticism from outside academics, since this inevitably involves people with, as they see it, a professional base of dubious appropriateness questioning teachers' professional competence (Hustler and Cuff, 1986; Hutchinson and Whitehouse, 1986). Some of the teachers in our research on the Discussion Paper spoke of their 'anger at some of the things that were said'. They felt demeaned as professionals, and exercised their own powers of critical appreciation in evaluating the paper. One of the teachers at Compton said she was willing to join in the research if it was going to be constructive and positive, but not if it was going to 'tear her to pieces'.

One answer is that if the research were truly collaborative this would not be a problem, for the teacher would have an equal share in the generation of any criticism. The point is illustrated by reactions to one of the papers on teacher style that I presented at Compton. The head's main comment was that he was surprised there was nothing 'critical' in the paper. The teacher who was the main subject of the paper, however, did find points of criticism in the paper, for example, 'the spelling test...I thought that was terrible....It's instructive to see yourself presented in this form. It makes you reflect on your teaching in a way that you otherwise wouldn't do.' The researcher's input here is to provide the material and the analysis for the teacher to make an informed judgement. This enables the teacher to have some control over the conclusions of the research and its practical applications.

This all has to be done within the context of career considerations, of both researcher and teacher. The researcher needs to disseminate, and particularly to publish, especially in high-status journals, for career purposes. The pressures are against experimental forms of dissemination, and against spending time on the later phases suggested above, which carry few points in ratings assessments. Equally, teachers for their part may be concerned about how the research is going to affect their careers. Some teacher reactions to the Discussion Paper showed how their professional identities and prospects as teachers were bound up in their interpretation (Woods and Wenham, 1994). At Compton, one teacher, who had been quite vociferous at the meeting, had earlier been keen for me to monitor a particular project she had initiated. She had been pleased with my report, which she felt 'captured the spirit of it'. She was applying for higher posts at the time, and the paper was a contribution to her curriculum vitae. But I was not invited to share other aspects of her teaching, nor did my good offices count for anything in the fateful meeting. One of the main concerns of the principal teacher in the research about the new research proposal was that she did not see 'how it would help her career'. The chances were, in fact, that it would damage it by distorting the truth as she knew it, and involve her in unwarranted criticism. Researchers could 'prove what they liked'. She felt that the proposal contained an underlying, unstated theory, and that we would simply select out material to fit it and 'prove' it. Considerations of politics, career, validity and pedagogy seem interconnected in her response. My research diary records that this in several respects was an uncomfortable day, but her reaction was

> really the development of the day about which I should feel pleased, for it really gets to the heart of collaboration and tests out not only one's good faith, but also all manner of hidden assumptions. These have to be purged.

I have tried to identify some of these assumptions as they apply to dissemination.

POSTSCRIPT

Let us end on a cheerful note. A reverse can lead to better things. From time to time, the researcher – if he or she is to continue – hits upon more felicitous conjunctures of factors. If the aim is collaborative research with a view to teacher empowerment and educational improvement, there can be no better feedback than a message like the following, received from a teacher who had been involved in the 'critical events' research (Woods, 1993a):

It feels very rewarding to me, and reassuring to my deepest ideals that you have written such a book. It somehow puts the limited happenings of that time within the wider inspirational and philosophical context that they originated from! Thank you again for supporting these ideals, and the creative endeavour of all those who strive to teach as 'artists' – especially in this time, when scant support is forthcoming for such efforts.

To receive such a letter makes it all seem worthwhile.

References

Abbs, P. (1989) 'Signs on the way to understanding', *Times Educational Supplement*, 10 November, p. 15.

Abbs, P. (1994) *The Educational Imperative: a defence of Socratic and aesthetic learning*, London, Falmer Press.

Acker, S. (ed.) (1989) *Teachers, Gender and Careers*, Lewes, Falmer Press.

Adelman, C. (1988) 'Looking at teaching', Unit C1 in Course EP228 *Frameworks in Teaching*, Milton Keynes, Open University.

Aggleton P. (1987) *Rebels Without a Cause*, Lewes, Falmer Press.

Alexander, R.J. (1984) *Primary Teaching*, London, Holt, Rinehart and Winston.

Alexander, R.J. (1992) *Policy and Practice in Primary Education*, London, Routledge.

Alexander, R.J., Rose, J. and Woodhead, C. (1992) 'Curriculum organisation and classroom practice in primary schools: a discussion paper', London, Department of Education and Science, HMSO.

Altheide, D.L. and Johnson, J.M. (1994) 'Criteria for assessing interpretive validity in qualitative research' in Denzin, N.K. and Lincoln, Y.S. (eds) *Handbook of Qualitative Research*, London, Sage.

American Sociologist. (1968) *Toward a Code of Ethics*, 3, pp. 316–318.

Anderson, G.L. (1989) 'Critical ethnography in education: origins, current status and new directions', *Review of Educational Research*, 59, 3, pp. 249–270.

Anning, A. (1986) '"Curriculum in Action" in action' in Hustler, D., Cassidy, D. and Cuff, E.C. (eds) *Action Research in Classrooms and Schools*, London, Allen and Unwin.

Anyon, J. (1981) 'Social class and school knowledge', *Curriculum Inquiry*, 11, 1, pp. 3–42.

Apple, M.W. (1986) *Teachers and Texts: a political economy of class and gender relations in education*, New York, Routledge and Kegan Paul.

Argyris, C. and Schön, D.A. (1976) *Theory in Practice: increasing professional effectiveness*, London, Jossey-Bass.

Arp 1885–1966 (1987) (museum catalogue of an exhibition), Minneapolis, MN, Minneapolis Institute of Arts.

Atkinson, M. (1977) 'Coroners and the categorization of deaths as suicides' in Bell, C. and Newby, H. (eds) *Doing Sociological Research*, London, Allen and Unwin.

Atkinson, P. (1990) *The Ethnographic Imagination: textual constructions of reality*, London, Routledge.

Bailey, F.G. (1977) *Morality and Expediency*, Oxford, Blackwell.

Baker, C. (1989) *Yacker 3: Australian Writers talk about their Work*, Sydney, Pan.

Baldwin, J.D. (1986) *George Herbert Mead: a unifying theory for sociology*, Beverly Hills, CA, Sage.

Ball, S.J. (1980) 'Initial encounters in the classroom and the process of establishment' in Woods, P. (ed.) *Pupil Strategies*, London, Croom Helm.

Ball, S.J. (1981) *Beachside Comprehensive*, Cambridge, Cambridge University Press.

Ball, S.J. (1984) 'Beachside reconsidered: reflections on a methodological apprenticeship' in Burgess, R.G. (ed.) *The Research Process in Educational Settings: ten case studies*, Lewes, Falmer Press.

Ball, S.J. (1990a) 'Self-doubt and soft data: social and technical trajectories in ethnographic fieldwork', *International Journal of Qualitative Studies in Education*, 3, 2, pp. 157–172.

Ball, S.J. (1990b) *Politics and Policy Making in Education*, London, Routledge.

Ball, S.J. (1993) 'Education markets, choice and social class: the market as a class strategy in the UK and the USA', *British Journal of Sociology of Education*, 14, 1, pp. 3–19.

Ball, S.J. and Bowe, R. (1992) 'Subject departments and the "implementation" of National Curriculum policy: an overview of the issue', *Journal of Curriculum Studies*, 24, 2, pp. 97–115.

Ball, S.J. and Goodson, I.F. (eds) (1985) *Teachers' Lives and Careers*, Lewes, Falmer Press.

Bandura, A. (1969) 'Social learning theory of identificatory processes' in Goslin, D.A. (ed.) *Handbook of Socialization Theory and Research*, Chicago, Rand McNally.

Barker, B. (1987) 'Visions are off the agenda', *Times Educational Supplement*, 3 December, p. 4.

Barone, T. (1990a) 'On the demise of subjectivity in educational inquiry', paper presented at the Annual Meeting of the American Educational Research Association, Boston, April.

Barone, T. (1990b) 'Using the narrative text as an occasion for conspiracy' in Eisner, E. and Peshkin, A. (eds) *Qualitative Inquiry in Education*, New York, Teachers College Press.

Becker, E. (1971) *The Birth and Death of Meaning*, 2nd edn, New York, Free Press.

Becker, H.S. (1963) *Outsiders: studies in the sociology of deviance*, Chicago, Free Press.

Becker, H.S. (1964) 'Personal change in adult life', *Sociometry*, 27, 1, pp. 40–53; also in Cosin, B. et al. (eds) (1977) *School and Society*, 2nd edn, London, Routledge and Kegan Paul.

Becker, H.S. (1967) 'Whose side are we on?', *Social Problems*, 14, pp. 239–247.

Becker, H.S. (1970) *Sociological Work*, Aldine, Chicago.

Becker, H.S. (1986) *Writing for Social Scientists: how to start and finish your thesis, book or article*, Chicago, University of Chicago Press.

Becker, H.S. (1994) '"Foi por acaso": conceptualising coincidence', *Sociological Quarterly*, 35, 2, pp. 183–194.

Becker, H.S., McCall, M. and Morris, L. (1988) 'Performing culture: local theatrical communities', performed at Northwestern University Theatre and Interpretation Centre, Evanston, IL, 15 January.

Becker, H.S., Geer, G., Hughes, E.D. and Strauss, A.L. (1961) *Boys in White*, Chicago, University of Chicago Press.

Bell, C. (1956) *Old Friends*, London, Cassell.

Bell, R.E. (1981) 'Approaches to teaching', Unit 15 of Course E200 *Contemporary Issues in Education*, Milton Keynes, Open University.

Bennett, N. (1976) *Teaching Styles and Pupil Progress*, London, Open Books.

Bennett, N. (1992) 'Never mind the sophistry', *Times Educational Supplement*, 14 February.

Berger, B.M. (1990) 'Looking for the interstices' in Berger, B. (ed.) *Authors of Their Own Lives*, Berkeley, CA, University of California Press.

Berger, P.L. (1966) *Invitation to Sociology*, New York, Doubleday.

Bernard, J. (1990) 'A woman's twentieth century' in Berger, B. (ed.) *Authors of Their Own Lives*, Berkeley, CA, University of California Press.

Bertaux, D. (ed.) (1981) *Biography and Society,* Beverly Hills, Sage.

Best, D. (1991) 'Creativity: education in the spirit of enquiry', *British Journal of Educational Studies*, 34, 3, pp. 260–278.

Bevlin, M. (1970) *Design Through Discovery,* New York, Holt, Rinehart and Winston.

Beynon, J. (1985) *Initial Encounters in the Secondary School*, Lewes, Falmer Press.

Biott, C., and Nias, J. (eds) (1992) *Working and Learning Together for Change*, Milton Keynes, Open University Press.

Bloom, L.R. and Munro, P. (1995) 'Conflicts of selves: nonunitary subjectivity in women administrators' life history narratives' in Hatch, J.A. and Wisniewski, R. (eds) *Life History and Narrative*, London, Falmer Press.

Blumenfeld-Jones, D. (1995) 'Fidelity as a criterion for practising and evaluating narrative inquiry' in Hatch, J.A. and Wisniewski, R. (eds) *Life History and Narrative*, London, Falmer Press.

Blumer, H. (1954) 'What is wrong with social theory', *American Sociological Review*, 13, pp. 542–554.

Blumer, H. (1962) 'Society as symbolic interaction' in Rose, A.M. (ed.) *Human Behaviour and Social Processes*, London, Routledge and Kegan Paul.

Blumer, H. (1976) 'The methodological position of symbolic interactionism' in Hammersley, M. and Woods, P. (eds) *The Process of Schooling*, London, Routledge and Kegan Paul.

Bogdan, R. and Taylor, S.J. (1975) *Introduction to Qualitative Research Methods*, New York, John Wiley.

Bolton, G. (1984) *Drama as Education*, London, Longman.

Bolton, G. (1994) 'Stories at work: fictional-critical writing as a means of professional development', *British Educational Research Journal*, 20, 1, pp. 55–68.

Bonnett, M. (1991) 'Developing children's thinking . . . and the National Curriculum', *Cambridge Journal of Education*, 21, 3, pp. 277–292.

Boswell, J. (1791) *The Life of Samuel Johnson*, London, James Blackwood.

Bourdieu, P. and Passeron, J.C. (1977) *Reproduction in Education: society and culture*, London, Sage.

Bowles, S. and Gintis, H. (1976) *Schooling in Capitalist America*, London, Routledge and Kegan Paul.

Boyle, M.L. and Woods, P. (1996) 'The composite head: coping with changes in the primary headteacher's role', *British Educational Research Journal*, 22, 5.

Bridwell-Bowles, L., Johnson, P. and Brehe, S. (1987) 'Composing and computers: case studies of experienced writers' in Matsuhashi, A. (ed.) *Writing in Real Time: modelling production processes*, Norwood, NJ, Ablex.

Brighouse, T. (1987) 'Goodbye to the head and the history man', *Guardian*, 21 July, p. 11.

Brown, S. and McIntyre, D. (1993) *Making Sense of Teaching*, Buckingham, Open University Press.

Bulmer, M. (1979) 'Concepts in the analysis of qualitative data', *Sociological Review*, 27, 4, pp. 651–677.

Bulmer, M. (1980) 'Comment on the ethics of covert methods', *British Journal of Sociology,* 31, 1, pp. 59–65.

Bulmer, M. (1982) 'The merits and demerits of covert participant observation' in Bulmer, M. (ed.) *Social Research Ethics*, London, Macmillan.

Bulmer, M. (1984) *The Chicago School of Sociology*, Chicago, University of Chicago Press.

Burgess, E.W. (1929) 'Basic social data' in Smith, T.V. and White, L.D. (eds) *Chicago: an experiment in social science research*, Chicago, University of Chicago Press.

Burgess, R.G. (ed.) (1982) *Field Research: a sourcebook and field manual*, London, Allen and Unwin.

Burgess, R.G. (1984a) *In the Field: an introduction to field research*, London, Allen and Unwin.

Burgess, R.G. (ed.) (1984b) *The Research Process in Educational Settings: ten case studies*, Lewes, Falmer Press.

Burgess, R.G. (1985a) 'The whole truth?: some ethical problems of research in the comprehensive school' in Burgess, R.G. (ed.) *Field Methods in the Study of Education*, Lewes, Falmer Press.

Burgess, R.G. (ed.) (1985b) *Field Methods in the Study of Education*, Lewes, Falmer Press.

Burgess, R.G. (1991) 'Sponsors, gatekeepers, members, and friends: access in educational settings' in Shaffir, W.B. and Stebbings, R.A. (eds) *Experiencing Fieldwork*, London, Sage.

Campbell, R.J. (1992) 'Scapegoats and the education debate', *Guardian*, 19 February.

Carr, D. (1994) 'Wise men and clever tricks', *Cambridge Journal of Education*, 24, 1, pp. 89–112.

Carr, W. (1989) *Quality in Teaching: arguments for a reflective profession*, Lewes, Falmer Press.

Carr, W. and Kemmis, S. (1986) *Becoming Critical*, Lewes, Falmer Press.

Casey, K. and Apple, M. W. (1989) 'Gender and the conditions of teachers' work: the development of understanding in America' in Acker, S. (ed.) *Teachers, Gender and Careers*, Lewes, Falmer Press.

Chanan, G. (ed.) (1973) *Towards a Science of Teaching*, Windsor, NFER.

Chandler, D. (1987) 'Are we ready for word processors?', *English in Australia*, 79, March, pp. 11–17.

Clark, C.M. (1992) 'Teachers as designers in self-directed professional development' in Hargreaves, A. and Fullan, M.G. (eds) *Understanding Teacher Development*, London, Cassell.

Clifford, J. (1986) 'Introduction' in Clifford, J. and Marcus, G.E. (eds) *Writing Culture: the poetics and politics of ethnography*, Berkeley, CA, University of California Press.

Clifford, J. (1988) *The Predicament of Culture*, Cambridge, MA, Harvard University Press.

Clifford, J. and Marcus, G. E. (eds) (1986) *Writing Culture: the poetics and politics of ethnography*, Berkeley, CA, University of California Press.

Cohen, S. (1968) 'Vandalism: its politics and nature', *New Society*, 12 December, pp. 316–317.

Cohen, S. (1981) *Folk Devils and Moral Panics*, 2nd edn, London, Martin Robertson.

Collingwood, R.G. (1966) 'Expressing one's emotions' in Eisner, E.W. and Ecker, D.W. (eds) *Readings in Art Education*, Lexington, MA, Xerox College Publishing.

Collins, J.L. and Sommers, E.A. (1985) *Writing On-Line*, Boynton/Cook.

Collins, R. (1989) 'Sociology: proscience or antiscience?', *American Sociological Review*, 54, pp. 124–139.

Connell, R.W., Ashenden, D.J., Kessler, S. and Dowsett, G.W. (1982) *Making the Difference: schools, families and social division*, Sydney, Allen and Unwin.

Connelly, F.M. and Clandinin, D.J. (1985) 'Personal practical knowledge and the modes of knowing: relevance for teaching and learning' in Eisner, E. (ed.) *Learning and Teaching and Ways of Knowing*, NSSE Yearbook, Chicago, University of Chicago Press.

Cook, M.C. (1992) *Freeing Your Creativity: a writer's guide*, Cincinnati, Ohio, Writers' Digest Books.

Cooper, P. and McIntyre, D. (1996) *Effective Teaching and Learning*, Buckingham, Open University Press.

Corrigan, P. (1979) *Schooling the Smash Street Kids*, London, Macmillan.

Cox, D.R. (1986) 'Computers and academic "survival": some questions', *Teaching English in the Two Year College*, October, pp. 178–183.

Dadds, M. (1992) 'Monty Python and the three wise men', *Cambridge Journal of Education*, 22, 2, pp. 129–141.

Dadds, M. (1995) *Passionate Enquiry and School Development: a story about teacher action research*, London, Falmer Press.

Darling, J. (1994) *Child-Centred Education and its Critics*, London, Paul Chapman.

Davey, A.G. and Mullin, P.N. (1982) 'Inter-ethnic friendship in British primary schools', *Educational Research*, 24, pp. 83–92.

David, T., Curtis, A. and Siraj-Blatchford, I. (1992) *Effective Teaching in the Early Years; fostering children's learning in nurseries and in infant classes*, Stoke-on-Trent, Trentham Books.

Davies, L. (1984) *Pupil Power: deviance and gender in school*, Lewes, Falmer Press.

Davies, L. (1994) *Beyond Authoritarian School Management*, Nottingham, Education Now.

Day, C.W. (1991) 'Roles and relationships in qualitative research on teachers' thinking: a reconsideration', *Teaching and Teacher Education*, 7, 5/6, pp. 537–547.

Day, C.W. (1995) 'Professional development and the role of teacher educators: fitness for purpose', *British Educational Research Journal*, 21, 3, pp. 357–369.

Dean, J.P. (1954) 'Participant observation and interviewing' in Doby, J., Sychman, E.A., McKinnet, J.C., Francis, R.G. and Dean, J.P. (eds) *An Introduction to Social Research*, Harrisburg, PA, Stackpole, pp. 225–252.

Dean, J.P. and Whyte, W.F. (1958) 'How do you know if the informant is telling the truth?', *Human Organisation*, 17, 2, pp. 34–38; also in McCall, G.J. and Simmons, J. (eds) *Issues in Participant Observation*, Reading, MA, Addison-Wesley.

Degenhardt, M.A.B. (1984) 'Educational research as a source of educational harm', *Culture, Education and Society*, 38, 3, pp. 232–252.

Delamont, S. (1992) *Fieldwork in Educational Settings: methods, pitfalls and perspectives*, London, Falmer Press.

Delamont, S. and Galton, M. (1986) *Inside the Secondary Classroom*, London, Routledge and Kegan Paul.

De Lyon, H. and Migniuolo, F.W. (eds) (1989) *Women Teachers: issues and experiences*, Buckingham, Open University Press.

Denscombe, M. (1980) 'Pupil strategies and the open classroom' in Woods, P. (ed.) *Pupil Strategies: explorations in the sociology of the school*, London, Croom Helm.

Denscombe, M. (1995) 'Teachers as an audience for research: the acceptability of ethnographic approaches to classroom research', *Teachers and Teaching: theory and practice*, 1, 2, pp. 173–191.

Denscombe, M., Szule, H., Patrick, C. and Wood, A. (1986) 'Ethnicity and friendship: the contrast between sociometric research and fieldwork observation in primary school classrooms', *British Educational Research Journal*, 12, 3, pp. 221–235.

Denzin, N.K. (1968) 'On the ethics of disguised observation: an exchange between Norman Denzin and Kai Erikson', *Social Problems*, 15, pp. 502–506.

Denzin, N.K. (1978) *The Research Act in Sociology: a theoretical introduction to sociological methods*, 2nd edn, London, Butterworth.

Denzin, N.K. (1992) 'The conversation', *Symbolic Interaction*, 15, 2, pp. 135–149.

Denzin, N.K. (1993) '"Rain man" in Las Vegas: where is the action for the postmodern self?', *Symbolic Interaction*, 16, 1, pp. 65–77.

Denzin, N.K. (1994) 'The art and politics of interpretation' in Denzin, N.K. and Lincoln, Y.S. (eds) *Handbook of Qualitative Research*, London, Sage.

Denzin, N.K. (1995) 'The experiential text and the limits of visual understanding', *Educational Theory*, 45, 1, pp. 7–18.

Denzin, N.K. and Lincoln, Y.S. (1994) 'Introduction' in Denzin, N.K. and Lincoln, Y.S. (eds) *Handbook of Qualitative Research*, London, Sage.

Denzin, N.K. and Lincoln, Y.S. (1995) 'Transforming qualitative research methods: is it a revolution?', *Journal of Contemporary Ethnography*, 24, 3, pp. 349–358.

Department of Education and Science (1983) *Teaching Quality*, London, HMSO.

Desforges, C. and McNamara, D. (1977) 'One man's heuristic is another man's blindfold: some comments on applying social science to educational practice', *British Journal of Teacher Education*, 3, 1, pp. 26–39.

Desforges, C., Cockburn, A. and Bennett, N. (1986) 'Teachers' perspectives on matching: implications for action research' in Hustler, D., Cassidy, A. and Cuff, E.C. (eds) *Action Research in Classrooms and Schools*, London, Allen and Unwin.

Dewey, J. (1929) *The Quest for Certainty: a study of the relation of knowledge and action*, New York, Minton, Balch.

Dingwall, R. (1980) 'Ethics and ethnography', *Sociological Review*, 28, 4, pp. 871–891.

Dollard, J. (1935) *Criteria for the Life History*, New York, Libraries Press.

Douglas, J.D. (1970) *Understanding Everyday Life*, Chicago, Aldine.

Draper, J. (1993) 'We're back with Gobbo: the re-establishment of gender relations following a school merger' in Woods, P. and Hammersley, M. (eds) *Gender and Ethnicity in Schools: ethnographic accounts*, London, Routledge.

Drummond, M.J. (1991) 'The child and the primary curriculum – from policy to practice', *Curriculum Journal*, 2, 2, pp. 115–124.

Dubberley, W. (1988a) 'Social class and the process of schooling – a case study of a comprehensive school in a mining community' in Green, A. and Ball, S. (eds) *Progress and Inequality in Comprehensive Education*, London, Routledge.

Dubberley, W. (1988b) 'Humour as resistance', *International Journal of Qualitative Studies in Education*, 1, 2, pp. 109–123.

Edson, C.H. (1988) 'Our past and present: historical inquiry in education' in Sherman, R.R. and Webb, R.B. (eds) *Qualitative Research in Education: focus and methods*, London, Falmer Press.

Edwards, D. and Mercer, N. (1987) *Common Knowledge: the development of understanding in the classroom*, London, Methuen.

Egan, K. (1992) *Imagination in Teaching and Learning: ages 8–15*, London, Routledge.

Egan, K. (1994) 'Tools for enhancing imagination in teaching' in Grimmett, P.P. and Neufeld, J. (eds) *Teacher Development and the Struggle for Authenticity: professional growth and restructuring in the context of change*, New York, Teachers College Press.

Eisenberg, J. (1995) 'The limits of educational research: why most research and grand plans in education are futile and wasteful', *Curriculum Inquiry*, 25, 4, pp. 367–80.

Eisner, E.W. (1979) *The Educational Imagination*, London, Collier Macmillan.

Eisner, E.W. (1985) *The Art of Educational Evaluation: a personal view*, Lewes, Falmer Press.

Eisner, E.W. (1991) *The Enlightened Eye: qualitative inquiry and the enhancement of educational practice*, New York, Macmillan.

Eisner, E.W. (1993) 'Forms of understanding and the future of educational research', *Educational Researcher*, 22, 7, pp. 5–11.

Eisner, E.W. (1995a) 'Is "the art of teaching" a metaphor?', keynote address, International Conference on Teacher Thinking, Brock University, Ontario, Canada, July.

Eisner, E.W. (1995b) 'What artistically crafted research can help us understand about schools', *Educational Theory*, 45, 1, pp. 1–6.

Elbaz, F. (1991) 'Research on teachers' knowledge: the evolution of a discourse', *Journal of Curriculum Studies*, 23, 1, pp. 1–19.

Elbaz, F. (1992) 'Hope, attentiveness, and caring for difference: the moral voice in teaching', *Teaching and Teacher Education*, 8, 5/6, pp. 411–432.

Eliade, M. (1959) *The Sacred and the Profane*, New York, Harcourt Brace.

Ellis, C. and Bochner, A.P. (1992) 'Telling and performing personal stories: the constraints of choice in abortion' in Ellis, C. and Flaherty, M. (eds) *Investigating Subjectivity: research on lived experience*, Newbury Park, CA, Sage.

Ellis, C. and Flaherty, M.G. (1992) (eds) *Investigating Subjectivity: research on lived experience*, Newbury Park, Sage.

Emihovich, C. (1995) 'Distancing passion: narratives in social science' in Hatch, J.A. and Wisniewski, R. (eds) *Life History and Narrative*, London, Falmer Press.

Erickson, F. (1986) 'Qualitative methods of research on teaching' in Wittock, M. (ed.) *Handbook of Research on Teaching*, New York, Macmillan.

Farberman, H.A. (1991) 'Symbolic interaction and postmodernism: close encounter of a dubious kind', *Symbolic Interaction*, 14, 4, pp. 471–488.

Festinger, L., Rieken, H.W. and Schachter, S. (1956) *When Prophecy Fails*, Minneapolis, University of Minneapolis Press.

Fielding, N. (1981) *The National Front*, London, Routledge and Kegan Paul.

Finch, J. (1986) *Research and Policy*, Lewes, Falmer Press.

Fine, G.A. (1994) 'Working the hyphens: reinventing the self and other in qualitative research' in Denzin, N. and Lincoln, Y. (eds) *Handbook of Qualitative Research*, London, Sage.

Fisher, W.R. (1992) 'Nature, reason and community' in Brown, R.H. (ed.) *Writing the Social Text: poetics and politics in social science discourse*, New York, Aldine de Gruyter.

Foster, P.M. (1990) *Policy and Practice in Multicultural and Anti-Racist Education: a case study of a multi-ethnic comprehensive school*, Milton Keynes, Open University Press.

Foucault, M. (1979) *A History of Sexuality*, Harmondsworth, Penguin.

Fullan, M.G. (1992) *Successful School Improvement*, Milton Keynes, Open University Press.

Furlong, J.V. (1976) 'Interaction sets in the classroom: towards a study of pupil knowledge' in Hammersley, M. and Woods, P. (eds) *The Process of Schooling*, London, Routledge and Kegan Paul.

Furlong, J.V. (1977) 'Anancy goes to school; a case study of pupils' knowledge of their teachers' in Woods, P. and Hammersley, M. (eds) *School Experience*, London, Croom Helm.

Gage, N. (1978) *The Scientific Basis of the Art of Teaching*, New York, Teachers College Press.

Galton, M. (1989) *Teaching in the Primary School*, London, David Fulton.

Gans, H.J. (1968) 'The participant observer as a human being: observations on the personal aspects of fieldwork' in Becker, H.S., Geer, B., Riesman, D. and Weiss, R.S. (eds) *Institutions and the Person*, Chicago, Aldine.

Gardner, H. (1983) *Frames of Mind: the theory of multiple intelligences*, New York, Basic Books.

Geertz, C. (1973) 'Thick description: toward an interpretive theory of culture' in Geertz, C. (ed.) *The Interpretation of Cultures: selected essays by Clifford Geertz*, New York, Basic Books.

Geertz, C. (1988) *Works and Lives: the anthropologist as author*, Stanford, CA, Stanford University Press.

Giddens, A. (1986) 'Action, subjectivity, and the constitution of meaning', *Social Research*, 53, pp. 529–545.

Gillborn, D. (1990) 'Sexism and curricular choice', unpublished paper, QQSE Research Group, University of Sheffield.

Gillborn, D. (1995) *Racism and Antiracism in Real Schools*, Buckingham, Open University Press.

Gipps, C.V. (1993) 'The profession of educational research', *British Educational Research Journal*, 19, 1, pp. 3–16.

Gitlin, A.D. (1990) 'Education research, voice and school change', *Harvard Educational Review*, 60, 4, pp. 443–466.

Glaser, B.G. (1978) *Theoretical Sensitivity: advances in the methodology of grounded theory*, Mill Valley, CA, Sociology Press.

Glaser, B.G. and Strauss, A.L. (1967) *The Discovery of Grounded Theory*, London, Weidenfeld and Nicolson.

Glaser, B. and Strauss, A.L. (1968) *Time for Dying*, Chicago, IL, Aldine.

Goodman, Y.M. and Goodman, K.S. (1990) 'Vygotsky in a whole-language perspective' in Moll, L.C. (ed.) *Vygotsky and Education: instructional implications and applications of socio-historical psychology*, Cambridge, Cambridge University Press.

Goodson, I.F. (1980) 'Life histories and the study of schooling', *Interchange*, 11, 4, pp. 62–76.

Goodson, I.F. (1991) 'Sponsoring the teacher's voice: teachers' lives and teacher development', *Cambridge Journal of Education*, 21, 1, pp. 35–45.

Gossett, P. (1996) *Programme Notes for* Mr Worldy Wise, London, Royal Opera House.

Gracey, H. (1972) *Curriculum or Craftsmanship: elementary schoolteachers in a bureaucratic system*, Chicago, University of Chicago Press.

Grant, L. and Fine, G.A. (1992) 'Sociology unleashed: creative directions in classical ethnography' in LeCompte, M.D., Millroy, W.L. and Preissle, J. (eds) *The Handbook of Qualitative Research in Education*, New York, Academic Press.

Greene, M. (1978) *Landscapes of Learning*, New York, Teachers College Press.

Grove, R.W. (1988) 'An analysis of the constant comparative method', *International Journal of Qualitative Studies in Education*, 1, 3, pp. 273–279.

Guba, E.G. and Lincoln, Y.S. (1981) *Effective Evaluation*, San Francisco, Jossey-Bass.

Guba, E.G. and Lincoln, Y.S. (1994) 'Competing paradigms in qualitative research' in Denzin, N. and Lincoln, Y.S. (eds) *Handbook of Qualitative Research*, London and New York, Sage.

Gusfield, J. (1990) 'My life and soft times' in Berger, B. (ed.) *Authors of Their Own Lives*, Berkeley, CA, University of California Press.

Hamill, P. (1988) 'A romantic in Cuba', *The Age Good Weekend*, August, pp. 42–51.

Hammersley, M. (1987a) 'Ethnography and the cumulative development of theory', *British Educational Research Journal*, 13, 3, pp. 283–296.

Hammersley, M. (1987b) 'Ethnography for survival?: a reply to Woods', *British Educational Research Journal*, 13, 3, pp. 309–317.

Hammersley, M. (1990) *Reading Ethnographic Research: a critical guide*, London, Longman.

Hammersley, M. (1992) *What's Wrong with Ethnography? Methodological explorations*, London, Routledge.

Hammersley, M. (1993) 'The rhetorical turn in ethnography', *Social Science Information*, 32, 1, pp. 23–37.

Hammersley, M. and Atkinson, P. (1995) *Ethnography: principles in practice*, 2nd edn, London, Tavistock.

Hammersley, M. and Scarth, J. (1993) 'Beware of wise men bearing gifts: a case study in the issue of educational research', *British Educational Research Journal*, 19, 5, pp. 489–498.

Hammond, R. (1984), *The Writer and the Word Processor: a guide for authors, journalists, poets and playwrights*, Sevenoaks, Hodder and Stoughton.

Hargreaves, A. (1978) 'Towards a theory of classroom strategies' in Barton, L. and Meighan, R. (eds) *Sociological Interpretations of Schooling and Classrooms*, Driffield, Nafferton.

Hargreaves, A. (1980) 'Synthesis and the study of strategies: a project for the sociological imagination' in Woods, P. (ed.) *Pupil Strategies*, London, Croom Helm.

Hargreaves, A. (1984a) 'Marxism and relative autonomy', Unit 22 in Course E205 *Conflict and Change in Education*, Milton Keynes, Open University.

Hargreaves, A. (1984b) 'The significance of classroom coping strategies' in Hargreaves, A. and Woods, P. (eds) *Classrooms and Staffrooms*, Milton Keynes, Open University Press.

Hargreaves, A. (1984c) 'Contrastive rhetoric and extremist talk' in Hargreaves, A. and Woods, P. (eds) *Classrooms and Staffrooms*, Milton Keynes, Open University Press.

Hargreaves, A. (1987) 'Past, imperfect, tense: reflections on an ethnographic and historical study of middle schools' in Walford, G. (ed.) *Doing Sociology of Education*, Lewes, Falmer Press.

Hargreaves, A. (1988) 'Teaching quality: a sociological analysis', *Journal of Curriculum Studies*, 20, 3, pp. 211–231.

Hargreaves, A. (1991) 'Restructuring restructuring: postmodernity and the prospects for educational change', unpublished paper, Ontario Institute for Studies in Education.

Hargreaves, A. (1993) 'Professional development and the politics of desire' in Vasquez, A. and Martinez, I. (eds) *Analyzing Education in the 90s: ethnographic perspectives, school socialization and minorities integration*, Barcelona, Fundacio La Caixa.

Hargreaves, A. (1994a) 'Towards a social geography of teacher education' in Shimahara, N.K. and Holowinsky, I.Z. (eds) *Teacher Education in Industrialized Nations*, New York, Garland.

Hargreaves, A. (1994b) 'Development and desire: a postmodern perspective' in Guskey, T. and Huberman, M. (eds) *New Paradigms and Practices in Professional Development*, New York, Teachers College Press.

Hargreaves, A. (1994c) *Changing Teachers, Changing Times*, London, Cassell.

Hargreaves, A. (1995) 'Transforming knowledge: blurring the boundaries between research, policy and practice', unpublished paper, Toronto, Ontario Institute for Studies in Education.

Hargreaves, D.H. (1967) *Social Relations in a Secondary School*, London, Routledge and Kegan Paul.

Hargreaves, D.H. (1976) 'Reactions to labelling' in Hammersley, M. and Woods, P. (eds) *The Process of Schooling*, London, Routledge and Kegan Paul.

Hargreaves, D.H. (1978a) 'Whatever happened to symbolic interactionism?' in Barton, L. and Meighan, R. (eds) *Sociological Interpretations of Schooling and Classroom: a reappraisal*, Driffield, Nafferton.

Hargreaves, D.H. (1978b) 'What teaching does to teachers', *New Society*, 9 March, pp. 540–542.

Hargreaves, D.H. (1980) 'The occupational culture of teachers' in Woods, P. (ed.) *Teacher Strategies*, London, Croom Helm.

Hargreaves, D.H. (1983) 'The teaching of art and the art of teaching: towards an alternative view of aesthetic learning' in Hammersley, M. and Hargreaves, A. (eds) *Curriculum Practice: some sociological case studies*, Lewes, Falmer Press.

Hargreaves, D.H., Hester, S.K. and Mellor, F.J. (1975) *Deviance in Classrooms*, London, Routledge and Kegan Paul.

Harris, A. (1976) 'Intuition and the arts of teaching', Unit 18 of Course E203 *Curriculum Design and Development*, Milton Keynes, Open University.

Hatch, J.A. and Wisniewski, R. (eds) (1995) *Life History and Narrative*, London, Falmer Press.

Heaney, S. (1980) *Selected Poems 1965–1975*, London, Faber & Faber.

Hedge, T. (1991) *Writing*, Oxford, Oxford University Press.

Hewitt, R. (1994) 'Expanding the literary horizon: Romantic poets and postmodern sociologists', *Sociological Quarterly*, 35, 2, pp. 195–213.

Hexter, J. (1971) *The History Primer*, New York, Basic Books.

Highet, G. (1951) *The Art of Teaching*, London, Methuen.

Hodgson, J. (1972) 'Drama as a social and educational force' in Hodgson, J. (ed.) *The Uses of Drama*, London, Eyre Methuen.

Holdaway, S. (1982) 'An "inside job": a case study of covert research on the police' in Bulmer, M. (ed.) *Social Research Ethics*, London, Macmillan.

Homan, R. (1980) 'The ethics of covert methods', *British Journal of Sociology*, 31, 1, pp. 46–59.

Hosford, P. (1984) *Using What We Know About Teaching*, Alexandria, VA, Association for Supervision and Curriculum Development.

Humphreys, L. (1975) *Tearoom Trade*, 2nd edn, Chicago, Aldine.

Hustler, D. and Cuff, E.C. (1986) 'Teachers' perceptions of the GIST project: an independent evaluation' in Hustler, D., Cassidy, A. and Cuff, E.C. (eds) *Action Research in Classrooms and Schools*, London, Allen and Unwin.

Hustler, D., Cassidy, A. and Cuff, E.C. (eds) (1986) *Action Research in Classrooms and Schools*, London, Allen and Unwin.

Hutchinson, B. and Whitehouse, P. (1986) 'Action research, professional competence and school organization', *British Educational Research Journal*, 12, 1, pp. 85–94.

Hutchinson, S. (1988) 'Education and grounded theory' in Sherman, R.R. and Webb, R.B. (eds) *Qualitative Research in Education: focus and methods*, Lewes, Falmer Press.

Jackson, P.W. (1990) 'Looking for trouble: on the place of the ordinary in educational studies' in Eisner, E.W. and Peshkin, A. (eds) *Qualitative Enquiry in Education: the continuing debate*, New York, Teachers College Press.

Jackson, P.W. (1992) *Untaught Lessons*, New York, Teachers College Press.

Jansen, G. and Peshkin, A. (1992) 'Subjectivity in qualitative research' in LeCompte, M.D., Millroy, W.L. and Preissle, J. (eds) *The Handbook of Qualitative Research in Education*, New York, Academic Press.

Jeffrey, R. and Woods, P. (1994) 'Creating atmosphere and tone in primary classrooms', paper presented at CEDAR International Conference, *Changing Educational Structures: Policy and Practice*, University of Warwick, 15–17 April. Forthcoming in Chawla-Duggan, H. R. and Pole, C. (eds) *Educational Change in the 1990s: perspectives on primary schooling*, London, Falmer Press.

Jeffrey, R. and Woods, P. (1995) 'Where have all the good times gone?', *Times Educational Supplement*, 9 June, p. 6.

Jeffrey, R. and Woods, P. (1996) 'The realities of Ofsted inspection', paper presented to the European Conference on Educational Research, Bath.

Johnson, J.M. (1993) 'Sociological practice', *Symbolic Interaction*, 16, 3, pp. 291–293.

Joyce, M. (1990) *Afternoon, A Story*, Cambridge, MA, Eastgate Systems.

Katovich, M.A. and Reese, W.A. (1993) 'Postmodern thought in symbolic interaction: reconstructing social inquiry in light of late-modern concerns', *Sociological Quarterly*, 34, 3, pp. 391–411.

Keddie, N. (1971) 'Classroom knowledge' in Young, M.F.D. (ed.) *Knowledge and Control*, London, Collier Macmillan.

Kelchtermans, G. (1991) 'Teachers and their career story: a professional development', paper presented at the Fifth Conference of the International Study Association on Teacher Thinking, Guildford, 23–27 September.

Kincheloe, J.L. and McLaren, P.L. (1994) 'Rethinking critical theory and qualitative research' in Denzin, N. and Lincoln, Y.S. (eds) *Handbook of Qualitative Research*, London and New York, Sage.

King, R.A. (1978) *All Things Bright and Beautiful*, Chichester, Wiley.

Kreiger, S. (1984) 'Fiction and social sciences', *Studies in Symbolic Interaction*, 5, pp. 269–286.

Lacey, C. (1970) *Hightown Grammar*, Manchester, Manchester University Press.

Lacey, C. (1976) 'Problems of sociological fieldwork: a review of the methodology of "Hightown Grammar"' in Hammersley, M. and Woods, P. (eds) *The Process of Schooling*, London, Routledge and Kegan Paul.

Lacey, C. (1977) *The Socialization of Teachers*, London, Methuen.

Laing, R.D. (1967) *The Politics of Experience*, Harmondsworth, Penguin.

Langer, S. (1967) *Mind: an essay on human feeling, vol. 1*, Baltimore, Johns Hopkins University Press.

Lather, P. (1986) 'Research as praxis', *Harvard Educational Review*, 56, 3, pp. 257–277.

Lawn, M. and Ozga, J. (1981) 'The educational worker: a reassessment of teachers' in Barton, L.E. and Walker, S. (eds) *Schools, Teachers and Teaching*, Lewes, Falmer Press.

Leader, Z. (1991) *Writers' Block*, Baltimore, Johns Hopkins University Press.

LeCompte, M.D. (1987) 'Bias in the biography: bias and subjectivity in ethnographic research', *Anthropology and Education Quarterly*, 18, 1, pp. 43–52.

LeCompte, M.D. and Preissle, J. (1993) *Ethnography and Qualitative Design in Educational Research*, 2nd edn, New York, Academic Press.

Lee, C. and Jackson, R. (1993) *Faking It: a look into the mind of a creative learner*, London, Cassell.

Lefebure, M. (1992) *The Lake Poets*, London, Tiger Books International.

Lemert, E.M. (1967) *Human Deviance, Social Problems and Social Control*, Englewood Cliffs, NJ, Prentice Hall.

Lewis, G. (1980) *Day of Shining Red*, Cambridge, Cambridge University Press.

Lieberman, A. and Miller, L. (1984) *Teachers: their world and their work*, Alexandria, VA, Association for Supervision and Curriculum Development.

Lincoln, Y.S. and Denzin, N.K. (1994) 'The fifth moment' in Denzin, N. and Lincoln, Y.S. (eds) *Handbook of Qualitative Research*, London and New York, Sage.

Lincoln, Y.S and Guba, E.G (1985) *Naturalistic Inquiry*, New York, Sage.

Lincoln, Y.S. and Guba, E.G. (1990) 'Judging the quality of case study reports', *International Journal of Qualitative Studies in Education*, 3, 1, pp. 53–59.

Llewellyn, M. (1980) 'Studying girls at school: the implications of confusion' in Deem, R. (ed.) *Schooling for Women's Work*, London, Routledge and Kegan Paul.

Lofland, J. (1971) *Analysing Social Settings*, Belmont, CA, Wadsworth.

Lofland, J. (1995) 'Analytic ethnography: features, failings and futures', *Journal of Contemporary Ethnography*, 24, 1, pp. 30–67.

Louden, W. (1991) *Understanding Teaching: continuity and change in teachers' knowledge*, London, Cassell.

Luscher, K. (1990) 'The social reality of perspectives: on G.H. Mead's potential relevance for the analysis of contemporary societies', *Symbolic Interaction*, 13, 1, pp. 1–18.

Mac an Ghaill, M. (1988) *Young, Gifted and Black*, Milton Keynes, Open University Press.

Mac an Ghaill, M. (1989) 'Beyond the white norm: the use of qualitative methods in the study of black youths' schooling in England', *Qualitative Studies in Education*, 2, 3, pp. 175–189.

Mac an Ghaill, M. (1994) *The Making of Masculinities*, Buckingham, Open University Press.

MacDonald, B. and Walker, R. (1975) 'Case study and the social philosophy of educational research', *Cambridge Journal of Education*, 5, 1, pp. 2–11.

Mackey, S. (1993) 'Emotion and cognition in arts education', *Curriculum Studies*, 1, 2, pp. 245–256.

Malinowski, B. (1922) *Argonauts of the Western Pacific*, London, Routledge and Kegan Paul.

Malinowski, B. (1926) *Myth in Primitive Psychology*, London, Routledge and Kegan Paul.

Marcus, G.E. (1994) 'What comes after "post"?' in Denzin, N. and Lincoln, Y. *Handbook of Qualitative Research*, London and New York, Sage.

Marland, M. (1975) *The Craft of the Classroom*, Exeter, NH, Heinemann.

Maslow, A. (1973) *Further Reaches of Human Nature*, Harmondsworth, Penguin.

Matza, D. (1969) *Becoming Deviant*, Englewood Cliffs, NJ, Prentice Hall.

Max, D.T. (1995) 'Fictions, facts and the future', *Guardian*, 3 January, p. 13.

McCall, G.J. and Simmons, J.L. (eds) (1969) *Issues in Participant Observation*, Reading, MA, Addison-Wesley.

McCall, M.M. (1990) 'The significance of storytelling', *Studies in Symbolic Interaction*, 5, pp. 269–286.

McCall, M.M. and Becker, H.S. (1990) 'Performance science', *Social Problems*, 37, pp. 117–132.

McCall, M.M. and Wittner, J. (1990) 'The good news about life history' in Becker, H.S. and McCall, M.M. (eds) *Symbolic Interaction and Cultural Studies*, Chicago, University of Chicago Press.

McLaren, P. (1986) *Schooling as a Ritual Performance*, London, Routledge and Kegan Paul.

McNamara, D. (1976) 'On returning to the chalk-face: theory not into practice', *British Journal of Teacher Education*, 20, 2, pp. 147–160.

Mead, G.H. (1929) 'The nature of the past' in Coss, J. (ed.) *Essays in Honour of John Dewey*, New York, Henry Holt.

Mead, G.H. (1934) *Mind, Self and Society*, Chicago, University of Chicago Press.

Mealyea, R. (1989) 'Humour as a coping strategy', *British Journal of Sociology of Education*, 10, 3, pp. 311–333.

Measor, L. (1983) 'Gender and the sciences: pupils' gender-based conceptions of school subjects' in Hammersley, M. and Hargreaves, A. (eds) *Curriculum Practice: some sociological case studies*, Lewes, Falmer Press.

Measor, L. (1989) 'Sex education and adolescent sexuality' in Holly, L. (ed.) *Girls and Sexuality: learning and teaching*, Milton Keynes, Open University Press.

Measor, L. and Woods, P. (1984) *Changing Schools: pupil perspectives on transfer to a comprehensive*, Milton Keynes, Open University Press.

Mercer, N. (1995) *The Guided Construction of Knowledge: talk amongst teachers and learners*, Clevedon, Multilingual Matters.

Middleton, S. (1987) 'Schooling and radicalization: life histories of New Zealand feminist teachers', *British Journal of Scoiology of Education*, 8, 2, pp. 169–189.

Miles, M.B. and Huberman, A.M. (1994) *Qualitative Data Analysis*, 2nd edn, London, Sage.

Mills, C.W. (1959) *The Sociological Imagination*, New York, Oxford University Press.

Moloney, R. (1994) 'Heart of Darkness', *Times Educational Supplement*, 30 September, p. xii.

Moore, A. (1992) 'Genre, ethnocentricity and bilingualism in the English classroom' in Woods, P. and Hammersley, M. (eds) *Gender and Ethnicity: ethnographic perspectives*, London, Routledge.

Mortimore, P., Sammons, P., Lewis, L. and Ecob, R. (1988) *School Matters: the junior years*, London, Open Books.

Motion, A. (1993) *Philip Larkin: a writer's life*, London, Faber & Faber.

Murphy, R. (1995) 'Research is rooted in the real world', *Times Educational Supplement*, 15 September, p. 26.

Murphy, R. (1996) 'Realising the potential of educational research', *British Educational Research Journal*, 22, 1, pp. 3–15.

Myerhoff, B. (1978) *Number Our Days*, New York, Dutton.

National Association of Headteachers (1992) 'Curriculum organization and classroom practice in primary schools: NAHT response', Haywoods Heath, NAHT.

Nespor, J. and Barber, L. (1995) 'Audience and the politics of narrative' in Hatch, J.A. and Wisniewski, R. (eds) *Life History and Narrative*, London, Falmer Press.

Newman, A.J. (1989) 'Review of McLaren, P. (1989) "Life in Schools: an introduction to critical pedagogy in the foundations of education", *International Journal of Qualitative Studies in Education*, 2, 3, pp. 269–270.

Newton, E. (1962) *The Meaning of Beauty*, Harmondsworth, Penguin.

Nias, J. (1989) *Primary Teachers Talking: a study of teaching as work*, London, Routledge.

Nias, J. (1991) '"Primary teachers talking": a reflexive account of longitudinal research' in Walford, G. (ed.) *Doing Educational Research*, London, Routledge.

Nias, J., Southworth, G. and Campbell, P. (1992) *Whole School Curriculum Development in the Primary School*, Lewes, Falmer Press.

Nisbet, R. (1962) 'Sociology as an art form', *Pacific Sociological Review*, Autumn.

Noddings, N. (1992) *The Challenge to Care in Schools: an alternative approach to education*, New York, Teachers College Press.

Olson, J. (1992) *Understanding Teaching: beyond expertise*, Milton Keynes, Open University Press.

Paget, M.A. (1990) 'Performing the text', *Journal of Contemporary Ethnography*, 19, 1, pp. 136–155.

Parekh, B. (1992) 'The hermeneutics of the Swann Report' in Gill, D., Mayor, B. and Blair, M. (eds) *Racism and Education*, London, Sage.

Parker, H.J. (1974) *View from the Boys*, Newton Abbot, David and Charles.

Parry, J. (1995) *Review of* Mr Worldy Wise, London, *Observer* 17 December, p. 10.

Patrick, J. (1973) *A Glasgow Gang Observed*, London, Eyre Methuen.

Paul, B.D. (1953) 'Interviewing techniques and field relations' in Kroeber, A.L. (ed.) *Anthropology Today: an encyclopaedic inventory*, Chicago, University of Chicago Press.

Peshkin, A. (1988) 'In search of subjectivity – one's own', *Educational Researcher*, 17, 7, pp. 17–22.

Phillips, D.C. (1990) 'Subjectivity and objectivity: an objective inquiry' in Eisner, E.W. and Peshkin, A. (eds) *Qualitative Inquiry in Education: the continuing debate*, New York, Teachers College Press.

Phillips, M. (1992) 'Rewriting the message', *Guardian*, 14 February, p. 20.

Plowden Report (1967) *Children and their Primary Schools*, Report of the Central Advisory Council for Education in England, London, HMSO.

Polanyi, M. (1958) *Personal Knowledge*, London, Routledge and Kegan Paul.

Polanyi, M. and Prosch, H. (1975) *Personal Knowledge in Meaning*, London, University of Chicago Press.

Pollard, A. (1982) 'A model of coping strategies', *British Journal of Sociology of Education*, 3, 1, pp. 19–37.

Pollard, A. (1984) 'Ethnography and social policy for classroom practice' in Barton, L. and Walker, S. (eds) *Social Crisis and Educational Research*, London, Croom Helm.

Pollard, A. (1985a) 'Opportunities and difficulties of a teacher-ethnographer: a personal account' in Burgess, R.G. (ed.) *Field Methods in the Study of Education*, Lewes, Falmer Press.

Pollard, A. (1985b) *The Social World of the Primary School*, London, Holt, Rinehart and Winston.

Pollard, A. (1990) 'Towards a sociology of learning in primary schools', *British Journal of Sociology of Education*, 11, 3, pp. 241–256.

Popper, K. (1968) *Conjectures and Refutations*, New York, Harper.

Porter, M. (1994) '"Second-hand ethnography": some problems in analyzing a feminist project' in Bryman, A. and Burgess, R.G. (eds) *Analyzing Qualitative Data*, London, Routledge.

Powell, M. and Solity, J. (1990) *Teachers in Control*, London, Routledge.

Preskill, H. (1995) 'The use of photography in evaluating school culture', *International Journal of Qualitative Studies in Education*, 8, 2, pp. 183–193.

Quantz, R.A. (1992) 'On critical ethnography (with some postmodern considerations)' in LeCompte, M.D., Millroy, W. and Goetz, J.P. (eds) *The Handbook of Qualitative Research in Education*, New York, Academic Press.

Quicke, J. (1992) 'Pupil culture and the curriculum', *Westminster Studies in Education*, 17, pp. 5–18.

Quicke, J. and Winter, C. (1993) 'Teaching the language of learning: towards a metacognitive approach to pupil empowerment', paper presented at the BERA Annual Conference, Liverpool.

Qvortrup, J. (1990) 'A voice for children in statistical and social accounting: a plea for children's right to be heard' in James, A. and Prout, A. (eds) *Constructing and Reconstructing Childhood*, London, Falmer Press.

Read, H. (1931) *The Meaning of Art*, reissued 1949, Harmondsworth, Penguin.

Richardson, L. (1987) 'Disseminating research to popular audiences: the book tour', *Qualitative Sociology*, 19, 2, pp. 164–176.

Richardson, L. (1990) *Writing Strategies: reaching diverse audiences*, London, Sage.

Richardson, L. (1993) 'Poetics, dramatics, and transgressive validity: the case of the skipped line', *Sociological Quarterly*, 34, 4, pp. 695–710.

Richardson, L. (1994a) 'Nine poems: marriage and the family', *Journal of Contemporary Ethnography*, 23, 1, pp. 3–13.

Richardson, L. (1994b) 'Writing: a method of inquiry' in Denzin, N. and Lincoln, Y. (eds) *Handbook of Qualitative Research*, London and New York, Sage.

Richardson, L. and Lockridge, E. (1991) 'The sea monster: an ethnographic drama', *Symbolic Interaction*, 14, pp. 335–340.

Riseborough, G.F. (1981) 'Teacher careers and comprehensive schooling: an empirical study', *Sociology*, 15, 3, pp. 352–381.

Riseborough, G.F. (1985) 'Pupils, teachers' careers and schooling: an empirical study' in Ball, S.J. and Goodson, I.F. (eds) *Teachers' Lives and Careers*, Lewes, Falmer Press.

Rist, R.C. (1980) 'Blitzkrieg ethnography: on the transformation of a method into a movement', *Educational Researcher*, 9, 2, pp. 8–10.

Robinson, B. (1985) *English, Language, and Education: microcomputers and the language arts*, Milton Keynes, Open University Press.

Rogers, C. (1983) *Freedom to Learn for the 80s*, New York, Macmillan.

Rollwagen, J.R. (1988) *Anthropological Film-Making*, Chur, Harwood Academic.

Rorty, R. (1979) *Philosophy and the Mirror of Nature*, Princeton, NJ, Princeton University Press.

Rosaldo, R. (1989) *Culture and Truth: the remaking of social analysis*, Boston, Beacon Press.

Rose, A.M. (1962) 'A systematic summary of symbolic interaction theory' in Rose, A.M. (ed.) *Human Behaviour and Social Processes: an interactionist approach*, London, Routledge and Kegan Paul.

Rose, D. (1990) *Living the Ethnographic Life*, London, Sage.

Rosenhan, D.L. (1982) 'On being sane in insane places' in Bulmer, M. (ed.) *Social Research Ethics: an examination of the Merits of Covert Participant Observation*, London, Macmillan.

Rosser, E. and Harré, R. (1976) 'The meaning of disorder' in Hammersley, M. and Woods, P. (eds) *The Process of Schooling*, London, Routledge and Kegan Paul.

Roth, J.A. (1962) 'Comments on "secret observation"', *Social Problems*, 9, 3, pp. 283–284.

Rowland, S. (1987) 'Child in control: towards an interpretive model of teaching and learning' in Pollard, S. (ed.) *Children and Their Primary Schools*, Lewes, Falmer Press.

Rowland, S. (1991) 'The power of silence: an enquiry through fictional writing', *British Educational Research Journal*, 17, 2, pp. 95–113.

Rubin, L.B. (1981) 'Sociological research: the subjective dimension', *Symbolic Interactionism*, 4, pp. 97–112.

Rudduck., J. (1985) 'The improvement of the art of teaching through research', *Cambridge Journal of Education*, 15, 3, pp. 123–127.

Rutter, M., Maugham, B., Mortimore, P. and Ouston, J. (1979) *Fifteen Thousand Hours*, London, Open Books.

Scarth, J. (1985) 'The influence of examinations on curriculum decision-making: a sociological case-study', PhD thesis, Department of Educational Research, University of Lancaster.

Schatzman, L. and Strauss, A. (1973) *Field Research: strategies for a natural sociology*, Englewood Cliffs, NJ, Prentice Hall.

Schensul, J.J. and Schensul, S.L. (1992) 'Collaborative research: methods of inquiry for social change' in LeCompte, M.D., Millroy, W.L. and Preissle, J. (eds) *The Handbook of Qualitative Research in Education*, New York, Academic Press.

Schnieder, J.W. (1991) 'Troubles with textual authority in sociology', *Symbolic Interaction*, 14, pp. 295–319.

Schön, D. (1984) 'Leadership as reflection-in-action' in Sergiovanni, T. and Corbally, J. (eds) *Leadership and Organizational Culture: new perspectives on administrative theory and practice*, Urbana, IL, University of Illinois Press.

Schön, D.A. (1983) *The Reflective Practitioner: how professionals think in action*, London, Temple Smith.

Schratz, M. and Walker, R. (1995) *Research as Social Change: new opportunities for qualitative research*, London, Routledge.

Schutz, A. (1967) *Collected Papers*, The Hague, Nijhoff.

Schwab, J.J. (1969) 'The practical: a language for curriculum', *School Review*, 78, pp. 1–24.

Schwalbe, M.L. (1993) 'Goffman against postmodernism: emotion and the reality of the self', *Symbolic Interaction*, 16, 4, pp. 333–350.

Schwalbe, M.L. (1995) 'The responsibilities of sociological poets', *Qualitative Sociology*, 18, 4, pp. 393–413.

Seidman, S. (1991) 'The end of sociological theory: the postmodern hope', *Sociological Theory*, 9, pp. 131–146.

Shaffir, W.B. and Stebbins, R.A. (eds) (1991) *Experiencing Fieldwork: an inside view of qualitative research*, London, Sage.

Shalin, D.N. (1993) 'Modernity, postmodernism and pragmatist inquiry: an introduction', *Symbolic Interaction*, 16, 4, pp. 303–332.

Sharp, R. and Green, A. (1975) *Education and Social Control: a study in progressive primary education*, London, Routledge and Kegan Paul.

Sharples, M. and Pemberton, L. (1992) 'External representations and the writing process' in Holt, P.O. and Williams N. (eds) *Computers and Writing: state of the art*, Boston, Kluwer Academic.

Shaughnessy, M.P. (1977) *Errors and Expectations: a guide for the teacher of basic writing*, New York, Oxford University Press.

Sherman, R.R. and Webb, R.B. (eds) (1988) *Qualitative Research in Education: focus and methods*, Lewes, Falmer Press.

Shulman, L.S. (1986) 'Those who understand: knowledge growth in teachers', *Educational Researcher*, 15, 2, pp. 4–16.

Shulman, L.S. (1987) 'Knowledge and teaching: foundations of the new reform', *Harvard Educational Review*, 57, 1, pp. 1–22.

Sikes, P., Measor, L. and Woods, P. (1985) *Teacher Careers: crises and continuities*, Lewes, Falmer Press.

Simon, B. (1988) 'Why no pedagogy in England?' in Dale, R., Fergusson, R. and Robinson, A. (eds) *Frameworks for Teaching*, London, Hodder and Stoughton.

Simon, B. (1992) Review article, *Curriculum Journal*, 3, 1, pp. 91–97.

Simon, B. and Willcocks, J. (eds) (1981) *Research and Practice in the Primary Classroom*, London, Routledge and Kegan Paul.

Simons, H. (1994) 'The paradox of case study', paper presented to the British Educational Research Association, 8–11 September, Oxford.

Siraj-Blatchford, I. (1993) 'Educational research and reform: some implications for the professional identity of early years teachers', *British Journal of Educational Studies*, 41, 4, pp. 393–408.

Smith, L.M. and Keith, P. (1971) *Anatomy of Educational Innovation*, New York, Wiley.

Smith, L.M., Dwyer, D.C., Prunty, J.J. and Kleine, P.F. (1988) *Innovation and Change in Schooling: history, politics and agency*, Book 3 of the trilogy 'Anatomy of Educational Innovation: a mid to long term re-study and reconstrual', London, Falmer Press.

Smith, L.M., Kleine, P.F., Dwyer, D.C. and Prunty, J.J. (1985) 'Educational innovators: a decade and a half later' in Ball, S.J. and Goodson, J.F. (eds) *Teachers' Lives and Careers*, Lewes, Falmer Press.

Smith, L.M., Prunty, J.P., Dwyer, D.C. and Kleine, P.F. (1987) *The Fate of an Innovative School*, Book 2 of the trilogy 'Anatomy of Educational Innovation: a mid to long term re-study and reconstrual', London, Falmer Press.

Smith, M.L. (1980) 'Solving for some unknowns in the personal equation', CIRCE occasional paper, Urbana, IL, University of Illinois.

Smithers, A. (1994) 'Research doesn't have to be dull', letter to *Times Educational Supplement*, 21 January, p. 21.

Smithers, A. (1995) 'Let usefulness be our yardstick for research', *Times Educational Supplement*, 8 September, p. 25.

Smyth, J. (1991) *Teachers as Collaborative Learners*, Milton Keynes, Open University Press.

Snow, D.A. and Morrill, C. (1995) 'New ethnographies: review symposium: a revolutionary handbook or a handbook for revolution?', *Journal of Contemporary Ethnography*, 24, 3, pp. 341–362.

Snyder, I. (1993) 'Writing with word processors: a research overview,' *Educational Research*, 35, 1, pp. 49–68.

Sockett, H. (1976) 'Approaches to curriculum planning', Unit 16 of Course E203 *Curriculum Design and Development*, Milton Keynes, Open University.

Sofer, A. (1994) 'Sense that is not common enough', *Times Educational Supplement*, 7 January, p. 88.

Soltis, J.F. (1989) 'The ethics of qualitative research', *International Journal of Qualitative Studies in Education*, 2, 2, pp. 123–130.

Sorel, G. (1950) *Reflections on Violence*, Glencoe, IL, Free Press.

Stake, R.E. (1981) 'A needed subjectivity in educational research', *Discourse*, 1, 2, pp. 1–8.

Stake, R.E. and Kerr, D. (1994) 'René Magritte, constructivism, and the researcher as interpreter', paper presented to the annual meeting of the American Educational Research Association, New Orleans, April.

Stanislavski, C. (1972) 'Emotional involvement in acting' in Hodgson, J. (ed.) *The Uses of Drama*, London, Eyre Methuen.

Stanley, J. (1986) 'Sex and the quiet schoolgirl', *British Journal of Sociology of Education*, 7, 3, pp. 275–286.

Stanley, J.R. (1989) *Marks on the Memory: the pupils' experience of school*, Milton Keynes, Open University Press.

Stebbins, R. (1980) 'The role of humour in teaching' in Woods, P. (ed.) *Teacher Strategies*, London, Croom Helm.

Stenhouse, L. (1975) *An Introduction to Curriculum Research and Development*, London, Heinemann.

Stenhouse, L. (1980) 'Curriculum research and the art of the teacher', *Curriculum*, 1, 1, Spring, pp. 40–44.

Stenhouse, L. (1985) *Research as a Basis for Teaching*, London, Heinemann.

Stone, L. (1981) *The Past and the Present*, Boston, Routledge and Kegan Paul.

Strauss, A. and Corbin, J. (1990) *Basics of Qualitative Research: grounded theory procedures and techniques*, Newbury Park, Sage.

Strauss, A. and Corbin, J. (1994) 'Grounded theory methodology: an overview' in Denzin, N.K. and Lincoln, Y.S. (eds) *Handbook of Qualitative Research*, London, Sage.

Strauss, A.L. (1959) *Mirrors and Masks: the search for identity*, Glencoe, IL, Free Press.

Strauss, A.L. (1987) *Qualitative Analysis for Social Scientists*, Cambridge, Cambridge University Press.

Swann Report (1985) *Education for All*, Report of the Committee of Enquiry into the Education of Children from Ethnic Minority Groups, Cmnd 9543, London, HMSO.

Sykes, A.T.M. (1965) 'Myth and attitude change', *Human Relations*, 18, 4, pp. 323–337.

Taylor, L. (1987) 'Interview with Bob Mullan' in Mullan, B. *Sociologists on Sociology*, London, Croom Helm.

Tesch, R. (1990) *Qualitative Research: analysis types and software tools*, London, Falmer Press.

Thomas, D. (ed.) (1995) *Teachers' Stories*, Buckingham, Open University Press.

Thomas, J. (1995) *Doing Critical Ethnography*, London, Sage.

Thomas, W.I. (1928) *The Child in America*, New York, Knopf.

Threadgold, M.W. (1985) 'Bridging the gap between teachers and researchers' in Burgess, R.G. (ed.) *Issues in Educational Research*, London, Falmer Press.

Tom, A. (1984) *Teaching as a Moral Craft*, New York, Longman.

Tom, A. (1988) 'Teaching as a moral craft' in Dale, R., Fergusson, R. and Robinson, A. (eds) *Frameworks for Teaching*, London, Hodder and Stoughton.

Tripp, D. (1993) *Critical Incidents in Teaching: developing professional judgement*, London, Routledge.

Trollope, J. (1994) 'Any questions?', *Observer Magazine*, 6 March, p. 46.

Troman, G. (1996) 'No entry signs: educational change and some problems encountered in negotiating entry to educational settings', *British Educational Research Journal*, 22, 1, pp. 3–15.

Troyna, B. (1994) 'The everyday world of teachers?: Deracialised discourses in the sociology of teachers and the teaching profession', *British Journal of Sociology of Education*, 15, 3, pp. 325–339.

Troyna, B. and Carrington, B. (1989) 'Whose side are we on? Ethical dilemmas in research on "race" and education' in Burgess, R. (ed.) *The Ethics of Educational Research*, Lewes, Falmer Press.

Troyna, B. and Foster, P. (1988) 'Conceptual and ethical dilemmas of collaborative research: reflections on a case study', *Educational Review*, 40, 3, pp. 289–300.

Tuchman, B. (1981) *Practising History*, New York, Knopf.

Turner, B.A. (1994) 'Patterns of crisis behaviour: a qualitative inquiry' in Bryman, A. and Burgess, R.G. (eds) *Analyzing Qualitative Data*, London, Routledge.

Turner, G. (1983) *The Social World of the Comprehensive School*, London, Croom Helm.

Turner, R.H. (1962) 'Role-taking: process versus conformity' in Rose, A.M. (ed.) *Human Behaviour and Social Processes*, London, Routledge and Kegan Paul.

Turner, V.W. (1974) *The Ritual Process: structure and anti-structure*, Harmondsworth, Penguin.

Tyler, S. (1986) 'Post-modern ethnography: from document of the occult to occult document' in Clifford, J. and Marcus, G. (eds) *Writing Culture*, Berkeley, CA, University of California Press.

Van Maanen, J. (1988) *Tales of the Field*, London, Sage.

Vulliamy, G. and Webb, R. (1993) 'Progressive education and the National Curriculum: findings from a global education research project', *Educational Review*, 45, 1, pp. 21–41.

Walker, R. (1986) 'The conduct of educational case studies: ethics, theory and procedures' in Hammersley, M. (ed.) *Controversies in Classroom Research*, Milton Keynes, Open University Press.

Walker, R. (1993) 'Using photographs in evaluation and research' in Schratz, M. (ed.) *Qualitative Voices in Educational Research*, London, Falmer Press.

Walkerdine, V. (1990) *Schoolgirl Fictions*, London, Virago.

Wallace, M. (1993) 'Discourse of derision: the role of the mass media within the education policy process', *Journal of Education Policy*, 8, 4, pp. 321–337.

Waller, W.W. (1932) *The Sociology of Teaching*, New York, Wiley.

Walmsley, L. (1935) *Foreigners*, London, Jonathan Cape.

Walsh, W. (1959) *The Use of Imagination: educational thought and the literary mind*, London, Chatto and Windus.

Wax, R. (1971) *Doing Fieldwork*, Chicago, University of Chicago Press.

Webb, E.J., Campbell, D.T., Schwartz, R.D. and Sechrest, L. (1966) *Unobtrusive Measures: nonreactive research in the social sciences*, Chicago, Rand McNally.

Webb, R. and Vulliamy, G. (1996) *Roles and Responsibilities in the Primary School: changing demands, changing practices*, Buckingham, Open University Press.

Werthman, C. (1963) 'Delinquents in school: a test for the legitimacy of authority', *Berkeley Journal of Sociology*, 8, 1, pp. 39–60; also in Hammersley, M. and Woods, P. (eds) *Life in School: the sociology of pupil culture*, Milton Keynes, Open University Press.

Whistler, T. (1988) *Rushavenn Time*, Brixworth, Brixworth Primary School.

Whitty, G.J. (1974) 'Sociology and the problem of radical educational change: towards a reconceptualization of the "new" sociology of education' in Flude, M. and Ahier, J. (eds) *Educability, Schools and Ideology*, London, Croom Helm.

Whyte, W.F. (1955) *Street Corner Society*, Chicago, University of Chicago Press.

Widdowson, H.G. (1983) 'New starts and different kinds of failure' in Freedman, A., Pringle, I. and Yalden, J. (eds) *Learning to Write: first language/second language*, London, Longman.

Willis, P. (1975) 'The expressive style of a motor-bike culture' in Benthall, J. and Polhemus, T. (eds) *The Body as a Medium of Expression*, London, Allen Lane.

Willis, P. (1977) *Learning to Labour*, Farnborough, Saxon House.

Willis, P. (1978) *Profane Culture*, London, Routledge and Kegan Paul.

Wilson, S. (1977) 'The use of ethnographic techniques in educational research', *Review of Educational Research*, 47, 1, pp. 245–265.

Winter, R. (1991) 'Fictional critical writing as a method for educational research', *British Educational Research Journal*, 17, 3, pp. 251–262.

Wolcott, H.F. (1990a) *Writing up Qualitative Research*, Newbury Park, Sage.

Wolcott, H.F. (1990b) 'On seeking – and rejecting – validity in qualitative research' in Eisner, E. and Peshkin, A. (eds) *Qualitative Inquiry in Education*, New York, Teachers College Press.

Wolcott, H.F. (1994) *Transforming Qualitative Data: description, analysis, and interpretation*, London, Sage.

Wolfe, T. (1973) *The New Journalism*, New York, Harper and Row.

Woodhead, C. (1992) 'Raise the standard bearers', *Guardian*, 11 February, p. 21.

Woods, P. (1979) *The Divided School*, London, Routledge and Kegan Paul.

Woods, P. (1985) 'Conversations with teachers: aspects of life history method', *British Educational Research Journal*, 11, 1, pp. 13–26.

Woods, P. (1986) *Inside Schools: ethnography in educational research*, London, Routledge and Kegan Paul.

Woods, P. (1987a) 'Life-histories and teacher knowledge' in Smyth, J. (ed.) *Educating Teachers – changing the nature of professional knowledge*, Lewes, Falmer Press.

Woods, P. (1987b) 'Ethnography at the crossroads: a reply to Hammersley', *British Educational Research Journal*, 13, 3, pp. 297–307.

Woods, P. (ed.) (1989) *Working for Teacher Development*, Cambridge, Peter Francis.

Woods, P. (1990a) *Teacher Skills and Strategies*, Lewes, Falmer Press.

Woods, P. (1990b) *The Happiest Days?: how pupils cope with school*, Lewes, Falmer Press.

Woods, P. (1990c) 'Cold eyes and warm hearts: changing perspectives on teachers' work and careers', *British Journal of Sociology of Education*, 11, 1, pp. 101–117.

Woods, P. (1993a) *Critical Events in Teaching and Learning*, London, Falmer Press.

Woods, P. (1993b) 'Towards a theory of aesthetic learning', *Educational Studies*, 19, 3, pp. 323–338.

Woods, P. (1993c) 'Managing marginality: teacher development through grounded life history', *British Educational Research Journal*, 19, 5, pp. 447–465.

Woods, P. (1993d) 'The charisma of the critical other: enhancing the role of the teacher', *Teaching and Teacher Education*, 9, 5/6, pp. 545–557.

Woods, P. (1994a) 'Adaptation and self-determination in English primary schools', *Oxford Review of Education*, 20, 4, pp. 387–410.

Woods, P. (1994b) 'Critical students: breakthroughs in learning', *International Studies in Sociology of Education*, 4, 2, pp. 123–146.

Woods, P. (1995a) *Creative Teachers in Primary Schools*, Buckingham, Open University Press.

Woods, P. (1995b) 'Intensification and stress in teaching', paper for conference on *Teacher Burnout*, Marbach, November.

Woods, P. and Jeffrey, R. (1996) *Teachable Moments: the art of teaching in primary school*, Buckingham, Open University Press.

Woods, P. and Pollard, A. (eds) (1988) *Sociology and Teaching*, London, Croom Helm.

Woods, P. and Sikes, P.J. (1987) 'The use of teacher biographies in professional self-development' in Todd, F. (ed.) *Planning Continuing Professional Development*, London, Croom Helm.

Woods, P. and Wenham, P. (1994) 'Teaching, and researching the teaching of, a history topic: an experiment in collaboration', *Curriculum Journal*, 5, 2, pp. 133–161.

Woods, P.J. (1993) 'Keys to the past – and to the future: the empirical author replies', *British Educational Research Journal*, 19, 5, pp. 475–488; also in Thomas, D. (ed.) (1995) *Teachers' Stories*, Buckingham, Open University Press.

Woods, P.J. (1995) 'Teacher biography and educational process', *Topic*, 14, pp. 1–9.

Worsley, P., Fitzhenry, R., Mitchell, J.C., Morgan, D.H.J., Pons, V., Roberts, B., Sharrock, W.W. and Ward, R. (1977) *Introducing Sociology*, 2nd edn, Harmondsworth, Penguin.

Wright, C. (1986) 'School processes – an ethnographic study' in Eggleston, J., Dunn, D. and Anjali, M. (eds) *Education for Some: the educational and vocational experiences of 15–18 year old members of minority ethnic groups*, Stoke-on-Trent, Trentham Books.

Wright, C. (1992) *Race Relations in the Primary School*, London, David Fulton.

Wu, D. (ed.) (1994) *Romanticism: an anthology*, London, Blackwell.

Yablonsky, L. (1968) *The Hippie Trip*, New York, Western.

Yang, Y. (1992) 'Supporting writing with an undo mechanism' in Holt, P.O. and Williams, N. (eds) *Computers and Writing: state of the art*, Boston, Kluwer Academic.

Young, M.F.D. (ed.) (1971) *Knowledge and Control: new directions for the sociology of education*, London, Collier Macmillan.

Zajano, N.C. and Edelsberg, C.M. (1993) 'Living and writing the researcher–researched relationship', *International Journal of Qualitative Studies in Education*, 6, 2, pp. 143–157.

Name index

Abbs, P. 22, 28, 30
Acker, S. 21, 48
Adelman, C. 21
Aggleton, P. 49
Alexander, R.J. 17, 30, 151, 152, 154–6, 166–7
Altheide, D.L. 8, 56–7
American Sociologist, The 65
Amis, K. 143
Anderson, N. 74
Anning, A. 18
Anyon, J. 35
Apple, M.W. 21, 25, 29, 156
Argyris, C. 124
Arp 1885–1966 85
Atkinson, J.M. 51
Atkinson, P. 51, 80, 105, 120, 124

Bailey, F.G. 155
Bain, A. 16
Baker, C. 143
Baldwin, J.D. 36
Ball, S.J. 7, 15, 48, 53, 69, 74, 120, 153
Bandura, A. 34
Barber, L. 150, 165–6
Barker, B. 141
Barone, T. 54, 59,78
Becker, E. 34
Becker, H.S. 10, 13, 32, 46, 48, 51, 68, 78, 86, 106, 133, 145, 148, 153
Bell, C. 140
Bell, R.E. 14
Bennett, N. 153, 154, 157–8, 167
Berger, B.M. 105
Berger, P.L. 38
Bernard, J. 143
Bertaux, D. 50
Best, D. 25
Bevlin, M. 135
Beynon, J. 69, 76, 84

Biott, C. 124
Bloom, L.R. 46
Blumenfeld-Jones, D. 58, 61, 81
Blumer, H. 32, 34, 37, 38, 70
Bochner, A.P. 85
Bogdan, R. 51
Bolton, G. 78, 86
Bonnett, M. 22
Boswell, J. 137
Bourdieu, P. 104
Bowe, R. 75
Bowles, S. 49
Brehe, S. 148
Bridwell-Bowles, L. 148–9
Brighouse, T. 14
Brown, S. 30
Bulmer, M. 7, 63, 64, 65, 70
Burgess, E.W. 7
Burgess, R.G. 51, 63, 64, 66, 120, 144

Campbell, R.J. 156, 158
Carr, D. 157
Carr, W. 23, 124
Carrington, B. 74
Casey, K. 21
Chanan, G. 29
Chandler, D. 139
Clandinin, D.J. 126
Clark, C.M. 126
Clarke, K. 154, 155, 166
Clifford, J. 13, 78–80, 87, 108, 166
Cohen, S. 69, 154
Collingwood, R.G. 27, 86
Collins, J.L. 147
Collins, R. 93
Connell, R.W. 158
Connelly, F.M. 126
Cook, M.C. 139, 143
Cooper, P. 31

Subject index